Collaborative Teaming

Teachers' Guides to Inclusive Practices

Collaborative Teaming

by

Martha E. Snell, Ph.D.
University of Virginia
Charlottesville

and

Rachel Janney, Ph.D.
Radford University
Radford, Virginia

with contributions from

Johnna Elliott, M.Ed.
Christine C. Burton, M.S.
Kenna M. Colley, Ed.D.
Maria Raynes, M.Ed.

Baltimore • London • Toronto • Sydney

Paul H. Brookes Publishing Co.
Post Office Box 10624
Baltimore, Maryland 21285-0624

www.brookespublishing.com

Typeset by Barton Matheson Willse and Worthington, Baltimore, Maryland.
Manufactured in the United States of America by Versa Press, East Peoria, Illinois.

All of the vignettes in this book are composites of the authors' actual experiences. In all instances, names have been changed; in some instances, identifying details have been altered to protect confidentiality.

Library of Congress Cataloging-in-Publication Data

Snell, Martha E.
  Collaborative teaming / by Martha E. Snell and Rachel Janney with contributions from Johnna Elliott . . . [et al.].
      p.   cm.—(Teachers' guides to inclusive practices)
  Includes bibliographical references and index.
  ISBN 1-55766-353-X
  1. Inclusive education—United States.   2. School support teams—United States.   3. Home and school—United States.   I. Janney, Rachel.   II. Elliott, Johnna.   III. Title.   IV. Series.
LC1201.S64   2000
378.14'8—dc21   99-43330
                                                                                                              CIP

British Library Cataloguing in Publication data are available from the British Library.

Contents

About the Authors

Martha E. Snell, Ph.D., is a professor in the Curry School of Education at the University of Virginia where she has taught since 1973. Her focus is special education and, specifically, the preparation of teachers of students with mental retardation and severe disabilities and young children with disabilities. Prior to completing her doctoral degree in special education at Michigan State University, she worked with children and adults with disabilities as a residential child care worker, a teacher, and a provider of technical assistance to school and residential programs. In addition to teaching coursework at the undergraduate and graduate levels, she currently coordinates the special education program, supervises teachers in training, provides in-service training to teachers and parents in schools and agencies, conducts research, serves on the boards of several community agencies serving people with disabilities, and is an active member of the American Association on Mental Retardation and TASH (formerly The Association for Persons with Severe Handicaps).

Rachel Janney, Ph.D., has worked with children and adults with disabilities in a number of capacities, including special education teacher, camp counselor, educational consultant, and researcher. She received her master's degree from Syracuse University and her doctorate from the University of Nebraska–Lincoln. Dr. Janney now teaches courses in special education, supervises student teachers, and coordinates the undergraduate program in special education at Radford University. She also serves as Co-director of the Training and Technical Assistance Center (T/TAC) for Professionals Serving Individuals with Disabilities at Radford University. The T/TAC, part of a statewide technical assistance network that is funded by the Virginia Department of Education, provides a variety of services and resources to special education teams in school divisions throughout southwest Virginia.

Dr. Snell and coauthor Dr. Janney have conducted several research projects in inclusive schools and classrooms. The focus of these projects has been on the ways that special and general education teachers work together to design and implement adaptations and accommodations for students with disabilities placed in inclusive settings. Both authors are frequent presenters of workshops on topics related to successful inclusive education.

Johnna Elliott, M.Ed., and **Christine C. Burton, M.S.,** are consulting teachers in a school division that serves all students in their neighborhood schools and provides individualized adaptations and accommodations to support students with disabilities alongside their peers within general education classrooms. As consulting teachers, they provide and coordinate an array of supports for students across all disability categories.

Kenna M. Colley, Ed.D., previously an elementary school inclusion specialist, is now the lead coordinator for the T/TAC at Radford University in Radford, Virginia. Her current role involves facilitating local school systems' improvement efforts, including enhancing their use of inclusive education practices.

Maria Raynes, M.Ed., previously an elementary school inclusion specialist, now provides technical assistance to teachers serving students with disabilities at the Training and Technical Assistance Center located at James Madison University.

Acknowledgments

Many colleagues, friends, families, and students merit recognition and deserve our thanks for their contributions to our knowledge of collaboration. Some of these individuals whose work we have learned from and built on include Michael Giangreco, Lynn Cook, Anita DeBoer, Susan Fister, Janet Freston, Marilyn Friend, David Johnson, Frank Johnson, Bev Rainforth, Jacque Thousand, Rich Villa, and Jennifer York-Barr.

We would also like to acknowledge our editors at Brookes Publishing: Scott Beeler, who helped get the "booklet concept" off the ground, and Lisa Benson and Kristine Dorman for their excellent editing and persistence in completing this series of booklets.

To all the educators, parents, and students who are working to create and maintain inclusive school environments: places where all students have membership, enjoy social relationships with peers, and have the needed supports to learn what is important for them to be successful in life

Collaborative Teaming

Chapter 1

An Overview of Collaborative Teaming

Twenty-three students attend Ms. Scott's second-grade class. On most days Ms. Scott begins class by asking the students to gather into a circle to share class news and to review what's in store for the day. Today, Daniel shares some news about a puppy that his family has just acquired. Daniel's classmates are eager to see the photos that he has brought in, and they laugh at the "facewash" photo of Daniel being licked by the puppy.

Rick, a 14-year-old who attends the local high school, takes general education classes and attends a one-to-one resource period. While Rick's classmates like the noise and chaos between every class, they understand that Rick dislikes it and may need their support or a teacher's support to make the transition between classes without "losing it." Some of Rick's peers have known Rick since middle school; although they recognize his talents, they also know when to "cut him a break."

These are not traditional scenes from second grade and high school; Daniel and Rick both have disabilities and receive special education support in general classrooms from collaborative teams.

Daniel's cerebral palsy has impeded his speech, making it necessary for him to use augmentative devices to communicate. Daniel also uses a wheelchair. Rick, a highly articulate adolescent, has been diagnosed with obsessive-compulsive disorder and pervasive developmental disorder. In both cases, Daniel's and Rick's teachers work closely with family members and other school staff to plan and implement programs that have been specifically designed to suit Daniel's and Rick's specific needs. The responsibility for teaching and monitoring progress is shared by the team members.

This booklet is about teachers who collaborate with each other and with other school staff, students, and families in order to individualize and deliver special education supports in the context of general classrooms and typical school activities. This booklet is written primarily for general and special educators who are serving or planning to serve students with disabilities in inclusive classrooms; however, it is a valuable resource for anyone working on or with a team (e.g., related services staff, administrators, family members).

The booklet describes the ways in which collaborative teaming facilitates the inclusion of students with disabilities in general education environments. In schools where inclusion is practiced, administrators and staff aim for several high standards:

- All students are members of general education classrooms in their neighborhood schools alongside their peers.
- Educational programs and special education supports are individually defined and implemented by teams.
- Special education supports follow students as they move through their daily school routines.

To reach these standards, teachers must work cooperatively while drawing on family members and other school staff members in the process. Collaborative teaming is so central to inclusive school programming that it can be viewed as "the glue that holds inclusive schools together." It is through collaborative teams that the educational programs and special education supports for individual students are planned and implemented; however, the range of supports that teams can plan for and provide is not limited to school work. Teams fill many functions in inclusive programs: They reduce barriers to participating in school activities, facilitate social interactions between students, build peer support, encourage the contribution of ideas by family members, embed related services into the school day, and design plans to ease students' transitions between grades and schools and into jobs or college. Likewise, the form that teams take to address these different team functions and types of support can vary. This booklet will primarily address collaborative teams that focus on students who need special education support; however, many of the principles of collaborative teaming that apply to these student-centered teams also apply to other types of teams that are formed within schools. Effective communication and trust are relevant whether a team is addressing a student with disabilities or selecting new textbooks.

This book begins with an overview of collaborative teaming in Chapter 1 and presents a way to view the various components involved in teaming. Chapter 2 addresses the first component, building team structure. This chapter describes how to organize collaborative teams and addresses the substantial roles that building administrators play when schools prepare for, initiate, and maintain inclusion. Chapter 3, which discusses "teamwork skills," delves into the basic elements of team members' work together. Chapter 4 describes problem-solving methods and ways to develop and implement action plans. Chapter 5 details collaborative teaching. Finally, Chapter 6 examines methods that teams use to improve communication among members and to address areas of disagreement and conflict. This booklet's content and case applications include rich contributions from teachers who work in inclusive school environments.

DEFINING TERMS

Collaborative Teaming

It is important to define some terms before the mechanics and methods of collaborative teaming are addressed. Perhaps the simplest definition of *collaborative teaming* is *two or more people working together toward a common goal. Work-*

ing includes setting goals, identifying problems, assessing students' needs and skills, exchanging information, brainstorming, problem-solving, making plans, and implementing and evaluating those plans. *Working together* means that *positive interdependence* exists among team members who agree both to pool and partition their resources and rewards and to operate from a foundation of shared values. Team members' interactions are cooperative, not competitive: Team members help each other and lend support to each other (Rainforth & York-Barr, 1997). A team's *common goals* are the goals on which teammates have reached a mutual agreement, not goals that have been determined by individual members. Figure 1.1 provides Johnson and Johnson's (1997) definition of a team. Figure 1.2 lists DeBoer's six key characteristics of collaborative teaming.

Much of the energy that can be observed in and around collaborative teams is produced from their operating philosophy: *If we work together, we can solve whatever problems we have* (Talbert, 1993).

Transdisciplinary Philosophy

Many collaborative teams for students with disabilities include members other than those from the teaching profession and from the students' families. In addition to general education and special education teachers, professional members might include physical therapists, occupational therapists, speech-language pathologists, guidance counselors, school psychologists, orientation and mobility specialists, adapted physical education specialists, counselors, interpreters for students with hearing impairment, nurses, and program administrators. In addition to family members, other nonprofessional members may include the stu-

---

"A team is a set of interpersonal relationships structured to achieve established goals . . . a team consists of two or more individuals who (1) are aware of their positive interdependence as they strive to achieve mutual goals, (2) interact while they do so, (3) are aware of who is and is not a member of the team, (4) have specific roles or functions to perform, and (5) have a limited life-span of membership."

Figure 1.1. Definition of a team. (From Johnson, D.W., & Johnson, F.W. [1997]. *Joining together: Group theory and skills* [6th ed.]. Englewood Cliffs, NJ: Prentice Hall.)

What the Research Says

DeBoer defined six key characteristics of collaborative teaming:

- "Collaboration is based on mutual goals" (p. 55): The team's short- and long-term goals are determined by the entire team. Mutual goals build team commitment from the beginning.

- "Collaboration requires parity among participants" (p. 55): When there is equality among team members, each member's contributions and role in decision making are valued and add to the team's outcomes. Parity among members makes team consensus more probable.

- "Collaboration depends on shared responsibility for participation and decision making" (p. 56): While all team members actively engage in deliberations and decision making, participation is not identical for all members. How a team shares its tasks depends on the team members' particular skills, work and team roles, and available time. Shared responsibility plus parity among team members contributes to both the achievement of team consensus and interdependence.

- "Collaboration requires shared responsibility for outcomes" (p. 57): Team success and failure are shared by all team members. If individual members take credit for team success or blame others for team failure, then participation and decision making have not been shared responsibilities.

- "Collaboration requires that participants share their resources" (p. 57): Teamwork means that each team member is responsible for sharing his or her particular resources, including information, equipment, and materials, with the rest of team.

- "Collaboration is a voluntary relationship" (p. 57): No one can be mandated to engage in a collaborative relationship with a team. Collaborative skills have to be learned and then practiced in order to be effective.

Figure 1.2.   Six key characteristics of collaborative teaming. (*Source:* DeBoer, 1995–1996.)

dent him- or herself, friends of the student, or a paraprofessional working with the student.

All team members play a part in achieving team goals regardless of how often they participate. As defined in Figure 1.3, *core teams* work together most frequently to achieve the team goals, while a student's *whole team* includes other team members who participate less frequently in the team meetings (Giangreco, Cloninger, & Iverson, 1998). Teams that are collaborative and include members of multiple disciplines are called transdisciplinary teams; their approach involves agreement that the multiple needs of students are interrelated (Rainforth & York-Barr, 1997). Both Daniel's and Rick's teams illustrate this transdisciplinary philosophy:

When Daniel shares his morning news with his classmates, he uses skills that have been shaped by the efforts of his team members. For example, to communicate in class circle,

Daniel first needs to be sitting upright with lots of support from a special "legless" chair. He then touches the symbols on a Cheaptalk communication device (Enabling Devices, Inc.) to activate a message corresponding to each symbol. Six of Daniel's team members— his classroom and special education teachers; his mother; and his occupational, physical, and speech-language therapists— worked together to design and refine this arrangement.

Rick and his team members (his classroom teachers, special education teacher, counselor, and parents) worked together to write Rick's behavioral support plan. This plan teaches school staff members who work with Rick ways to prevent his disruptive behavior, to teach him appropriate behavior, to respond to difficult situations, and to handle a behavioral crisis if one should occur.

Teaming Terminology	
Core team	*Core team* members include those members most directly responsible for the student, who work together daily or almost daily to plan, implement, and evaluate a student's educational program. Core members usually consist of a student's general and special education teachers, paraprofessionals (if involved), and family members. While it is unusual for family members to be physically present daily with other core members, their input can be heard regularly through mutually determined ways (e.g., telephone calls, traveling notebook, etc.).
Whole team	The *whole team* includes core members plus team members who participate with the student or team less often, yet are important to the achievement of team goals. These team members have less frequent regularly scheduled contacts with core team members and the focus student (Rainforth & York-Barr, 1997).
Role release	"A process of transferring information and skills traditionally associated with one discipline to team members of other disciplines" (Rainforth & York-Barr, 1997, p. 19).
Pull-out services	Supports from special education staff or team members other than classroom staff are provided for specific students apart from the general education classroom. The student in need is "pulled out" of the general education setting but may be accompanied by other classmates. If used, pull-out requires team collaboration to be effective.
Pull-in services	Supports from special education staff or team members other than classroom staff are provided for specific students in the context of ("pulled in") a general education classroom or in a class or school activity.
Collaborative teaching	Also called team teaching or co-teaching, *collaborative teaching* refers to two or more team members teaching a class together. When special and general educators teach together, the motivation is often more effective instruction of a diverse group of students.

Figure 1.3. Teaming terminology.

Role Release

Role release is an important concept for collaborative teamwork. At the simplest level, role release means that team members step out of their usual roles to become either teachers of other team members or learners taught by other team members.

- To be a teacher of other team members requires sharing the knowledge and expertise of one's position as a teacher, parent, therapist, and so forth at times when this information is relevant to the team's goals.

- To be a learner and benefit from other team members' experiences requires the belief that each team member's knowledge and perspectives are valuable to other team members and will assist the team in reaching their goals.

Rick's classroom teachers are eager to learn how to prevent his disruptive behavior; when he becomes anxious, Rick can change quickly from being a talented student to being so disruptive that an entire class session is lost! During team meetings, Rick's classroom teachers learn new methods of behavior management from the special education teacher and the school counselor, including behavior rehearsal, peer support, organizational support, and social stories. The classroom teachers then share their expertise to help shape these new methods into strategies that will work in their classrooms.

Role release involves sharing and recognizing the expertise of fellow teammates. It is most likely to occur 1) when teams are operating in a cooperative atmosphere of trust and support and 2) when teams are working toward achieving a common goal (Thomas, Correa, & Morsink, 1995).

Delivering Special Education Support

Traditionally, schools have provided special education apart from the general education classroom by either 1) pulling a student out of a general classroom into tutoring sessions or resource rooms or 2) teaching students in self-contained classrooms which only serve students with disabilities. Typically, these approaches have not been coupled with sharing of information or ideas between general education and special education teachers. These traditional approaches contrast with the collaborative practices of 1) pull-in, 2) collaborative teaching or co-teaching, and 3) pull-out with collaborative teaming (Figure 1.3). According to from DeBoer and Fister (1994, p. 11), one can better understand how these approaches operate by assigning phrases and speakers:

1. Self-contained classes = "I do it all by myself" (says the special educator).

2. Resource or pull-out = "I do the special part by myself" (says the special educator).

3. Consultation = "Someone else does it" (says the general education teacher).

4. Pull-in, co-teaching, and collaborative teaming = "We do some or much of it together" (say the general education and special education teachers).

Teams' goals center upon facilitating student learning and membership within classes, school activities, and peer groups. Teams plan ways to "deliver" special education that maximize learning and membership. Thus, the most frequently used "delivery approaches" involve pulling in supports and teaching collaboratively and less often involve pulling the student away from class activities.

Collaborative teams need to maintain a dual focus in order to deliver special education supports to students. A collaborative team must direct its attention and effort toward the student(s) who it is supporting and

toward the team itself. Examples of student-centered efforts include

- Developing a student's schedule or program

- Designing needed accommodations and adaptations

- Finding ways to ensure consistency and quality among school staff implementing a team's support plan

- Problem-solving about specific issues that arise

- Co-teaching

- Planning for successful transitions within and between schools, as well as successful transitions out of school

To address student needs, team members interact with each other by consulting, planning, problem-solving, and "touching base" with other team members throughout the school day (Figure 1.4). Team members carry out team-generated plans that provide support to the student(s) within the context of scheduled class activities. These plans are implemented both as the team members teach other students and as they work with the included student(s) alone.

Examples of team-centered efforts include:

- Understanding other team members' roles and talents

- Clarifying the team's values

- Learning to communicate effectively among team members

- Identifying and resolving concerns

- Reaching consensus on decisions

- Developing trust

To address team needs, team members should take time to celebrate their successes; to relate to each other as individuals and teammates; to process their teaming skills by self-reflection, self-assessment, observation, and monitoring skills that are weak; and to discuss and use skill-building strategies.

Collaborative teaming means:	. . . But does NOT mean:
• Learning from each other	• One-way learning
• Teaching each other	• One-way teaching
• Being trusting *and* trustworthy	• Being trusting *or* trustworthy
• Attending to and building teaming skills	• Ignoring communication problems
• Identifying common goals and working toward them	• Team goals are determined by individuals or competitively
• Using problem-solving approaches to resolve team-identified concerns	• Settling for solutions that are not team generated
• Communicating face to face and keeping team members current	• Leaving members not involved in a decision out of the communication loop
• Using agendas and time limits for scheduled sessions	• Wasting time *or* being so business-like that warm, personal exchange is lost
• Reviewing notes from past sessions	• Losing track of team decisions
• Sharing notes with absent team members	• Letting those absent become excluded
• Collaborating "on the fly" as well as in "sit-down" sessions	• Waiting for "sit-down" meetings to make decisions
• Making decisions by team consensus	• Making decisions by coercion or default
• Developing shared values over time through team self-examination and growth	• One rigid set of values *or* widespread divergence of beliefs about the team process

Figure 1.4. What collaborative teaming is and is not. (Adapted with permission from DeBoer, A., & Fister, S. [1995–1996]. *Working together: Tools for collaborative teaching.* Longmont, CO: Sopris West. All rights reserved.)

TEAM MEMBERS AND TEAM INTERACTIONS

The core members of most collaborative teams are teachers (the classroom teacher(s) and special educator(s) who serve the included student) and family members. The classroom teacher(s) and the special educator(s) primarily share the responsibility for teaching the focus student; however, other professional or paraprofessional team members sometimes contribute by teaching or by monitoring the student's performance during a teaching activity or routine.

The contributions that family members make to the core team are equally weighty. The family's perspective on the student may differ from that of the school's and, therefore, may provide a more accurate and complete picture of the student's abilities and needs.

Also, the family's perspective, along with their outlook on their child's educational priorities, is often rich with implications for in-struction and should influence team decisions about goals and programs.

Family members are part of the core team because they are the constant in their child's life: the "historians" of what has occurred and the observers of what is current in their child's life beyond school (Salisbury & Dunst, 1997). Limiting family members' involvement to attending formal meetings (eligibility and IEP meetings) or to giving consent for decisions means that their input either is too little or comes too late. The family's perspective, in addition to being listened to, understood, and respected by the other team members, should influence the child's program development (Soodak, in press). Professionals need to make sure to recognize family members as experts on their child.

Figure 1.5 shows members of the core team and the whole team. In addition to general and special educators and family members, several other individuals may be included on the core team. For example, when

the included students reach adolescence, they should participate as members of their own team so that they can offer their perspectives directly. Students may become more self-determined and feel more in control of their lives if they directly participate in planning their educational programs. Typically, focus students should participate in meetings during which key decisions are made, but not in all of the team meetings. In some cases, a paraprofessional may be added to the core team because a student's support needs are extensive. Finally, if there are other people who play a constant and critical role in the student's life, they, too, can become regular core members.

The speech-language therapist is a core member of Daniel's team because of her active involvement in developing his communication system. Because she is based in the school building, she makes daily contact with Daniel and his classroom teacher.

Rick attended his individualized education program (IEP) meeting with his entire team at the end of his freshman year when the focal point became his transition goals. Since then, Rick's viewpoints have been crucial in shaping his long-term goals for academics and job training.

The most active members of the core team will always be teachers and family members. Because family members are not available for face-to-face interactions as often as teachers are, many team discussions will only involve a small cluster of two or more people. Family members are, however, a part of the core team, so their input needs to be ongoing; they need to be involved in decision-making, and they should receive regular updates on how the team is implementing any decisions regarding the student. Teachers need to work with the family members to identify how communication will occur and how much and what types of involvement the family wants to

---

The whole team includes . . .

The core team plus others who work with the student:

- Additional family members

- Other teachers (e.g., academic classes, PE, Music, Art, Computer)

- School nurse

- Related services personnel

Speech-language pathologist (SLP), Occupational therapist (OT), Physical therapist (PT)

> **The core team includes . . .**
>
> - General education teacher(s)
> - Special education teacher
> - Family member(s)
> - *Sometimes* Paraprofessional(s), if involved with student
>   Focus student, when older
>   Others (highly involved)

- Vision/hearing Consultant

- Administrator

- Adapted PE teacher

- Peer(s)*

- Psychologist

- Guidance counselor

*(May or may not sit down with team)

Figure 1.5.   The core team and the whole team.

maintain. There is no "right" formula or frequency for participation by family members; instead, participation is determined with each individual family member and is allowed to change over time. Team interactions occur both during sit-down meetings and during spontaneous, "on the fly" exchanges:

- Sit-down meetings involve two or more team members. These meetings are held away from students and outside of scheduled class time, though not necessarily before or after school. The time, location, and agenda for a sit-down meeting are planned, even if only minimally. The meeting may involve many team members or only those members who are on the agenda or who are available. For students who receive special education services, more formal collaborative team meetings may center around planning a student's IEP, while less formal and more frequent team meetings address specific student needs, classwork modifications, and teacher concerns.

- Informal, "on the fly" interactions among a subset of the team take place frequently during the school day. During "on the fly" encounters, members "touch base" on the implementation of team plans and student progress and make adjustments to those plans. Interaction times may be planned or spontaneous and may occur during or after school. Students are often present and class activities may be ongoing but are under control.

While family members often participate in sit-down meetings, they are less likely to be a part of "on-the-fly" interactions during school hours. However, family members and teachers often take advantage of any spontaneous opportunities to quickly update each other and exchange information. These "on the fly" meetings might happen when parents drop off or pick up their child from school, at PTA meetings and school events, or during chance encounters in the community.

When the whole team is large, as is the case with Daniel's team, collaboration becomes challenging. Getting people together in one location and at one time is difficult enough, but keeping the whole team current on the daily or weekly interactions of the core team may seem impossible. (Strategies to organize teams and build teamwork skills are discussed in Chapters 2 and 3.)

Ms. Scott, Daniel's second-grade teacher, and Ms. Colley, the special education teacher, meet once or twice a week before school, sometimes with Ms. Johnson, the paraprofessional who supports Daniel and others in his classroom. On days when the occupational therapist and the physical therapist come into the classroom, both teachers touch base with them. Interaction with the speech-language therapist is easier because she does not travel between schools. Daniel's mom often picks him up after school and arrives a little early to check in with Daniel's teachers; if only Ms. Johnson is available, then Ms. Johnson shares Daniel's mother's comments with Ms. Scott and Ms. Colley. Daniel's teachers and his family exchange additional information via a notebook that Daniel carries back and forth from school every day. Every month the whole team meets to review progress and current issues.

COMPONENTS OF COLLABORATIVE TEAMWORK

It is helpful to view collaborative teamwork as a set of different, yet overlapping, components. The five components pictured in Figure 1.6 occur somewhat sequentially as a team forms and develops; however, each component maintains its importance even after its implementation. For example, in addition to an initiative from the principal to get the team underway, most lasting teams rely on some administrative support to organize and sustain themselves over time. Once a team is organized, it will make numerous decisions about a student or students during the school year and will also work to improve in-

---

Building team structure

- Set school policy on teaming.
- Define team purpose and focus.
- Establish team membership.
- Create and protect time and space.
- Support teams and teamwork.

Learning teamwork skills

- Listen and interact well.
- Develop shared values.
- Define team roles and responsibilities.
- Establish team meeting process and schedule.
- Prepare for and conduct meetings.
- Give and receive information.
- Make decisions by consensus.
- Team effectively "on the fly."
- Reflect on the team process.

Taking team action

- Problem-solve team concerns.
- Collaborate to design programs.
- Deliver coordinated programs.
- Assess student progress.
- Review and revise team action plans.

Teaching collaboratively

- Understand collaborative teaching.
- Plan at the school level.
- Understand tested organizational models and instructional strategies.
- Consider collaborative teaching strategies suited to grade level.
- Plan between collaborative teachers.
- Evaluate outcomes.

Improving communication and handling conflict

- Know and trust each other.
- Communicate accurately and unambiguously.
- Be sensitive to diverse cultures.
- Foster staff–family interaction.
- Take time to process group skills.
- Resolve conflicts and problems.

Figure 1.6.   Components of collaborative teaming.

terpersonal communication and address conflict within the team. When teams add new members at the beginning of each school year, the reconfigured team should take some time to review teamwork skills.

Daniel's core team will change when he goes to third grade and Ms. Scott is no longer a team member; however, many other members will remain the same. Most of the general education teachers on Rick's team will change when he moves into tenth grade, and vocational staff will be added to the team.

On both teams, the members who remain (special education teachers, family members, the related services staff for Daniel, and the counselor for Rick) plan team building activities to prepare the newly reconstituted teams for the beginning of the school year.

The ensuing chapters in this booklet are organized to address the following components:

1. Building team structure

2. Learning teamwork skills

3. Taking team action

4. Teaching collaboratively

5. Improving communication and handling conflict

This section will briefly describe each of these components.

Building Team Structure

Building team structure primarily relates to the formation and organization of collaborative teams. This component addresses the following questions:

- What is the team's purpose?
- What responsibility and authority does the team possess?
- On which student or students will the team focus?
- Who should be included on the core and whole teams?

These questions are more challenging to answer when schools are first initiating collaborative teams. As teachers gain experience with collaborative teaming they will find ways to modify the team structure to increase efficiency and effectiveness and to suit changing team members. Teaming experience usually improves collaborative teams.

The administrative leadership in the school (and perhaps also the central office administration, special education in particular) plays an important part in these first two components: building team structure and learning teamwork skills. Administrators often lay the foundation for inclusion and teaming, but they rely on teachers and staff to shape the school's vision or mission and to define many of the details for organizing teams. For example, many principals instill the value of collaborative teaming by the ways in which they share decision making with teachers and run faculty meetings. They also bring in resources to strengthen staff teaming skills, and they work with and rely on teams to plan supports for students. Principals may also assist in finding time for teams to meet and in protecting

those times. Because the two biggest barriers to collaborative teaming are negative staff attitudes and a lack of time, the principal's ability to influence the collaborative team process in these ways is crucial (Karge, McClure, & Patton, 1995).

Learning Teamwork Skills

There is agreement among experts on collaborative teaming that teaming skills are learned, not instinctual. The implication of this view is that training helps teams during their early stages of formation. Initially, team members need guidance and time to get to know each other's values, talents, faults, fears, and hopes. Team members then focus on discovering the values that they share regarding education and on defining both their team's role in furthering student learning and their individual roles and responsibilities in the process. Exploring various models for running team meetings (e.g., agenda, time frame, leadership roles, problem-solving methods) can help teams create their own teaming process to suit their purposes and goals.

Making decisions by consensus is a critical teamwork skill that may be more time-consuming than deciding by majority vote or by having a "team leader" decide. Team members should not learn to avoid conflict but, instead, should learn to focus on presenting their positions clearly and listening to other team members' viewpoints (Johnson & Johnson, 1997). Barriers such as group size, inadequate discussion time, unprepared or self-centered members, a lack of information, and conflicting goals all can contribute to a team's failure to reach a consensus on decisions.

Finally, teams must continue to function well outside of the meeting times when they work to implement their plans. Members need to continue to communicate, problem-solve, and make decisions about refining plans outside of the scheduled team meetings. Successful team functioning is not automatic but depends on trust, equal status, open-mindedness, and good communication skills; it improves with guidance, practice, and self-assessment.

Taking Team Action

In addressing student needs, teams apply their creative energy to several key areas: solving team concerns, collaborating to design programs, delivering coordinated programs, assessing student progress, and reviewing and revising team action plans. The cycle that teams use to take action is ongoing throughout the school year, occurs within and outside of team meetings, and seems to follow several predictable steps: identify the problem, gather information, generate potential solutions, evaluate potential solutions, implement a plan, and evaluate the implemented plan (Snell & Janney, in press). Even though many people routinely engage in brainstorming and problem-solving, teams often benefit from instruction and guided practice in using several efficient problem-solving approaches. Designing instructional programs for students that are geared toward individualized educational objectives in academic and social areas often requires team members to gather assessment information for consideration in identifying the supports that a student needs to learn. Additional data may need to be gathered to evaluate the success of the team's plans in promoting student learning. Team members may work together to observe student performance and collect data, to bring assessment data back to the team, and to analyze the data for ways to improve the student's educational program.

Teaching Collaboratively

When team members take action together in classrooms, they often choose from the several different approaches that were defined previously. For example, if the team is using the pull-in approach, they schedule planned supports and services to be provided in the classroom or during class activity.

Rick's counselor and his special education teacher take turns spending time with Rick before school assemblies and during activities when added support seems necessary. Sometimes, they pull Rick aside and rehearse the upcoming event (e.g., where he

will sit, what will happen during the event and afterward). Early in the school year, these team members visited several classes and quietly reminded Rick to use his daily agenda or to check his work organizer. During team sessions, team members modeled prevention methods for teachers to use with Rick.

Team members also may apply a co-teaching approach, whereby specialized teachers (special educator, adapted physical educator), and, occasionally, therapists, counselors, or other team members, teach cooperatively with classroom teachers. Co-teaching may extend temporarily over a unit:

Daniel's physical therapist works with the entire second grade when a science unit on the body and movement is taught; she teaches the students about Daniel's positioning equipment and his needs for physical support.

Co-teaching also may be scheduled on a regular basis in a classroom:

Rick's special education teacher usually works with several small groups during general math class; consequently, while she monitors Rick's progress, she can also assist others in the class who are having difficulty with math.

Teams create their own variations of co-teaching to address the support that students need to function successfully in a general education classroom.

For some students, teams may use yet a third approach: pull-out services with collaborative planning. Students should be removed from general education classrooms for instruction only when teams agree on the purpose, the time frame, and the need. Oftentimes, rather than removing a single student with disabilities from the general education classroom, a small mixed group of classmates could benefit from pull-out services. Teams who plan to use pull-out do so for a number of reasons:

- Students have functional skill goals in their programs that require instruction on and around school grounds or in the community (e.g., street crossing, making purchases, learning a job).

- Students have needs in personal care skills and require privacy.

- A student's learning in the classroom can be furthered with intermittent, intensive tutoring in small groups or alone.

Pull-out requires initial planning up front, as well as ongoing communication about student progress with team members who are not directly involved with the pull-out services. Team planning for individual students means that students will have their own personalized supports delivered through suitable collaborative teaming approaches.

Daniel's team members created an individually designed plan for supporting Daniel that suits his IEP objectives and meshes both with Daniel's second-grade schedule and with staff schedules (Figure 1.7). Pull-out is used only for 6-week assessment checks by the physical therapist and for Daniel's daily personal needs. Pull-in instructional support and co-teaching occur daily and involve Daniel's special education teacher, his therapists, and the teaching assistant. Co-teaching occurs during language arts groups.

Improving Communication and Handling Conflict

For most teams, the formation of quality interpersonal relationships between team members is the most difficult facet of teaming. Effective teamwork depends on team members getting to know each other personally and professionally. Trust between team members emerges from familiarity and positive teamwork. Trust builds an atmosphere of comfortable interdependency and mutual respect, which is highly conducive to productive teamwork. Sometimes, teams will need to identify barriers that are inhibiting team functioning. For example, when members are insensitive to cultural diversity (in each other or in their students), anger can arise, which blocks communication and trust. Family members who feel like outsiders instead of team members may not feel comfortable making contributions, causing school staff to complain about a lack of parental "involvement."

Different perspectives on learning and on a particular student can result in conflict between team members; however, conflict or differences of opinion that result from members' "slant on things" can also be a great asset to a team. As Rainforth and York-Barr noted, "a primary reason for group, as opposed to individual, problem-solving is that differences in perspective can result in higher quality solutions to complex challenges" (1997, p. 295). To achieve these benefits, team

Team Support Approaches			
Student	Collaborative planning with pull-out	Collaborative planning with pull-in	Co-teaching
Daniel	Every 6 weeks: PT checks Daniel's movement and equipment. M-F: All staff use pull-out for bathroom skills.	M-F: OT, PT, speech-language teacher and special education teacher are scheduled to be in second-grade classroom.	M-F: Special education teacher teaches with Ms. Scott during language arts groups.

Figure 1.7.   Teaming approaches used with Daniel by team members.

members need to work through conflict constructively by engaging in trusting communication about their differences.

Team processing is crucial to maintaining healthy communication among team members. Teams regularly take meeting time to assess how well they are doing both in accomplishing student outcomes and interpersonally. In taking time to reflect on their collaborative process, team members might start a meeting by celebrating their successes since their last meeting. During the meeting, they might pause to ask, "How are we doing as a team?" and, "How are we doing on our student-focused tasks?" (Thousand & Villa, 1992). As teaming issues arise, experienced teams will shift their focus from the student to themselves in an attempt to resolve the blocks to communication that have arisen. Although ongoing team evaluation is not easy, it is essential to the health of team functioning. Teams must take time to explore their actions, to celebrate their successes, and to smooth their rough edges.

THE BENEFITS OF COLLABORATIVE TEAMING

Today's classrooms are filled with students who are diverse in their skills and entry knowledge, their motivation to learn, their home life and past experiences, and their languages. An array of teachers and consultative professionals with complementary talents is needed to promote learning in these classrooms, thereby making communication and collaboration between teachers essential. But, are teachers motivated to work together, or are they just "scared into" doing so because of the challenges students bring to their classrooms? Judith Little (1990), a researcher who has ob-

served in many schools, found that the intellectual, emotional, and social demands of teaching do, in fact, motivate teachers to team with other teachers.

In the 1990s, as inclusion has increased, many authors have reported the pivotal advantages of planning and creating solutions within a collaborative team (e.g., Johnson & Johnson, 1997; Rainforth & York-Barr, 1997; Thousand & Villa, 1992). These benefits include the following:

1. Shared decision-making appears to yield better decisions and results.

2. Both teachers and administrators appear to be motivated by the increase in shared decision-making and power.

3. Collaborative teaming is reported to enhance teachers' satisfaction with their jobs; they enjoy the regular exchange of resources and expertise, the sense of belonging, the freedom from isolation, and the intellectual stimulation.

4. When team members have been instrumental in forming a plan, they report that they are more committed to the plan's implementation and success.

5. Communication and collaborative skills are viewed as essential abilities for being effective in most jobs today.

Team members provide educational supports using a variety of approaches. Each support approach (e.g., collaborative teaching, pull-in support, and, less often, pull-out support with teaming) entails cooperative exchange and decision-making between team members and allows for the provision of necessary supports. The benefits of collaborative teaming for students and team members far outnumber the costs.

Chapter 2

Building Team Structure

"When we started Quincey that first year in summer school, he couldn't sit for 3 minutes without yelling or fussing and moving all over the place. So, as far as learning to listen and behave like his peers, he's come a long way. Now, he seems to be paying attention, although not always to me. I notice him watching the other children's reactions to me, and I think that's good for him, too. He has ways to communicate now, whereas he didn't before.

"That first summer, we were just learning to be a team. We didn't know each other, and some of us didn't even know Quincey very well; but, we all knew that if we could just get him communicating, it would help him so much. We knew there was no magical thing that would make him communicate overnight; we had to figure it out." (Quincey's third-grade teacher)

What is the next step once a school community has made the decision to include all students in the mainstream? Although there is no formula or any rigid set of steps that works in all cases, there are some definite actions that schools can take to facilitate students' success in general education environments, including building a structure for collaborative teams to work in school environments as one of the initial actions. The content of this chapter is organized around five tasks that are fundamental to building a collaborative team structure (see Figure 1.5). The school that Quincey attended had worked through each of these five tasks before Quincey entered the third grade; consequently, Quincey's core team understood their roles, though they were still learning how to fill them. After several months of school, Quincey's collaborative team functioned well together, and they were taking actions that resulted in Quincey's successful participation in third grade (these actions are described in subsequent chapters).

DEVELOP SCHOOL POLICY ON TEAMING

Administrative Leadership and Negative Attitudes

Many school systems have begun giving teachers important roles in decision-making. Principals often involve their staff in the hiring of new teachers and administrators as well as in school budget planning, curriculum improvements, and self-study activities. In the early preparation phase, before inclusive programs and collaborative teams are implemented, the building administrator's leadership is crucial in getting staff to examine their values, to understand inclusion, and to learn how collaborative teaming aids in the inclusion of students with disabilities in general education. With the support of building administrators, teaching and professional support staff need to play a major role in developing the school's values regarding inclusion and collaboration, in addition to defining a structure that will support collaborative teaming.

In Chapter 1, we discussed teachers' negative attitudes toward the teaming process as the predominant factor that hinders collaboration (Karge et al., 1995). What are some possible reasons for these attitudes?

1. A lack of clarity about what inclusion is and why the school is advocating for it

2. Limited interaction with students who have disabilities

3. Fears about having students with special needs in class

4. Lack of knowledge of what collaborative teaming entails or past bad experiences with teaming

5. Anticipation that teaming will be time-consuming and concern about having adequate time

Additional causes of teachers' negative attitudes toward teaming can be found in the failure of the school community to 1) self-

examine its stance on inclusion or 2) work with staff to develop and implement a teaming structure for the school. The process involved in adopting inclusive practices and implementing collaborative teams in a school can be broken down into three phases: 1) preparation phase: schools prepare for inclusion and teaming; 2) implementation phase: students are included and teams are being used to plan, problem-solve, and implement student supports; 3) maintenance phase: teams are in use and relied on by building administrators and staff; self-evaluation and improvement are ongoing.

Building administrators play a critical role in each phase. This next section addresses specific actions that administrators, in cooperation with other school staff, can take to develop a school policy on teaming. Figure 2.1 provides a checklist of some of the different phases of these actions.

Phases of Policy Development and Administrative Support for Teams

Administrators fill important support roles for teams as school policies on inclusion and collaborative teams are developed. As described next, their roles and the actions they take are modified to fit the phase of development: preparation, implementation, and maintenance.

Preparation In many schools, principals and assistant principals initiate discussions with staff members in regard to potential school improvements and inclusion. These discussions often lead to recommendations by the staff members for collaborative teaming. Sometimes, district policy changes have helped to initiate inclusion and to make teaming a recommended districtwide practice; however, before there can be schoolwide adoption of a structure and a procedure for team development, schools (and districts) need to examine their reasons for serving students inclusively and develop a mission statement or a shared purpose. Schools should not begin to form collaborative teams without first taking

some time to examine their values and beliefs. Shared values provide a firm foundation for the creation of collaborative teams.

To define a common mission or shared values, building administrators often schedule an in-service day and explore questions such as, "What are our beliefs regarding learning and regarding the students whom we serve?" or, "What is our purpose?" Sometimes, forums are held during which parents and other members of the school community who are interested in inclusion can voice their concerns and obtain answers to their questions. Information on inclusion is usually supplied in response to any concerns or questions that are raised and, consequently, a vision for a school begins to develop. Teachers and staff, along with representative parents and students, then work toward consensus on the school's mission or vision. Mission statements become a primary guide for those who design a school's major goals and its instructional program and activities in that they often clarify the need for collaborative teams (Roach, 1995). Figure 2.2 provides examples of several mission statements.

Another effective action that administrators can take during the preparation phase is to provide positive, personal experiences that challenge existing beliefs and attitudes (Giangreco, Dennis, Cloninger, Edelman, & Schattman, 1993). In fact, what seems to have the strongest effect on negative attitudes about disability is information plus interaction with individuals who have disabilities. Thus, schools may find it helpful to listen to teams from other schools who have been successful with inclusion and collaboration, to view illustrative videos on these topics, and to visit schools that practice inclusion and then evaluate these experiences as a group. Perhaps even more powerful than learning about methods of inclusion and collaboration are direct experiences with adults and students who have disabilities. Giangreco and his colleagues tracked the changes in the perspectives of 19 general education teachers who

Phase			Actions that may be taken
P	**I**	**M**	
X			• Plan times for open dialogue at the district level and the school level about inclusive education and its benefits and challenges.
X	X		• Arrange for staff to view and learn more about inclusive school models (e.g., visits, videos, panels from schools). Participate in these workshop sessions with staff.
X	X	X	• Attend workshops on inclusion and related topics as collaborative teams; process in-service content as teams
X	X		• Recognize that staff have varying levels of comfort, understanding, and values about inclusion; provide time for staff to learn and experience the new philosophy and gain comfort with the changes inclusion brings.
X	X		• With teachers, plan for a schoolwide program on ability awareness or "climate for learning" to emphasize themes of appreciation and understanding of diversity.
X	X		• Be alert to staff morale and use team-building activities during the school year to promote collegiality.
X			• Engage staff in creating a common definition of their school community—one that addresses what it is (or is becoming) and why. Expand this definition into a mission statement to guide school improvement.
X	X	X	• Involve all stakeholders in reaching mutual decisions
X	X	X	• Identify school- and grade-level inclusion goals, and support taking small steps towards those goals.
X	X	X	• Make use of "round robin" brainstorming at meetings to hear all voices.
X	X	X	• Recognize that listening and being empathic may be more useful than solving a problem.
	X	X	• Recognize and celebrate successes.
	X	X	• Be alert and responsive to staff needs as they change over time.
	X	X	• Make consultative services available to general educators and collaborative teams.
	X	X	• Know that support takes different forms and functions for different classroom teachers; develop a school/district menu of support options.
	X	X	• Encourage staff/teams to share their ideas and resources with others.
	X	X	• Orient new staff to school philosophy and progress; link them with strong teams.
	X	X	• Find ways to record, share, and publicize student success stories.

P = Preparation: As schools are preparing for inclusion
I = Implementation: As teams are being planned and implemented
M = Maintenance: Once teams are in use

Figure 2.1.   A building administrator's checklist for building collaborative teaming during preparation, implementation, & maintenance phases. (*Sources:* Hennen, Opatz, Perlman, & Read [n.d.]; NICHCY, 1995; and Roach, 1995.)

had a student with extensive support needs included in their classrooms (with the necessary individualized supports pulled in). They identified a positive "transformation" in 17 of the 19 teachers; the teachers changed from being uninvolved and noninteractive with the student, to taking ownership, increasing their involvement with the students, and, finally, changing their language from cautious and negative to positive and optimistic. These transformations were gradual and progressive rather than fast and abrupt. Teachers credited their transformations to several things: teamwork and shared goals, the efforts of the special education staff, recognition and validation of their contributions, and the pres-

Voices from the Classroom

The mission statement of one school system in Virginia identified five rules to follow in their integration of students with special education needs:

1. "We accept the responsibility for the success of every student.
2. We believe in the inherent dignity and worth of each individual.
3. We believe every student can learn.
4. Projecting a segregated attitude within an integrated setting will not work.
5. What we are doing is consistent with what we want, believe, and know about children and educational best practice." (Roach, 1995, p. 8)

Mission statements can be written for entire states, as has been done in Michigan and New Mexico, for example. Michigan's broad mission statement for student outcomes applies to all school districts:

- "A person who values and is capable of learning over a lifetime
- A person capable of applying knowledge in diverse situations
- A competent and productive participant in society" (National Association of State Board of Education [NASBE], 1992, p. 9)

The vision statement for the New Mexico State Department of Education reads in part: "... We believe education must challenge all students to reach their potential" (NASBE, 1992, p. 20). Ultimately, the faculty and administrators of each school need to examine their school's philosophy and, then, establish consensus on the elements of their philosophy that define their unique mission.

Figure 2.2. Examples of mission statements.

ence of the child with disabilities (Giangreco et al., 1993).

The in-service training planned for schools during this phase needs to be tailored to match the staff's concerns in addition to their skills; therefore, administrators should work closely with teachers and inclusion specialists to plan each training session. (Inclusion specialists are individuals who have extensive firsthand experience with inclusive programs; they may be employed by the school district or hired as consultants to advise schools.) Giangreco and his colleagues (1993) found that traditional preparatory training for teachers that addressed the inclusion of students with extensive support needs in general education classrooms was not as beneficial as expected. Some teachers thought that their initial fears about inclusion kept them from absorbing the information offered in these traditional preparatory workshops. These same teachers identified two beneficial methods for alleviating their fears:

- Direct experience working with a child with disabilities (who comes to class with the essential supports)

- Nontraditional ongoing training about inclusion and teaming ("Nontraditional" meaning that both the content of training and the timing of its delivery were atypical)

The most influential of these nontraditional training practices identified by teachers included the following:

1. Hearing about the feelings and experiences of other teachers in inclusive classrooms

2. Learning about the elements of inclusion that were critical to starting the school year: teamwork, ways to interact with and what to expect from the included student(s), roles and schedules of the special education staff, and methods of involving class members in creative problem solving

3. Learning about successful approaches from experienced teachers (e.g., cooperative groups and activity-based teaching, group strategies, ways to use and adapt typical materials and class activities for included students)

These valuable nontraditional training methods were implemented during the preparation phase once class placement decisions were made and before the school year started.

Implementation   Because they exercise ultimate control over school schedules and space, school administrators play an important role during the team implementation phase. Basic questions need to be addressed, such as, "Why will we form teams (team purpose)?" "When will teams meet?" and, "Where will we meet?" During the implementation phase, building administrators will continue to listen and respond to the obstacles teams face as they form and develop. With teachers' input, principals will arrange in-service training and consultation on teaming topics that refine teachers' emerging skills (e.g., problem solving, reaching consensus, teamwork skills) and that address implementation issues (e.g., ideas for teaching and assessing collaboratively, improving family participation).

During both the implementation and maintenance phases, it is often valuable for building administrators to hold regular discussions with staff regarding their successes and concerns with inclusion. The meetings provide another collaborative forum for problem-solving that involves the principal and extends to all staff. In one elementary school, for example, the principal holds monthly staff discussions on inclusion progress; he begins these sessions by giving each staff member an opportunity to share a success story that pertains to inclusion. The remainder of the time is then devoted to quick group problem-solving using an issue/action format:

- One person volunteers to take notes on large poster paper.
- Staff members take turns and share successes.

- Staff members take turns and briefly describe a single concern they may have.
- The principal facilitates fast-paced brainstorming from the group.
- Needed actions are determined and given target completion dates, and responsible staff members are identified.
- The next meeting starts with quick updates regarding these actions.

As school staff members take turns sharing issues or asking for support with particular students or difficulties, the rest of the staff members gain a broader view of inclusion and teaming issues. A loose time structure of 6 minutes per teacher enables all kindergarten through fifth-grade teachers to share and obtain immediate feedback, in the form of four to five suggestions, from the other group members. Their schoolwide inclusion meetings are over within an hour. The responsibility of taking notes with an Issue/Action Planning form rotates among the staff members. Once notes from the large paper are rewritten onto notebook paper and copied, each meeting has a record and decisions can be reviewed. The principal actively provides suggestions and support. The outcomes of these collaborative group sessions include positive solutions and shared celebrations about progress. Sometimes such a forum can give a team the boost it needs to move forward, either by assisting in the resolution of a concern or by giving staff members a feel for other teams' progress and issues. Figure 2.3 shows the notes from an actual "issue/action" meeting (a blank Issue/Action Planning Form is included in Appendix A).

Maintenance   In the maintenance phase, some actions that administrators have taken during preparation or initiation (e.g., issue/action problem-solving at the school level, "prescriptive" in-service training) will continue, while other actions will be added or discontinued. The emphasis during this phase is on the refinement and evolution of the collaborative team's function and process. Team functions and outcomes need to be visibly integrated into the standard school procedure

Issue/Action Planning Form

Team/Student/Group: _Inclusion Support Mtg._   **Date:** _November 2, 1998_

Team members present: _Rob, Brenda, Ray, Kari, Sue, Maryanne, Norine, Alice, Jan, Ruth,_

Kathy, Joslyn , Sarah, Flo, Bert

Issue	Planned Action	Person(s) Responsible
1. Novels on tape needed, especially for students with LD in 3rd/4th	Check w/ library for the blind; student in building has these services & can share—catalogs available	Kenna get catalogs to Maryanne
2. Self-esteem builders for classrooms	Guidance counselor get info. for classroom teachers—get list of teachers—put in mailbox	Brenda
3. Absenteeism that is chronic—2 students in 5th grade—at IEP's	Teacher share action plan w/asst. principal & he will write letter	Rob/Kari
4. Weed wacker during class times disturb 2nd grade, esp. child w/autism	Call maintenance dept. (principal) for before/after school weed wacking only!	Ray
5. Problems in many rooms w/underachievers; students who are not SE identified—"at-risk"	Need remediation ideas: • Contact spec. ed. office for ideas • Counseling groups w/guidance • Parent Volunteers in classroom	Kenna Brenda Sue

Figure 2.3. Issue/Action Planning Form.

so staff members see the significance of their work. Improvement of team function will continue to be a priority during this phase, though in-service training might shift to more focused topics including communication, co-teaching, handling team conflict, and transitions between grades and schools.

DEFINE TEAM PURPOSE AND FOCUS

The overall purpose of collaborative teams is to promote student learning and success in school. Student-level teams, which are the focus of this book, are groups of people organized to address the learning needs and priorities of individual students or groups of students (York-Barr, 1996). Teams may choose a narrow or wide focus in addressing these student-centered purposes. For students with numerous support needs, the team's focus is often on that particular student; other times, teams may work to address the needs of all students from a single classroom who require extra support to be successful.

• *Individual student teams:* Teams organized to address the needs of single students. When a student is eligible for special education,

this team also is involved in planning and reviewing the individualized education program (IEP).

• *Classroom/Grade-level teams:* Teams formed to address support issues pertaining to individual students in a classroom or to an entire grade level (see Figure 2.4).

Quincey, who has been diagnosed as having autism, is a member of Carla Breedon's fourth-grade class. In addition to his classroom teacher, Quincey's core team includes Ms. Colley (special education teacher), his parents, and his speech-language pathologist. The core team meets once a month with frequent verbal exchange between meetings. Quincy's teachers meet weekly but interact daily as they work together to implement and adapt classroom instruction and school activities for Quincy. Also, on a monthly basis, Ms. Breedon meets with the other fourth-grade teachers and Ms. Colley to address student-focused, grade-level issues.

Although these two arrangements for collaborative teams (teams formed around a single student and those formed for entire classrooms or grade levels) are the primary focus of this book, there are several other ways teams can organize to fulfill their purpose and focus on students:

• Multigrade teams: When a school is small (with only one to two classrooms per grade level), multigrade teams might be an option (e.g., K–first-grade team, second- and third-grade team, fourth- and fifth-grade team). Although this arrangement helps with transition and facilitates continuity of collaboration, the size of the team and the number of students on whom the team focuses may prevent adequate attention to individual students or classrooms (Figure 2.5).

• Department teams: Secondary school teachers may choose to organize themselves into teams by academic department. When special education staff are active members (or regular drop-ins) on these teams, the learning and success of students with special needs who are enrolled in general education classes in that department can be promoted.

• Ad hoc problem-solving or teacher assistance teams: These teams consist of teachers and other professional support staff who meet to address specific students who are exhibiting difficulties; teams take action before formal consideration for special education services ("pre-referral") and may, consequently, avoid referring a student to special education (Porter, Wilson, Kelly, & Den Otter, 1991; Pugach & Johnson, 1988; West & Idol, 1990).

• Related services teams: These teams include teachers and therapists whose focus is limited to the students who receive the team's related services and the issues surrounding those services (e.g., scheduling, types of therapy support).

Teams also can form to address short- or long-term system-level and building-level

Voices from the Classroom

At Collingwood Elementary, a K–5 grade school of about 475 children, most special education teachers are assigned to a combination of grade level teams, while special education teachers assigned to the fifth-grade work with no other grade levels. One special education teacher who is trained across categories of special education works with the fifth-grade team. This teacher attends weekly fifth-grade team meetings during which many issues on students and inclusion are discussed among the teachers; she also attends weekly individual planning meetings (for the students with the most significant needs) during which she meets with a single fifth-grade teacher regarding a particular student. These meetings last about 15–20 minutes.

Figure 2.4. How special education teachers are assigned to grades in one elementary school. (Contributed by Kenna Colley.)

Voices from the Classroom

Two approaches have been used to organize teachers into teams in elementary schools: a *grade by grade organization* (in larger schools) or a *grade clustering organization* (in smaller schools). Greenfield Elementary, a small K through fifth-grade school, applied a grade clustering approach and teamed up the fourth- and fifth-grade teachers with one special education teacher and one paraprofessional. This group met together every 2 weeks; related services personnel, "special" teachers (art, music, P.E., etc.), the counselor, and the principal rotated among the team meetings or attended when specifically requested. The school also organized two similar teams for grades K–1 and 2–3. In elementary schools, such as Greenfield, where special education teachers have *cross-categorical training* (i.e., across different disability areas), they may serve a variety of students and rotate across multiple grades to lend support to students. However, staff in inclusive elementary schools usually prefer to have a special education teacher assigned to one specific grade level so familiarity and trust develop.

Figure 2.5.   Grade clustered teams in a small elementary school.

goals. System-level goals may include writing a curriculum, planning textbook changes, or studying the ways in which related services are delivered to students. Building-level teams address school-specific issues, such as designing plans to involve families, site-based decision-making, studying staff development needs, and designing a discipline plan. The general principles for building teams, learning teamwork skills, taking team action, improving communication, and evaluating outcomes apply across all three types—systems-level, building-level, and student-level—of team arrangements.

Figure 2.6 illustrates the variety of collaborative teams that can be implemented in inclusive schools in order to plan education programs for students and to collaborate on related changes within schools and at the systems level. The configuration of collaborative teams chosen by a particular school should relate to classroom, school, and system needs in addition to the phase of inclusion and team development that the school system or individual school is in.

ESTABLISH TEAM MEMBERSHIP

Who should be chosen as team members to provide support to a given student or group of students? Teams should consist of those people who work closely with the student and know him or her well. For students who have IEPs, team members should be those service providers listed on the plan who work with the student. We have already defined the core team members as those who play major roles in planning, implementing, and overseeing a student's daily education schedule; they include the general educator(s), special educator, family member(s), and sometimes others. A student's whole team is often larger; in addition to the core team members, it includes other people who are needed in the educational process but whose involvement is required less frequently.

Three questions can be used to identify who should be on a student's core and whole or extended teams (Thousand & Villa, 1992, p. 77):

- *Who has the talent and expertise that the team must have to make the best decisions for that student(s)?* To make informed decisions about students, teams depend on having the needed expertise and experience so they can identify, understand, and resolve concerns that arise.

- *Who is affected by the team's decisions?* Those affected by team decisions need to have a voice. For example, this means that students should be represented by family members when they are younger and, when older, by peers and directly through their own participation. If a paraprofessional is heavily in-

	Examples in inclusive schools		
Collaborative team level	*Elementary School*	*Middle/Junior High School*	*High School*
Student-Level	• Individual student teams • Classroom teams • Grade level teams • K–1, 2–3, 4–5 teams	• Individual student teams • Grade level teams	• Individual student teams • Department teams (math, English, science, social studies, vocational, health & PE)
School-Level	• Site-based committee • Inclusion team • GIRDLE meeting[1] • Issue-Action Planning Team	• Site-based committee • Inclusion Team	• Site-based committee • Departmental heads
Systems-Level	• District Inclusion Team • "Rocket Scientists" Team[2] • Consulting Teacher Team[3]		

[1] GIRDLE (Getting Into Really Discussing Learning and Experiences) meeting—A monthly meeting of all teachers aimed at problem-solving and voicing new ideas. Teachers submit issues; two are selected which seem to be the most pressing. Those whose issues have been selected have 5 minutes to present the issue, answer questions about the issue, and then listen as the invited guest while the other teachers brainstorm ideas to address the issue. The meeting is limited to 60 minutes. Snacks are served; the special education consulting teacher facilitates. Guests invited are from outside the school and are chosen to share new ideas or information on pressing problems. Another method involves one person describing an issue to the group, with whining allowed.
[2] A team whose members include special education teachers, representatives from related services (e.g., OT, PT, speech-language, adapted PE), and general education teachers who meet at a district level to discuss and resolve concerns.
[3] A team whose members include all of the consulting special education teachers in a district; they meet, give and obtain information, discuss and resolve issues regarding inclusion, and take ideas back to their schools.

Figure 2.6. Examples of collaborative teams used at elementary, middle, and high school levels. (With contributions from Johnna Elliott and Cynthia Pitonyak.)

volved in service delivery, he or she needs to have a voice as well.

• *Who has an interest in participating?* People who are excited about contributing to a student's educational program often bring energy, ideas, and creativity to the team, even if their involvement might not be as great as other core members.

When students need more services than a small core team can provide, member selection is not as simple. The bottom line for determining who should participate on a student's team is that team membership be directly related to the student's needs.

Rainforth and York-Barr (1997) addressed several factors that require careful consideration when deciding who will be a core or whole team member for a given student or for a set of students.

How Many Members Should Be on a Team?

Generally, smaller teams require less energy to gather together and fewer schedules to coordinate; consequently, they make communication easier. Members of smaller teams are more familiar with one another, which leads to more task involvement and a greater sense of responsibility (Johnson & Johnson, 1997). Larger

teams, however, often translate into more resources and greater expertise; however, coordination, accountability, and contribution by individual members may actually be reduced. Oftentimes, general education teachers are overwhelmed by too many team members serving the same student.

A study of team membership for students with multiple disabilities found that team size ranged from five to eleven members (Giangreco, Dennis, Edelman, & Cloninger, 1994). In secondary schools, teams get even larger:

Rick, who is a ninth grader, is served by seven general education teachers (one from each of his general education classes), a number of teaching assistants who alternate across his day, and several special education teachers (one of whom oversees Rick's vocational training in the community). The guidance counselor and school psychologist are extended team members, and Rick's parents both work closely with the team as core members. Because 15 people provide support for Rick, about the only time everyone is in the room together for a meeting is when they are discussing Rick's IEP. A lot of communication is done in writing so that team members can provide input even if they can't be at the more frequent planning meetings. Johnna, Rick's lead special education teacher, knows that "whenever we have a planning meeting, almost everyone will have a conflicting meeting or two; therefore, we ask for everyone's input first and then give each team member information about the meeting's outcome. If it's an IEP meeting, the outcome is an Issue/Action Plan or a Program-at-a-Glance. Once each team member is informed about the meeting outcome, I touch base with everyone and we work on-the-fly to make things happen."

Johnson and Johnson (1997) reported that all teams that were judged to be effective ranged in number from 2 to 25 members; however, most of the effective teams had fewer than 10 members. When teams are constructed with core team members who meet frequently and whole team members who meet less often and have good communication between the two groups, many of the advantages of both smaller (core) teams and larger (whole) teams can be realized (Giangreco, 1996).

How Involved Can a Team Member Be?

The degree to which a team member can become involved on a particular student's team is a function of several factors, including the access he or she has to the student and the school, the distance that the member must travel to serve the student, and the "caseload" of students whom the member already serves. To be a contributing team member, a person has to know the student and environment and relate to the other team members, all of which require physical presence and interaction. Sometimes, potential team members who do not have adequate access to the student or the environment will serve as consultants to the core team (i.e., they visit "on demand" and focus on a specific student issue) or will offer input to the team through individual family or professional members.

Corrie, who is a regional specialist on autism, participates periodically on Quincey's team. Because she serves several school districts, Corrie often is not available; however, when she is available, she contributes valuable information on autism to the core team members and adds new strategies to the core team's program plans.

What Skills and Knowledge Do Potential Team Members Have?

A third consideration for the selection of team members is their knowledge and skill level. Some experts suggest that team members should be selected based on their expertise, skills, and potential for learning new skills, not because of their position or personality (Johnson & Johnson, 1997). When there is overlap in ability and experience, though not in actual job title, among team members,

it often is better to select a smaller team of members who have excellent access to the student than to have a larger team with redundant skills. Sometimes, team members will have training and experience that bridge different categories of disability (in special education, this is referred to as *cross-categorical training*). These individuals often are more versatile in the supports they provide, particularly on classroom or grade-level teams or with students who have multiple disabilities.

The guiding principle for selecting team members is to balance these factors: teaming efficiency, team members' time available to work with students and other team members, and the match between members' abilities and students' needs (Figure 2.7).

CREATE AND PROTECT TIME AND SPACE FOR TEAMING

After team membership has been established, team members will address two questions: How much time is needed to meet? and, Where will we find the time? The next section describes guidelines for team members to answer these questions.

Time Needed for Teams to Meet

How much meeting time is needed for a team to support a student with special needs? Al-though there is no actual numerical answer to this question, several general guidelines exist for determining the amount of time teams need both for "sit-down" meetings and for "on-the-fly" communications:

1. Students who have more complex disabilities, less supportive families, and/or display atypical or disruptive social behavior usually need more support and, consequently, require more involvement and time from team members.

2. The core team members of students with high support needs often meet weekly and communicate daily.

3. The core team members of students with fewer support needs may meet every 1–3 weeks but communicate at least weekly and often several times a week.

4. When paraprofessional staff are involved in the support, they should communicate daily with the special education and the general education teachers.

5. When related services staff are involved in the support, they should communicate with the classroom staff (general education teacher and paraprofessional or special education teacher if present) whenever they are scheduled with the student and should give verbal or written com-

---

Rule: Balance efficiency, time available, and diversity of knowledge and skill

1. Select only one to be a member if two or more team members overlap in their skills.
2. Select the member who can address multiple challenges or student needs.
3. Select the person with better access to the student, if two or more potential members have similar competencies.
4. Identify a member with ongoing student involvement and provide technical assistance, If none of the potential members have adequate knowledge/skills to address a priority area.
5. Let two members with similar but non-overlapping skills work together and teach each other with the goal of a divided caseload (gives more time for involvement with individual students).
6. Focus on matching student challenges and needs with competencies of team members.

Note: The type/amount of services provided must match the IEP.

Figure 2.7.   Guidelines for selecting support personnel as team members. (From Rainforth, B., & York-Barr, J. [1997]. *Collaborative teams for students with severe disabilities: Integrating therapy and educational services* [2nd ed.] [pp. 262–264]. Baltimore: Paul H. Brookes Publishing Co.; adapted by permission.)

ments to the special education teacher on a pre-planned basis.

6. Schools and teams decide on written approaches to preserve the decisions made in meetings (e.g., Issue/Action Person Responsible notes, meeting minutes) and to share the decisions with team members.

7. Family members and teachers decide how they will communicate (e.g., in person before or after school, traveling notebook, telephone, voice-mail, e-mail) and how often, as well as what meetings families will/can attend.

Communication among team members between meetings must also be planned and valued. The preceding guidelines for meeting frequency are only general rules, and most teams will adopt the general principle, "Meet when there is a reason to meet and let the agenda drive the meeting."

Finding the Time to Plan

Probably the biggest challenge for most teams is finding the time to meet (e.g., Idol, 1990; Karge et al., 1995; West & Cannon, 1988). General and special education teachers may not have common planning times. Often, special education teachers in elementary schools have no planning time. Paraprofessionals, if part of the team, sometimes have contracts that do not pay after-school hours or have after-school duties or other jobs. Related services staff frequently rotate across schools. Although it is the nature of the job that teachers and school staff working in public schools will always find their time short and scheduling difficult, there are some solutions.

First, building administrators and teachers need to confront both sides of the time problem, including the shortage of available time and schedule conflicts. Meeting times for teams will always be influenced by building-wide scheduling decisions. Principals can facilitate team scheduling by understanding the value of team meetings and, with teacher assistance, exploring ways to make time available and to coordinate staff schedules.

Second, numerous creative approaches exist that can make use of in-school planning time before after-school or before-school time is tapped. It is sometimes helpful for school staff to develop a list of planning options that they regularly add to and review, such as those found in Figure 2.8. Figure 2.9 describes one school's plan to designate one day every 2 weeks as Collaboration Day.

Third, scheduling therapists for longer, blocked time periods in schools increases the likelihood that they will be available to meet with core teams. Scheduling therapy becomes difficult for included students because they are no longer clustered in self-contained classrooms. Block scheduling of therapy (occupational, physical, vision and mobility, and speech-language) refers to "allocating longer periods of time than usual (e.g., a half or full day instead of 30–45 minutes) to provide the time and flexibility needed to work in and move between the learning environments in which students with disabilities are integrated" (Rainforth & York-Barr, 1997, p. 267). By going to a particular school less often but staying longer, therapists reduce travel time between and within buildings and create teaming possibilities by being available before and/or after school or during planning periods.

Fourth and finally, it is true that many of us are used to inefficiency when we meet in groups or committees, much like Milton Berle's comment that "A committee is a group that keeps minutes and loses hours!" Teams are not meant to function like committees. Efficiency is often the best antidote to a shortage of time. Several practices (discussed in more detail in Chapters 3 and 4) will increase the efficiency of even short periods of available time:

1. Teams should use and mutually enforce a regular schedule and process for meetings.

2. Team members must be respectful of each others' time by adhering to time limits: Start on time, stay on task, and end on time.

3. Teams should use an agenda, take notes, share notes with all members, and use notes to review progress.

Create Time

- Dismiss school early periodically.
- Meet during independent work time, rest (in early grades), recess (while TAs or parents supervise class), or planning periods.
- Involve peers periodically in team meetings, and hold meetings as a class activity.
- Identify and preserve a regularly scheduled time, convenient to all team members, to plan, problem-solve, and discuss topics of concern.
- Ask special education teachers to join grade level team meetings to collaborate on issues of instruction and curriculum for students with support needs.
- Assign teaching assistants to specific grade levels, and have them use their flex time to attend grade level team meetings.
- Use faculty meetings on alternate weeks for team meetings.
- Use part or all of some faculty meetings for sharing or for problem-solving; have the principal facilitate.
- Schedule meeting time on a school-wide basis so common prep time can be scheduled for all members of grade-level teams.
- Plan, schedule, and use Collaboration Days during the school year.
- Create early release days (e.g., create five/year by increasing each school day by 5 minutes; create 1 day weekly by adding 15 minutes to daily students' schedules 4 days each week.
- For one day each week, schedule a common lunch period; ideally this lunch period should be scheduled before or after a common prep period.
- Combine classes for a period to free up a teacher for teaming.
- Plan special events (by grade level or for the entire school) on a monthly basis that are operated by nonschool staff; this frees up staff members for team meetings.

Coordinate Schedules

- Have principals and teachers design a school teaming schedule.
- Designate and coordinate planning times for grade/department planning meetings.
- Re-structure school planning teams (grade level and department) so special education teachers are members.
- Establish common lunch or recess schedules by grades.
- Use parallel block scheduling (Snell, Lowman, & Canady, 1997) to create meeting times.
- Have principals arrange master schedule so a given grade level has back-to-back "specials" twice a week to assist in planning.
- Have PTA/PTO advocate with school board for some compensated team planning time.
- Hire a floating, trained, substitute teacher to rotate among classes and free up 30–45 minute blocks of the classroom teacher's time.
- Use school funds to cover compensatory time.
- Advocate annually with central office when the school calendar is planned to have professional time reserved for teaming.

Figure 2.8.   Ideas for scheduling and creating team meeting time. (Sources: DeBoer & Fister, 1995–1996; Hennen, Hirschy, Opatz, Perlman, & Read, n.d.; Rainforth & York-Barr, 1997.)

When these three practices are applied, a great deal can be accomplished in a 30-minute period. What is not accomplished can be formally saved until the next meeting.

SUPPORT TEAMS AND TEAMWORK

If changes, such as the change to inclusion and the use of collaborative teams, are going to be meaningful and sustained in schools, building administrators need to be more than simply "in support" of them. Figure 2.10 provides an example of the way in which a principal can positively affect the inclusion process. Researchers report that principals need to become directly involved with the change process; those who participate half-heartedly will find that little progress is made (Fullan, 1991). Principals are not a homoge-

	Using Collaboration Days to create team meeting time
Planning	Special educators identified a common day among themselves during which they could meet with a variety of staff (e.g., guidance, OT, nurse, speech); they selected that day as Collaboration Day, targeting Thursdays every other week to match their 2-week rotation schedule. They then presented the idea to staff and asked if they would be willing to fit a collaboration session into their schedules.
Scheduling	Once there was interest, teachers each identified three schedule preferences for the day, and a schedule was developed using the teachers' preferred times. Meeting lengths for teachers were determined by the number and intensity of students and student needs. Meeting lengths ranged from 20 to 35 minutes. Initially, a sub was hired using prep day money to cover classes. In the second year, two changes were made: 1) the planning team scheduled collaboration sessions during times when members of the special education team could meet without needing sub coverage and when teaching assistants (TAs) could provide coverage while teachers or students were in other activities, and 2) all Collaboration Days for the year were scheduled in September.
Implementing	Each session began by having a special educator facilitate the discussion and another person take minutes. Minutes were used to record agenda items, key points, and action plans; they served to guide team actions and to monitor team progress. Session topics were rotated so all focus students could be addressed regularly. Food was provided! When possible, TAs attended; they used their flex time for early departure on other days. Staff members listed on students' IEPs were scheduled to attend the sessions that pertained to those students. A common meeting place was chosen, and a copy of the collaboration schedule and who would be attending was posted.
Outcomes	Teacher evaluations indicated their support. In subsequent meetings, music and PE teachers were also included. Some teachers were scheduled weekly to discuss students with more support needs.

Figure 2.9. Collaboration days. (From Hennen, L., Hirschy, M., Opatz, K. Perlman, E., & Read, K. [1996]. *From vision to practice: Ideas for implementing inclusive education.* Minneapolis, MN: Institute on Community Integration, University of Minnesota; adapted by permission.)

neous group. Some researchers have found that administrators who exhibit initiator and manager styles of leadership are the most effective at implementing change. Actions taken by principals with these styles of leadership reflect both a willingness to collaborate with staff and an ability to delegate responsibilities among team members (Fullan, 1991). Typical actions of building administrators who manage with initiator and leadership styles often include the following:

1. Clarify and support the innovation (inclusion and teaming) through consultation with teachers and reinforcement of their efforts.

2. Work in collaborative ways with others involved in the change: Send support notes to staff, hold regular problem-solving sessions with staff, use shared decision-making in meetings, and have conversations about team progress.

3. Have their finger "on the pulse of the school": These principals are frequently seen in the hallways and the classrooms, even teaching a class; they are knowledgeable about every significant innovation in the school.

4. Be actively involved in the school's work without being controlling of staff: Monitor pupil progress by implementing a systematic policy of record keeping and review data, but have teachers keep the records; be involved in curriculum decisions and in influencing content, but do not taking control.

5. Implement strategies to transform the school's culture: Take action to improve the culture and to reinforce change, foster staff development, frequently communi-

Voices from the Classroom

"We've had a very supportive administration . . . he's (the principal) real interested in the kids and he's there. He's not telling Nate (a kindergartner with many support needs) to be quiet in the hallway. There are other schools that I have been in where, honestly, Nate would have been shipped out the first week! Teachers see him as giving them opportunities to make mistakes without that being viewed as negative—that has really freed them up."

"He really buys into the team concept, that it's a joint effort, and he wants to make sure that those who are here less often are playing by the same rules. He sort of sets the tone and the purpose (for our team meetings)."

Figure 2.10.   A special educator on administrative support for teaming.

cate about values and cultural norms, share power and responsibility, and use symbols to express cultural values. (Fullan, 1991, pp. 160–161)

Both the principal's "background" work and visible modeling make a difference in whether collaborative teaming continues in schools as a healthy, functional process or dies an early death. Hargreaves describes a high school principal who consistently supported a collaborative culture:

The modest and unassuming principal . . . modeled what he most expected of his staff. He praised them, sent them notes to thank them, was always visible around the school to see and hear them, and often bought them corsages or other little gifts to show how much he valued them. When a teacher needed his advice, he willingly offered it. When he himself needed help, he unashamedly asked for it. And when teachers wanted to spend their preparation times planning together, he fixed the schedule to fa-

cilitate it. He promoted rituals and ceremonies . . . to bring the school and the community together. He encouraged experiments in cross-grade groupings of students and links between their teachers to bring teachers together. And he himself sometimes taught classes to show the importance of bringing the principal and students together. In response, . . . teachers broke down the barriers, worked closely together and learned a lot from each other. They didn't just collaborate on things initiated from the outside, but also on projects they developed themselves. (Hargreaves, 1994, p. 194)

Perhaps the central role of administrators in supporting collaborative teaming is to recognize that collaboration is a "predictor for success in school reform" (Friend & Cook, 1990, p. 69). The extent to which schools can create conditions needed for successful collaboration will determine how meaningful inclusion becomes within a school community. Principals play a major role in creating and maintaining these conditions.

Chapter 3

Learning Teamwork Skills

"How did things get so crazy so fast? School has only been in session for 2½ weeks, and almost every day I come into this school, I have a new student on my caseload [for adaptive PE]. Initially, there were five, now there are eight, and I just learned there'll be two more next week! I need planning time with the PE teacher, but he's always busy. I also have to talk to the physical therapist, but she's never here when I am. I know she is doing the same things with some of my kids, but when are we ever going to have time to figure out the overlap? I only have a few minutes with the classroom teachers, but then I'm usually preoccupied with keeping track of the students. There are just too many adults, too many kids, and not enough time." (An adapted PE teacher in an elementary school)

"Our high school had a rather traditional, experienced, English teacher who took a 4-year break when his wife had triplets and, then, he returned to a transformed school. He had never really had students with disabilities in his classes, and when he came back, he had students with IEPs in every class he taught. Although kids with IEPs meant good special education support, it also meant other people coming and going all the time. In our school, special educators are used to co-teaching in English classes; however, this teacher was used to teaching by himself. It was like a time warp for him. Since he came back, there have been many issues we have had to work through, including co-teaching, individualizing class expectations, and having more flexibility with test formats. The most difficult issue, however, was his attitude. Initially, he justified his traditional approaches this way: 'If these kids [with disabilities who are included] want to be in the big league, they have to learn to play that way.'" (A special education teacher in a high school)

In both of these situations, inclusion and teaming are failing to operate together. The adapted PE teacher and her colleagues, all of whom were serving the same students, were not talking to each other because no team structure was in place; no precedent existed for forming teams to deliver coordinated programs. In the high school scenario, all of the teachers, with one exception, had moved with the flow and development of collaborative teams; they had a team structure and they applied their teaming skills to deliver coordinated programs to students in general education classes. This single teacher did not value teamwork or have teaming skills; as a result, his teaching methods conflicted with, and even blockaded, his colleagues' efforts to support the included students.

This chapter addresses an array of nine basic teamwork skills, from arranging and conducting team meetings (e.g., define a team process, schedule and hold meetings) to attending to the interpersonal aspects of participating in meetings. These nine skills are clustered together because they all are required to start a collaborative team. Subsequent chapters will expand upon team processes (e.g., problem-solving methods), the actions teams take (e.g., co-teaching), and the interpersonal skills teams use (e.g., improving communication and addressing conflict) to be effective.

LISTEN AND INTERACT WELL

One of the best ways to understand effective interaction among team members is to spend time with experienced teams and watch them work together. Effective teams don't necessarily avoid conflict; instead, they minimize conflict, recognize it when it occurs, and establish strategies to address it. Smoothly functioning teams spend most of their time cooperatively engaged in "student-focused" discussion and working toward common goals. They typically use many strategies to communicate effectively, and they rely on one or several processes to identify and resolve problems.

Effective teams also regularly shift the focus to themselves as a team to address and build teaming skills, improve relationships among

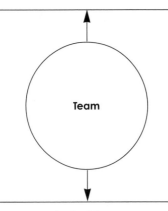

Team Focus

1. Build team skills.
2. Improve relationships.
3. Address and resolve conflicts.

Team

Student Focus

1. Identify common goal or problem.
2. Share information.
3. Brainstorm ideas.
4. Evaluate ideas against team criteria.
5. Select and develop solution.
6. Develop an action plan.

Figure 3.1. Team and student focus.

members, and resolve conflict (Figure 3.1). Observation of teams who alternate their student focus with a team focus reveals the following predictable characteristics (Dinnebeil & Rule, 1994; Dunst, Johanson, Rounds, Trivette, & Hamby, 1992; Johnson & Johnson, 1987; Thousand & Villa, 1992):

1. Positive interdependence and mutual respect (*"We are in this together and we can all contribute."*)

2. Frequent, focused, face-to-face exchange

3. The use of processes to facilitate communication and shared decision-making (e.g., problem identification, problem solving, consensus on decisions, conflict management)

4. The use of methods for being responsible and accountable (e.g., setting an agenda, identifying a time and length for meetings, keeping written records of decisions, updating those who are absent, following-up on team decisions)

5. Team trust derived from trusting one another and being trustworthy

Basic Communication Skills and Outward Behavior

There are several basic strategies of effective interpersonal communication. These strategies strongly influence whether many of the other teamwork skills that this chapter addresses will be successful. Positive interaction starts with the outward behavior of teammates and polite consideration of others. In fact, DeBoer and Fister (1995–1996) reported that, in most interactions, information is communicated most powerfully through one's facial expressions and body language. Voice (i.e., pitch, tone, and timing) is the second most powerful means for communicating information; actual words are the least effective means. The following rather basic communication guidelines reflect the power that non-verbal communication and facilitative listening have on one's interactions with others:

- *Attend to your own and your teammates' verbal and nonverbal behavior; look for your teammates' responses to your behavior:* These outward behaviors include the orientation of your body toward others to whom you are speaking or listening, eye contact, facial expressions, the way in which you gesture or touch others, response time, whether you interrupt, and the volume and tone of your voice.

- *Listen first and then respond in ways that facilitate the exchange* (DeBoer, 1995): There are five common methods to respond to teammates' comments that act to promote interaction: 1) Encouraging ("Mm-hm"); 2) paraphrasing without judgment ("What you are saying is . . ." "Your sense is . . ."), then listening to the speaker's approval, modification, or clarification of your para-

phrase; 3) clarifying without judgment ("Are you saying that . . . ?") and then listening for the speaker's explanation or comment; 4) reflecting on the person's feelings ("You are really frustrated with Rick"), then listening for confirmation or correction; and 5) perception checking ("You sound like you've almost had it with Rick; have you?") and then listening for confirmation or correction.

- *Avoid interrupting others when they are speaking.*

- *Contribute in ways that do not waste team time:* Make your points succinctly and steer clear of lengthy anecdotes.

- *Speak clearly and use a vocabulary that others can understand.*

- *Use team members' names.*

Although these six basic communication guidelines are rather ordinary, they are not necessarily ones that team members automatically practice. These skills need to be habitual enough to withstand disagreement and discussions of challenging issues that teams must face.

Questioning and Leading Methods of Communication

Questioning and leading methods of communication can provide team members with additional effective ways to speak to one another. Methods of questioning include open- and close-ended questions, as well as direct and indirect questions (DeBoer, 1995). Some of these methods reflect strategies that have been developed by counselors and consultants to 1) invite others to listen, and 2) move through the difficult times of stalled interaction and disagreement. DeBoer (1995) refers to these strategies as "inviting" questions:

- Use *open-ended questions* to encourage people to describe their perspective; be aware that close-ended questions may communicate a need to agree (DeBoer, 1995). Open-ended questions do not seek specific answers; they are broad and invite people to share their views, feelings, and ideas. Open-ended questions usually begin with *how* and *what* and allow team members to explain their ideas or explore further:
  "How does this math adaptation for Jennifer seem to you?"
  "That was a helpful overview of the problem; now, how do you want to begin?"
  "Nora, you seem a little discouraged today. What's concerning you?"

- Close-ended questions need to be used carefully, as they can leave colleagues with the feeling that they must agree or be rejected. Close-ended questions are narrow, often seek a yes or no response or specific information, and usually begin with *are, do/don't, have, should, will, can, when,* and *where;* close-ended questions focus discussion around a specific response.
  "You appear uneasy about this idea, are you?"
  "It's clear that Tina is not really disruptive, don't you agree?"
  "You don't think that all kids can learn with a lecture approach, do you?"

- Use indirect questions to create a cooperative climate (DeBoer, 1995). Indirect questions are not really questions but statements that ask without appearing to ask; listeners understand that their response is being sought:
  "I guess that this approach will be difficult to use."
  "I am curious to know if these adaptations will look okay to Katie's friends."
  "It must be difficult to plan for three reading groups."
  "Please share your impressions about this grouping plan."

- Be aware that direct questions may create a nonequitable climate (DeBoer, 1995). Direct questions are open or closed but are clear questions with a rising intonation and a question mark at the end:
  "How hard would it be to use this adaptation in your class?"
  "Yes, it is hard to plan for three reading groups, isn't it?"
  "What do you think about this grouping plan?"

Figure 3.2 lists additional examples of questioning strategies.

Carefully use leading strategies (DeBoer, 1995) (e.g., explaining, encouraging, assuring, suggesting, agreement and disagreement statements, and spontaneous humor). These strategies do not work if 1) you have not first thoroughly listened to the team member or 2) you do not fully trust the person.

- Use an explaining strategy to state your position:

  "Here is the picture I get, although I'm not sure it's fully accurate. Joy (the speech-language therapist) feels we should not teach Quincey to use the photo book at lunch time because he just needs to eat and be with his peers; however, Mary (Quincey's teaching assistant) thinks she should and is seeking your support. You feel caught between them and want to get team agreement."

- Use an encouraging strategy to keep the interaction going:

  "You certainly have been trying to use some new methods this semester."

- Use an assuring approach to build confidence:

  "I know that we can solve this problem as a team."

- Use suggesting cautiously to present tentative ideas as one equal talking to another:

  "Here is an idea I think may work with Rick's English assignment, but you may be in a better position to know if it will work."

- Use agreement or disagreement statements to indicate your opinion of whether another team member is right or wrong.

  "What you have shown us about Bryce's performance on his tests and all that you have reported on his opinion of changing his testing accommodations tells me that your ideas are going to work."

  "I can't really see how that approach will work with William at this point, but I really appreciate the frustration you must be feeling."

- Use spontaneous humor to relieve tension and create a connection between yourself and your teammates:

  "Can you imagine if we needed to pick a leader out of this group of strong personalities? There would be no followers!"

  "They say that making mistakes is part of the process—and if that's right, we should be getting gold stars!"

These methods for asking questions and leading interactions build on the six basic

---

1. To obtain identification or objective information:
   "How many students do you have in your class?" (closed)
2. To clarify when a person is being vague or evasive:
   "I am unclear with the term 'spina bifida'; could you please explain?" (indirect)
3. To define the problem more precisely before designating interventions:
   "What strategies does Katie use when she does not understand the Earth Science content?" (open)
4. To clarify, step-by-step, a course of action that has been taken or will be taken:
   "What did we agree needed to be done after we did a needs assessment?" (open)
5. To request feedback about whether you accurately expressed your intent:
   "I need your help. What did you understand me to say?" (open)
   "I'd be interested to know if my confused remarks seem to make any sense!" (indirect)
6. To explore an important thought or feeling in more depth:
   "You mentioned 'too little time'; please tell me more about that." (indirect)
7. To facilitate someone who is expressing anger and seems hesitant to continue:
   "Mary . . . anything else you need to say?" (closed, but with open intent)
   "Please continue." (indirect)
8. To encourage others to talk when you sense there are issues left unstated:
   "Anything else that needs to be said before we continue?" (closed, but with open intent)

Figure 3.2. Appropriate ways to use questions. (Reprinted with permission from DeBoer, A. [1995]. Working together: The art of consulting and communicating. Longmont, CO: Sopris West. All rights reserved.)

communication skills previously listed. These approaches are not automatic; they must be studied and practiced to be learned.

Signs of Difficulty

There are many signs that indicate that teams are challenged by their shortcomings with communication (Briggs, 1993; Senge, Roberts, Ross, Smith, & Kleiner, 1994). Some of these signs include

- Nonverbal behaviors suggest that attending and listening skills are missing (e.g., members have poor eye contact with each other; do not face each other as they speak; appear tense, rushed or preoccupied; do not engage in active listening).

- Speaking skills are poor (e.g., rambling, speaking too quietly), and there is little evidence of verbal skills (e.g., using encouraging words/phrases, clarifying ideas through restatement, checking for agreement).

- Team members are overly cautious and make many conditional statements.

- Words are mismatched with speaking tone and mannerisms.

- Team members rarely acknowledge one another.

- Viewpoints are stated as facts or formed into questions (see also Figure 3.3).

When these behaviors occur during team exchanges, it is a sign that the team must shift its focus inward and evaluate team communica-

tion. Outside observers can be very helpful in obtaining unbiased comments and honest feedback on team dynamics. Viewing videotapes of both model and problem teams at work can be an excellent method of isolating, observing, discussing, and practicing collaborative communication skills (e.g., a helpful "before and after" videotape and guide on teamwork skills has been developed by Garner, Uhl, & Cox, 1992a, 1992b). The issue of team evaluation will be discussed in greater detail in Chapter 6.

It is difficult to improve interpersonal skills quickly; the previous listing of nonverbal and verbal strategies is far from comprehensive. Team members must pay attention to the ways in which they interact with each other in order to reach their goals without becoming sidetracked by unnecessary hurt feelings, misunderstandings, or disputes.

DEVELOP SHARED VALUES AND GROUND RULES

In addition to positive, flexible communication that involves all team members, a second essential characteristic of teams, according to parents and teachers, is having a set of common philosophical beliefs and *shared values* (Figure 3.4). These principles and beliefs may pertain to teaching and learning, student motivation, disability, inclusion, interpersonal communication, and working together. Examples of important shared values often agreed on by teams include the following:

- Judging and evaluating ("You should . . .")
- Conveying superiority ("I'm better than you")
- Certainty ("My mind's made up")
- Advising when not requested ("Why don't you try . . .")
- Controlling/manipulating
- Diagnosing others' feelings ("The reason you feel this way . . .")

- Prying or interrogating ("Why did you do that?")
- Warning or threatening
- Lecturing or arguing ("Don't you realize?")
- Inappropriate praising ("You've made so much progress")
- Ridiculing
- Diminishing ("Cheer up")
- Stereotyping ("Those parents . . .")

Figure 3.3.   Barriers to effective communication. (From Briggs, M.H. [1993]. Team talk: Communication skills for early intervention teams. *Journal of Childhood and Communication Disorders, 15*(1), 33–40; adapted by permission.)

What the Research Says

When 226 teacher team members and 397 parent team members were asked by several researchers to respond to the question "What things enhance the ability of your team to collaborate?," two team traits were closely agreed upon and frequently referenced (Dinnebeil, Hale, & Rule, 1996. p. 334–5):

1. *The team's ways of working together* (half of the team members' comments fell into this category): Team members had effective communication that was conducted in flexible ways; was characterized by honesty, positive tone, and tactfulness; and enabled the exchange of information that was both relevant to the child and contributed by all members.
2. *The team's shared philosophical beliefs and values* (a quarter of team members' comments fell into this category): Shared principles guided the relationship, such as value of parent perception and knowledge, optimism about the child's potential, mutual respect and trust, and sensitivity to each others' feelings.

Figure 3.4.   Effective team characteristics. (From Dinnebeil, L.A., Hale, L.M., & Rule, S. [1996]. A qualitative analysis of parents' and service coordinators' descriptions of variables that influence collaborative relationships. *Topics in Early Childhood Special Education, 16,* 322–347.)

- *We value the knowledge and unique perspectives of Quincey's parents and siblings; they are the constants in Quincey's life.*

- *We are optimistic about Quincey's potential.*

- *We respect and trust each other and show it in a variety of ways.*

- *We make better decisions when we work together, and we sink or swim together.*

- *We are sensitive to each others' feelings.*

It is useful for teams to take time together to allow individual members to describe their values and work toward the identification of a small set of shared values. Shared values help identify the bonds that make a team cohesive; however, instead of being rules that members may have to work to achieve, shared values reflect team members' similarities in philosophy, beliefs, and outlook on life. A list of these values forms a common ground from which teams can begin. (Chapter 4 describes team criteria for selecting solutions to identified problems; these criteria will link back to a team's shared values.)

Setting Ground Rules

Discussion of team values often influences the ways in which team members interact with each other. Some authors (Johnson & John-

son, 1997; Thousand & Villa, 1992) suggest that teams follow discussions of shared values with an activity to develop *ground rules* for interaction and team conduct. Ground rules are informal directives set by the team that reflect each team member's view of conditions that enable comfortable and honest communication. Ground rules help team members strike a balance between 1) completing the work or tasks of the group and 2) keeping the relationships among team members positive and rewarding (Rainforth & York-Barr, 1997). Some of the more critical rules of conduct cited by Johnson and Johnson include

- Attendance: no interruptions to make or take telephone calls

- Discussion: everyone participates, no exceptions

- Confidentiality: nothing discussed leaves the room without team permission

- Analytic approach: facts are essential for reaching informed decisions

- End-product orientation: all members have tasks and all complete them

- Constructive confrontation is good but not finger pointing

- Contributions: all members perform real work (1997, pp. 521–523)

One way for a team to compile ground rules involves each team member's writing down his or her answer to the question, *"What would it take for me to feel safe communicating openly and honestly in this group?"* Responses to the question are anonymously compiled into a single list by a nonteam member; the resulting list can become the group's ground rules for teamwork. No group member is asked to identify or defend the rule(s) he or she contributed; however, team members may need to explain or restate a particular rule if other team members do not seem to understand it. The following are some examples of the ways that different people answered this question after being organized into new teams:

- *Give me ample time to state and develop my ideas without being interrupted.*
- *Take our team work seriously. Stay on task.*
- *Keep our deliberations within the group unless we agree to share them.*
- *Take time to be nice and to celebrate our successes.*
- *Be aware of what we "say" with our body with regard to listening and accepting.*
- *Don't "put down" my ideas just because I don't have the same experience you do.*
- *Ask me to clarify if you don't understand me.*
- *Encourage everyone to have their say.*
- *Don't give false praise.*

Another trigger question that can be used to identify ground rules is, *"What does it take for our team to get its work done?"* To accomplish their work teams need to identify and use some concrete processes (e.g., roles and responsibilities, process), but they also need basic operating rules or standards to guide the work. Typically, functioning teams have established ground rules that relate to time and participation, such as

- *Everyone's participation is important.*
- *Meeting times are a priority; we begin on time and end on time.*
- *Actions taken by team members are team-generated.*

Both the values a team shares and the ground rules or conduct rules by which the team decides to operate are specific to that team; values and rules cannot be standardized. Once identified, written out, and shared with team members, team values and rules should be used. Teams should also revisit their ground rules or shared values periodically to reaffirm them and revise any that have changed. As the comfort level of a team grows, these rules could also be examined openly and revised as a group.

Signs of Difficulty

In order for Daniel's mom to meet face-to-face with her son's whole team every 6 weeks, she has had to balance schedules perfectly including work and child care. Her input in weekly core team meetings has been primarily verbal (i.e., telephone calls, "on-the-fly" conversations, and daily log), but very active. At the first whole team meeting of the year, everyone but Daniel's mom was late, which meant they started late, finished late, and Daniel's mom was late picking up her kids at child care. Ms. Scott apologized to Daniel's mom as she hurried out the door; but it was clear that one of the primary ground rules that the team had established several weeks before had been broken by everyone but the mom: "Start and end on time." As Daniel's mother was leaving, both teachers looked at each other and knew that the team needed to reaffirm their agreement with Daniel's mother or risk losing her trust and input. They spent the next 15 minutes brainstorming ways they could guarantee to start and end on time. That evening, Ms. Colley called Daniel's mom to apologize and share the team's plans for being as prompt as she had been.

There are some indicators of potential problems with ground rules (Senge et al., 1994) to which team members need to be alert:

- Team members slip up on priority ground rules.

- Very few people follow the ground rules.

- No one remembers the ground rules.

- Too many topics are taboo, or important topics are routinely avoided.

- Disagreement exists about what the team designates as acceptable and unacceptable behavior.

- Irritating behaviors occur: Members miss meetings, arrive late, leave early, or don't participate.

Groups should review their ground rules or even start with a clean slate and write new rules if one or several of these indicators occur. It is often effective to ask an impartial observer to attend the team meeting and tune into the behavior of members as rules are ignored and teamwork slows down. Without relevant ground rules, teaming becomes inefficient and noncollaborative, and members' motivation for teaming erodes.

DEFINE TEAM ROLES AND RESPONSIBILITIES

School Changes Lead to Role Changes

Staff roles change frequently in collaborative schools (West, 1990). Collaborative teachers are more likely to seek help from other teachers and from support staff than are teachers who work alone. Collaborative teachers are also apt to plan instruction together and solicit help from family members. General education teachers are usually in charge when general and special educators share planning and teaching responsibilities to serve students with special education needs in general classrooms: They have command of the content and primary responsibility for the class. In contrast, special educators bring their complementary skills of designing teaching programs suited to nontypical students. As Chris Burton said, "General educators are the content specialists who know the curriculum; special educators are the access specialists who make instruction accessible to everybody in the classroom" (personal communication, September, 1997).

Collaborative teaming requires that team members learn how to communicate, plan, and deliver coordinated services jointly. The question is not only, *"Who will do what on teams?"* but also, *"How can team members determine their parts and avoid issues of territoriality"* (e.g., stepping on each others' toes, squabbling about "my turf, your turf," competing rather than cooperating)? Several years ago, team members in an elementary school that was practicing inclusion were asked about the duties they and their teammates filled with inclusion, as compared to the days when students with disabilities were "pulled out" for services (Snell et al., 1995). Different team members were asked about their own roles and responsibilities and each others' roles (e.g., general and special educators, related services staff, the building administrator, paraprofessionals). Several things became evident:

- Their roles had changed because of inclusion.

- They felt positive about these changes.

- Staff agreed about what their roles were.

Finally, each team member included him- or herself in sharing the responsibility of promoting peer involvement with the focus students. The specific themes these staff members described in their role changes are listed in Figure 3.5.

Because role changes can cause considerable concern among staff and because some role changes should be expected in inclusive schools, it is important that team members be actively involved in defining changes. Therefore, an initial step in building teamwork is to think about, discuss, define, and clarify team members' roles and responsibilities concerning the student(s) with disabilities and other students in a classroom or activity.

Self-Perception of Strengths and Weaknesses Personal style and perception of strengths and weaknesses influence how team members envision their jobs and professional duties. The duties that teachers elect to fulfill will change 1) when they gain experience with

Responsibilities of General Educators	Responsibilities of Teaching Assistants
• Treat the child like other students. • Model for peers. • Develop and use adaptations. • Function as a team member. • Serve as the child's primary teacher. • Be flexible.	• Implement team-generated plans. • Work with other students. • Be part of the team. • Know and work well with the target child. • Help the child fit into the class.

Responsibilities of General Educators

- Treat the child like other students.
- Model for peers.
- Develop and use adaptations.
- Function as a team member.
- Serve as the child's primary teacher.
- Be flexible.

Responsibilities of Special Educators

- Serve as the inclusion facilitator and case manager.
- Work with general education teachers.
- Collaborate.
- Make curricular adaptations.
- Teach and supervise the teaching assistant.
- Provide information on the child.
- Develop, assist in implementing, and supervise behavior programs.
- Work with peers.

Responsibilities of the Principal

- Initiate and be active in a school integration committee.
- Prepare teaching staff for the change to inclusion.
- Provide teacher support when needed.
- Address the concerns of parents and others about inclusion.
- Participate in problem-solving around specific children.
- Handle the logistics that affect inclusion.

Responsibilities of Teaching Assistants

- Implement team-generated plans.
- Work with other students.
- Be part of the team.
- Know and work well with the target child.
- Help the child fit into the class.

Responsibilities of Related Services Providers

- Reduce pull-out services and use opportunities to work in the context of the class activities.
- Provide equipment that helps the child participate in class activities.
- Have flexible schedules that allow therapy to be provided during the most relevant times (e.g., physical therapy during physical education).
- Based on the teacher's unit topics or lesson plans, weave therapy into the planned class activities.
- Come prepared with adaptations and "be able to jump in and do whatever the class is doing."
- Be sensitive enough to know when to stay and when to leave.

Responsibilities for All Team Members in Promoting Peer Involvement

- Answer questions.
- Model appropriate interactions.
- Monitor interactions unobtrusively.
- Include students in peer planning groups.
- Help peers problem-solve.
- Assign buddies.
- Use cooperative learning groups.

Figure 3.5.   Changing roles in inclusive schools. (From Snell, M.E., Raynes, M., Byrd, J.O., Colley, K.M., Gilley, C., Pitonyak, C., Stallings, M.A., VanDyke, R., William, P.S., & Willis, C.J. [1995]. Changing roles in inclusive schools: Staff perspectives at Gilbert Linkous Elementary. *Kappa Delta Pi Record, 31*, 104–109. Adapted by permission of Kappa Delta Pi, an International Honor Society in Education.)

a broader diversity of students in inclusive programs, 2) as the team to which they belong works to support various students, and 3) as the team's composition changes. DeBoer and Fister (1995–1996) suggested activities in which teams can engage to facilitate this process.

1. In-service training is provided for grade-level teams or for entire schools on topics such as effective teaming, collaborative problem solving, and methods of pulling in

special education services and co-teaching. Training helps teachers and other team members define the skills that are needed to include students and presents teachers with different models for planning and delivering coordinated special education supports. Training ensures that team members are better equipped to match new team responsibilities to their talents.

2. Special education teachers meet individually with general education teachers to de-

termine the general education teachers' preferences for teaming roles and responsibilities.

3. Team members identify and share their responses to questions about their strengths/resources and needs/fears regarding inclusion and teaming: What skills, talents, knowledge, and experiences do I bring to the team? What are my emerging skills? What supports and resources do I need? What supports can I provide? What situations do I find stressful? What fears do I have about inclusion and teamwork?

4. Team members identify and discuss their styles of working in a group (e.g., achiever, persuader, risk-taker, supporter, analyst, optimist, worrier).

Jennifer is a fifth grader whose team experienced these early team building steps. (Take a moment to read over Jennifer's abbreviated IEP, or Program-at-a-Glance, in Figure 3.6).

Student Snapshot

 Jennifer is an expressive and energetic fifth grader at Roundhall Elementary who experienced trauma during birth, resulting in some degree of neurological impairment. Her seizure disorder causes significant short-term memory difficulties that affect learning; however, she responds well to "memory jogging" strategies such as personal calendars, numberlines, or math facts charts. Her academics skills (e.g., reading, math, and spelling) are on a mid-first-grade level. Jennifer uses several accommodations, such as the previously mentioned "memory joggers" and a calculator, in addition to the use of oral and typed responses in place of written responses.

A full-time teaching assistant (Ms. Nelson) works with Jennifer and other students in the classroom. Jennifer participates in Ms. Harris's classroom in all but three daily periods; these periods include daily one-to-one tutorials in reading with Ms. Ager the special education teacher; alternate activities in place of social studies twice weekly with a small group of students and Ms. Nelson, and speech/phonemic awareness with the speech teacher twice weekly.

Jennifer is extremely social and works well with her peers with little adult involvement during cooperative activities. She is involved in school activities and frequently invites friends to her home to play. Her classmates, who have known Jennifer since first grade, have come to understand Jennifer, her talents, her personality, and her needs for support. They understand why she engages in "sensory overload" behaviors periodically, which show as high frequency hand and arm movements. "Sensory breaks" are provided across the school day to give Jennifer opportunities to release energy in appropriate ways. Jennifer has made great improvements in her ability to attend to group directions, take turns in group activities, participate in multiple-step tasks, pay attention to other's social cues, and socialize and take turns with peers.

Jennifer's core team includes her mom and dad, Ms. Ager, and Ms. Harris. Before the school year started, Ms. Ager discussed with the classroom teacher her preferences for teaming roles and responsibilities. Ms. Harris thought she'd feel comfortable carrying out team ideas when Jennifer was in the classroom for whole- or small-group instruction, but she wanted the assistant (Ms. Nelson) to implement the daily reading tutoring. At the same time, Ms. Harris was concerned that the teaching assistant would need some supervision; therefore, the team decided that Ms. Ager would observe every other Friday. Both teachers wanted to take part in assessing Jennifer's progress, so they decided to take turns testing her on alternate Fridays. Jennifer's parents liked this plan because they knew the reading tutorials and Jennifer's progress would be well supervised.

Role and Responsibility Worksheet Discussions about roles and responsibilities can be further facilitated by using a matrix that lists team members across the top and typical re-

Program-at-a-Glance

Student: _____Jennifer_____ **Date:** __9/1/98___ **Grade:** __5__

IEP Objectives (briefly)

Math:

- *"Count on" for addition to 15.*
- *"Count on" for subtraction from 15.*
- *Use calculator—add and subtract from 25.*
- *Identify coins and match to values.*
- *Compare two digit numbers.*
- *Match time to hour, ¹/2 hour, and to events.*
- *Identify month, day, year.*

Reading and Writing

- *Decode c-v-c words.*
- *Decode short vowel words with blends and digraphs.*
- *Write two related sentences in journal.*
- *Use correct beginning, ending, and medial vowels in writings.*

Academic/ Social Management Needs

School Independence and Peers

- *Carry out routine errands around the school.*
- *Approach peers to initiate task.*
- *Complete cooperative task with peer without adult prompting.*

Transition to Middle School

- *Visit class in November.*
- *Use middle school photos in classroom activities.*

Accommodations

- *Calculator*
- *Number line*
- *Manipulatives in math*
- *"Money" chart (modification of 100's chart)*
- *Personal Schedule*
- *Personal Calendar*

*Special education assistant teaches the 1:1 or 1:2 reading tutorial for 40 minutes every day with Jennifer. She participates in reading group with class.

Comments/Special Needs

- *"Beat the clock" system works well to speed performance.*
- *Peers are the best way to provide behavior models and help with organizational issues.*
- *Have a full-time teaching assistant in her classroom who serves the whole class.*

Figure 3.6. Jennifer's Program-at-a-Glance. (Contributed by Maria Raynes.)

sponsibilities for delivering coordinated programs on the left-hand side. Figure 3.7 provides an example of such a worksheet that Jennifer's fifth-grade team used in planning their roles to support her. Notice that the responsibilities are truly shared among Jennifer's team members but that the person(s) with the primary responsibility for a task is identified.

On Jennifer's team, Ms. Harris, the classroom teacher, has taken primary responsi- *bility for scheduling IEP conferences, just as she does for scheduling other parent conferences. Ms. Ager, the special educator, seeks input from the classroom teacher, instructional assistant, and Jennifer's mom on all aspects of adaptation but takes the primary responsibility herself.*

When the focus is on secondary students, such as Rick, the worksheet will need to be expanded to include other general education

Team Roles and Responsibilities

Classroom: _Ms. Harris's fifth grade_   **Date:** _9/1/98_

School: _Roundhill Elementary_

Teaching and Support Team Members:

Classroom Teacher: _Ms. Harris_   **Instructional Assistant:** _Ms. Nelson_

Special Ed. Teacher: _Ms. Ager_   **(Other):** _Mr. & Ms. Mays_

Key: x = Primary responsibility
        Input = Input into decision-making and/or implementation

Roles and Responsibilities	Who is Responsible?				
	Classroom Teacher	Special Ed. Teacher	Instructional Assistant	Parent	Other:
Developing lessons, units	x	input		input	
Adapting curriculum	input	x		input	
Adapting teaching methods	x	x	input	input	
Adapting materials	input	x	input	input	
Monitoring student progress	x(daily in class; biweekly tutorials)	x(reports; biweekly tutorials)	x(data log)	input	
Assigning grades	x	x			
Assigning duties to/ supervising assistants	x(daily in class)	x(training) x(observe tutorials)			
Scheduling team meetings: a. IEP teams b. core planning teams	x input	input x		input input	
Daily or weekly communication with parents	x	input	input	x	
Communication and collaboration with related services		x (case manager)	input (notes, logs)	input	
Facilitating peer supports	x	x (peer planning)	input	input	

Figure 3.7.   Team roles and responsibilities. (From Ford, A., Messenheimer-Young, T., Toshner, J., Fitzgerald, M.A., Dyer, C., Glodoski, J., & Laveck, J. [1995, July]. *A team planning packet for inclusive education.* Milwaukee, WI: The Wisconsin School Inclusion Project; adapted by permission.)

teachers who are team members and who share responsibilities.

Focus should be redirected to the assignment of roles and responsibilities whenever a new member joins the team or the team reforms at the beginning of a new school year. The question to ask is, *"How can we make this team work in this school for these students?"* When students move from one school to another, a student's team may need to be completely reformed. Teams can smooth these major transitions by meeting with new team members well before the change.

By next year, Jennifer's team will be reformed and will have all new members except for Jennifer's parents. Therefore, in addition to the typical duties listed on the team's worksheet, Jennifer's team has been focusing on Jennifer's transition to middle school next year. To prepare for Jennifer's team change and move, Ms. Ager, Ms. Harris, and Jennifer's mom met in October with several staff members from Oak Grove Middle School (i.e., the special educator and

two general education teachers who will have Jennifer for math, English, and social studies). To give the new staff members a glimpse of Jennifer's talents at the initial meeting, the teachers showed a short video the class had made of themselves engaged in several activities. The current team agreed that Ms. Ager would make connections with Oak Grove to arrange for a class tour of the school in November. In the spring, the combined teams will meet to plan Jennifer's IEP.

Teams have "shared ownership" of the students on whom they focus although special education teachers ultimately are responsible for knowing and implementing special education procedures consistent with school policy and state law. In classrooms that are truly inclusive, however, the special education teacher does not have primary responsibility for every item on the team role and responsibility checklist, and the general education teacher is not left to figure things out alone (see Figure 3.8).

---

1. Specify the desired student behavior/outcome and explain why the behavior is important for the student.
2. Outline the intervention sequence and provide a rationale for its design.
3. Explain the sequence and steps to the team member learner. Emphasize no more than two or three of the most important aspects of the intervention.
4. Demonstrate the intervention sequence in the situation in which the intervention will actually be used.
5. Ask the team member learner to review the demonstration and written sequence. Assist in reinforcing critical aspects of the intervention.
6. Provide an opportunity for the team member learner to demonstrate the intervention sequence at least three times. It may be helpful to try the intervention with another team member and/or in a simulated setting. For teaching to be complete, however, the learner must demonstrate the intervention with the student in the setting where support is required.
7. Provide instructive feedback and reinforce successive approximations. Provide specific and positive feedback about correct intervention procedures. Provide corrective feedback only on the critical aspects of the intervention that were not demonstrated correctly.
8. Review, discuss, and revise the written procedures so they function as a useful prompt for correct implementation of the intervention.
9. Ask if the team member learner has any questions, suggestions, or concerns or if he or she would like to demonstrate the procedures again.
10. Encourage the team member learner to initiate contact if questions or comments arise. Arrange for follow-up interactions.

Figure 3.8.   A sequence for teaching other team members. (From Rainforth, B., & York-Barr, J. [1997]. *Collaborative teams for students with severe disabilities: Integrating therapy and educational services* [2nd ed., p. 289]. Baltimore: Paul H. Brookes Publishing Co.; reprinted by permission.)

ESTABLISH TEAM MEETING PROCESS AND SCHEDULE

It is helpful for team members to answer several questions to establish the team process they will use:

- What do we want to accomplish in our team meetings?

- How will we proceed during our meetings?

- When and how often/long will we meet?

- Where will we meet?

- How will our process be suited to the focus student's family members?

What Do We Want to Accomplish in Our Team Meetings?

What occurs during meetings is closely related to 1) team roles and responsibilities and 2) students' status as class/school members and their progress as learners. For example, if and when teams have concerns about students' academic progress or membership, these concerns can be aired during team meetings and teams can determine whether to take action to address them. Most student-centered teams direct their energies toward facilitating student learning and membership within classes, school activities, and peer groups. For example, they develop lessons; adapt curriculum, teaching methods, and materials; assess student progress; assign grades; and address interaction issues. Teams use agendas as their primary strategy for defining the tasks they need to accomplish:

- An agenda, even if just verbal, is established prior to a team meeting (or in the first minutes of a meeting) and provides the reason(s) for meeting.

- The agenda is reviewed at the beginning of the meeting; revisions are made until the team agrees on the content, number and order of items, and time needed for each item.

- Once reviewed and agreed on, the agenda is used to guide the meeting.

- Agendas include student-focused items and team-focused items (e.g., celebrations, processing).

- At the end of the meeting, any important agenda items that have not been addressed in addition to other items that have cropped up during the meeting are placed on the agenda for the next meeting.

How Will We Proceed During Our Meetings?

Teams use several general procedures to address agenda items:

- At the beginning of the meetings, have team members volunteer to fill roles that will help the group accomplish their tasks and allow leadership to be distributed among team members. These roles should rotate each meetings (Figure 3.9).

- Teams proceed through their agenda in a previously determined fashion.

- Team members apply a variety of procedures to each agenda item as needed: They may define the issue or concern, share and discuss information relevant to an issue or concern, brainstorm potential solutions, evaluate ideas and select acceptable options, make decisions through group consensus, and/or translate these decisions into action plans.

- As a record of the meeting, teams develop or adapt a meeting form that reflects their procedures and facilitates note-taking. Meeting note forms may be simple (such as the Issue/Action Form in Figure 2.2) or more complex, such as the Collaborative Team Meeting Worksheet (see Figure 3.10). Complex forms provide both a guide for meeting procedures and a form for recording team decisions, agenda items for the next meeting, and other important information (e.g., meeting date, members present/absent, agenda items, times per item, role assignments).

Team Role	Role Description
Note: All team members participate in the meeting while also filling one of the following roles.	
Facilitator	This team member expedites the meeting process and promotes the participation of all members though encouragement.
Time keeper	This team member watches the time and warns fellow members when the designated time for each agenda item is almost over and is finished.
Recorder	This team member writes down team meeting details (e.g., people present, agenda items, roles) and takes notes on relevant information and team decisions. Sometimes, two recorders may be selected: one to take notes that are visible to team members, and another to complete the written minutes.
Jargon Buster	This team member is alert to terms used by members that may not be understood by other members and signals the user to explain or define the terminology in simpler or more complete terms.
Processor or observer	This team member pays attention to the teaming process and the way in which members work together collaboratively.
Other	Praiser/supporter, direction and role definer, information and opinion giver, energizer, encourager of participation, interpersonal problem solver, tension reliever, refreshment provider, comprehension checker, summarizer.

Figure 3.9.   Roles team members take to accomplish team tasks and distribute leadership. (Source: Johnson & Johnson, 1997.)

When and How Often/Long Will We Meet?

Teams need to determine a meeting frequency and duration that suits team members and allows enough time to address team goals. Once frequency and duration have been established, teams should identify a regular time to meet. Whole team meetings times should be scheduled less often and be less flexible; core team meetings should be scheduled more often, and their times may need to be more flexible. The following guidelines may assist teams in planning this part of their process:

• Meet only when there is something to meet about (i.e., when there is a clear purpose). "No purpose, no meeting" (Parker, 1994, p. 167)! (See Figure 3.11.)

• Meetings must be "timely" so current and serious student or staff issues can be promptly addressed (Thousand & Villa, 1992).

• Meet when the time is right (e.g., necessary material and information is available, key members can attend) (Parker, 1994).

• When a team meeting is held to discuss new information, consider distributing printed information before the meeting or instead of holding the meeting.

• Regularly held meetings (e.g., 4 o'clock on Tuesdays) are predictable and easier to schedule.

• Schedule meeting times early in the year for the whole school year or at least an entire semester (Rainforth & York-Barr, 1997); unnecessary meetings can simply be canceled.

• Meetings must be long enough for team members to address the essentials (e.g., build relationships, celebrate, organize, discuss, problem-solve, plan, process the discussion). Skilled core teams can accomplish these essentials in meetings as short as 20–30 minutes.

• Teaming procedures require high-energy thinking and interaction and can be exhausting, especially after a long school day; therefore, experts recommend that meetings be kept under an hour. Twenty- or thirty-minute meetings often allow many issues to be adequately addressed (Thousand & Villa, 1992).

• Sometimes there is no agenda or one that can wait. Consider canceling meetings

Collaborative Team Meeting Worksheet

Members present:	Date: _____	Others who need to know:
_____	Members absent:	_____
_____	_____	_____
_____	_____	_____
_____	_____	_____
_____	_____	_____
	_____	_____

Roles:	This meeting	Next meeting
Timekeeper	_____	_____
Recorder	_____	_____
Facilitator	_____	_____
Jargon Buster	_____	_____
Processor or Observer	_____	_____
Other: _____	_____	_____

Agenda

	Items	Time Limit
1.	Celebrations _____	_____
2.	_____	
3.	_____	
4.	_____	
5.	How are we doing? _____	
6.	_____	
7.	_____	
8.	_____	
9.	How did we do? _____	

Minutes of Outcomes

Action Items	Person(s) Responsible?	By when?
1. How we'll tell others who need to know:		
2. _____		
3. _____		
4. _____		
5. _____		

Agenda Building For Next Meeting

Date: _____   **Expected agenda items**:

Time: _____   1. _____   3. _____

Location: _____   2. _____   4. _____

Figure 3.10. A collaborative team meeting worksheet. (From Thousand, J.S., & Villa, R.A. [1992]. Collaborative teams: A powerful tool in school restructuring. In R.A. Villa, J.S. Thousand, W. Stainback, & S. Stainback [Eds.], *Restructuring for caring and effective education: An administrative guide to creating heterogenous schools* [pp. 73–108]. Baltimore: Paul H. Brookes Publishing Co.; adapted by permission.)

Figure 3.11.   Meetings without a purpose. (DILBERT reprinted by permission of United Feature Syndicate, Inc.)

when you can do without; team members will be grateful (Parker, 1994).

Teams initially may construct long agendas, thinking they can accomplish more than they actually can; over time, as team members learn to use the process and procedures and to work with each other, teams increase their productivity without increasing their meeting time (Thousand & Villa, 1992).

Where Will We Meet?

A meeting locale that is free from distractions greatly contributes to team productivity; unfortunately, many schools are crowded or simply do not have suitable meeting rooms. Physical comfort factors of meeting locales—a pleasant location that is quiet and has comfortable chairs, a seating arrangement that facilitates face-to-face communication, a table surface to ease notetaking and examination of materials, and refreshments to provide needed energy and create a collegial atmosphere—can often motivate team members to attend team meetings.

Most teamwork should be kept confidential within the team; therefore, a meeting location where other staff members or students cannot hear or observe the meeting is important. Teachers' lounges are not good places to meet! Likewise, teams work best without interruptions. Staff members may need to post signs on meeting room doors to prevent unwelcome interruptions and explore how to

lower or eliminate the school intercom volume in the meeting room.

Some teams prefer to use two team recorders: one to take notes on a worksheet or a laptop and another to take notes on a blackboard or on large newsprint that can be taped to the wall for all members to see. It is particularly advantageous to display the meeting notes on the wall or blackboard when the team is large; remarks are easily referred back to, memory need be relied on less, and progress made on action plans can be easily reviewed. If the team uses a second recorder to take notes on a blackboard or newsprint for the group, a blackboard and chalk or an easel, markers, tape, and newsprint will need to be available in the meeting location. Ideally, when a school becomes inclusive, they should designate private, comfortable space for collaborative teaming meetings and equip them with the materials necessary to support the team's work.

How Will Our Process Be Suited to Family Members?

Teams that include family members need to ensure that their team meeting process works for the focus student's family in addition to the staff. The practices described in the previous section are still pertinent (i.e., the team should still choose roles, use an agenda, brainstorm and settle on solutions, and periodically self-evaluate). Sometimes, teams will need to accommodate family members who may not be familiar with or well-practiced in using

typical collaborative practices. Teachers will then need to individualize their approach to suit the family members' level of sophistication, interaction styles, and preferences. For example, parents may or may not want to fill a role during the meeting. Some family members who initially discounted their value to the team process gained new confidence upon realizing that other team members respected their knowledge about their child. Getting input from families is crucial; consequently, team members may need to adopt family-sensitive practices that enable the focus students' families to feel comfortable and to contribute.

If parents are able to meet regularly with the core team, communication prior to each meeting enables a check on the time and place and a review of the agenda. When family members cannot meet regularly, pre-meeting communication is still valuable because it allows current family input to be considered; communicating with family members following the meeting helps keep the student's family linked to the team process.

During meetings, team members will find that the following practices communicate sensitivity to the concerns and perspectives of family members:

1. Regularly remind team members of the confidentiality of the meeting content (e.g., team minutes should be treated as confidential, minutes should summarize general outcomes and planned actions rather than list specific details about students, team outcomes should not be shared with staff members who are not part of the team unless previously agreed on by the team).

2. Teach and prompt teaming procedures by using simple guidelines for problem-solving methods; for example, use large notetaking pages with the key problem-solving steps written at the top (e.g., What's the Concern?, Important Facts Include . . . , Brainstorm Possible Solutions, Choose a Solution, What's Our Action

Plan?). Hand out a printed list of team roles and their definitions, or post a large listing on the wall where you meet.

3. Strive to generate an action plan for implementing solutions.

4. Attend to interpersonal aspects: Be aware of how your outward behavior in meetings communicates interest or disinterest (e.g., eye contact, careful listening, facial expressions).

   Avoid professional jargon, or "bust" jargon when it occurs by providing clear explanations of the term to team members.

   Look like and be a good listener; monitor dominance by staff members.

   Seek the input of family members by posing open-ended questions one at a time (*"What makes sense to you about Quincey's plan for interacting with his classmates?" "How do you feel about these ideas to encourage Jennifer to pay attention in class?"*), waiting for a response, and listening to their comments.

   Recognize that both agreement and disagreement are part of the teaming process but that team consensus is the goal.

5. End meetings on time, but also be sure to review major outcomes and plans, thank team members, and establish a time for a follow-up meeting or contact.

If there are cultural and/or language differences between the team's staff members and family members, staff should take steps to prevent those differences from becoming barriers. Strategies should be individualized to suit teams and family members. The following are examples of such strategies:

1. The composition of the student's team could be reconfigured to include a staff member of the same culture, one who speaks the family's native language, or one who is well-informed and can heighten the awareness of other staff members.

2. Staff members could ask a family member to share information regularly on the student's home and culture; this practice en-

Daniel's core team meets weekly, at 3:30 on Mondays, for 30 minutes. Team members "touch base" at least once daily and problem-solve issues that arise between meetings. Daniel's mom is sometimes part of the scheduled meetings, but usually her concerns/advice are expressed in the daily log that moves between Daniel's home and school. The two teaching assistants who work with Daniel (one in the morning and one in the afternoon) do not usually attend team meetings due to their schedules; however, they are asked about issues beforehand and are kept updated.

For meetings, the classroom and special education teachers target potential discussion topics, such as ways to build peer support, how to teach Daniel to use a daily schedule (with objectives for each activity), and ideas to improve team communication with and between the two assistants who work with Daniel. Daniel's related services specialist (i.e., OT, PT, speech therapist, and vision teacher) give updates to the special education teacher twice a month during individual 15-minute meetings; this information is shared with Daniel's second-grade teacher, and the teacher's concerns that need the specialists' expertise are shared with the specialists.

The team sets an agenda for each meeting, uses an informal problem-solving approach, aims for consensus on all decisions, writes action plans for team members to implement, and makes and shares meeting minutes.

Figure 3.12.   How Daniel's team works.

lightens staff, communicates appreciation, and assists staff in relating to the family and student more meaningfully (Figure 3.12).

3. Staff could seek in-service training on multicultural sensitivity, curriculum adaptations and cultural diversity relating to parents, or characteristics of social friendships among children and adolescents of minority cultures (Almanza & Mosley, 1980; Townsend, 1998; Townsend, Lee, Thomas, & Witty, 1996).

PREPARE FOR AND CONDUCT TEAM MEETINGS

A team's initial meetings make important impressions on members; therefore, the initial team leaders, organizers, and supporting administrators should strive to make the team's first meeting successful (Katzenbach & Smith, 1993). Initial meetings should focus on team-building activities such as redefining the school's mission into goals that are specific to the team, defining shared values, identifying ground rules, determining members' roles and responsibilities, and clarifying the teaming process members will use. Once teams have established these fundamentals, they are ready to tackle specific issues concerning students. Initial meetings and group interactions often determine team members' impressions of how successful a team will be. Whether all members attend (particularly anyone seen as being in charge or an organizer), show up on time, play by the established rules of conduct, participate, and stay the entire session, are good indicators of whether team members will view initial sessions as successes. Team members tend to focus on the person perceived as being in charge, observing their behavior more closely than their words and making predictions about the future of the team based on these impressions (Johnson & Johnson, 1997).

Conducting Meetings

Although meetings are conducted according to the team process members have designed, this design will be fairly similar for all collaborative teams that focus on students. Every team member must take some responsibility if meetings are to run both efficiently and effectively; success is not simply a matter of having a good facilitator. Whether the agenda addresses team building, student issues, or team issues or a combination of these topics, a certain sequence should be followed:

1. Team members take a few minutes to socialize with each other.

2. Someone (perhaps a predesignated facilitator) opens the meeting.

3. Team members assign roles, unless previously done.

4. The facilitator leads a discussion about agenda items (i.e., clarity, priority, and team time required to address each item).

5. The facilitator leads a review of action plan progress; team celebrates successes.

6. Using team process, the facilitator provides structure and helps members focus on each agenda item as time allows.

7. The time keeper repeatedly reminds team of meeting's schedule.

8. Members filling other roles play their part (e.g., jargon buster, notetaker, process observer, encourager).

9. Members work to process the functioning of the team.

10. The facilitator brings the meeting to a close and summarizes outcomes.

11. Notes taken by the recorder are disseminated to team members.

Preparation for Meetings

At the conclusion of a team meeting, most members leave with a defined part in one or several action plans. Review the team minutes from Daniel's meeting in Figure 3.13.

When they left the previous meeting, each team member had a copy of meeting minutes which listed "new issues and responsibilities." All had a part in implementing or assisting with Daniel's use of his communication switch, adjusting the wheelchair foot rests, using the slant board, or getting Daniel to participate in the "coat off and hung" routine. Each member came to the October 15th meeting prepared to report the status of these "old issues." Likewise, when they left that meeting, members had

---

Student: _Daniel_   **Date:** _10/15/98_

Members Present: _Judy Scott (classroom teacher), Kenna Colley (special educator), Moe Johnson (morning assistant), Sue Evans (OT), Danielle Seale (Daniel's mother), Georgia Allen (speech-language)_

Members Absent: _Jim Harris (afternoon assistant), Pita Thomas (PT)_

Old issues and "to-do" list reviewed

1. Communication switch works and Daniel is using it (Georgia & Sue).
2. Wheelchair footrests have been adjusted (Danielle, Pita).
3. Slant board helps Daniel's visual attention to materials (Sue & Judy).
4. Daniel is making progress on coat on/off and hanging it up (partial participation) (Danielle, Sue, Judy, Kenna, Moe).

New issues and responsibilities (person)

1. Regular recordings need to be made by peers for the CheapTalk communication device (Judy, Georgia).
2. Teach staff/peers how to offer choices: give meaningful options, position choices close, know what to say and how long to wait (Kenna, Georgia).
3. Monitor peer assistance with equipment placement; peers should help only when Daniel is out of equipment (Pita, Sue, Judy).
4. Weekly peer support group will start next week (Kenna with Joan Washington, counselor).

Next Meeting Date: _11/19/98_   Place: _Judy's classroom_   Time: _2:45–3:45_

Figure 3.13. Team meeting minutes. (Contributed by Kenna Colley.)

signed on for new responsibilities to carry out before the next meeting, responsibilities that evolved from team discussion and resolution of their agenda items.

Most of us can recall meetings that were unproductive because no one came prepared. Participants who had promised to bring materials or information or to report on a student's progress with program changes showed up empty-handed. When team members come to a meeting unprepared, team morale is low and team effectiveness suffers; however, when members take action between meetings and come prepared to report on their role in addressing "old issues," the team moves forward with its plans.

A consistent lack of preparation by one or more team members is a clear indication of team trouble and requires team processing. There are many reasons for team members to be unprepared and teams need to analyze the causes. Some questions can be posed to help with this process:

- Are team members overloaded with too many competing commitments?

- Are team responsibilities distributed unevenly?

- Are responsibilities (action plans) unworkable or poorly defined?

- Are those responsible for action plans in agreement with the plans (was consensus reached)?

- Are team members in agreement on their team's general goals and purpose?

- Do team members share and operate by a common set of values?

Clarifying Team Goals

As facilitators conduct team meetings and members participate, all are alert to team goals. Team goals can be either

- Broad, overall goals (reflected in shared values and roles and responsibilities)

- Immediate goals (reflected in ongoing action plans and current meeting agendas)

A review of the eleven general steps involved in conducting a meeting, listed on page 51, reveals the degree to which team goals are integrated with meeting process. Awareness of and attention to both levels of team goals is evident in almost every step of conducting a team meeting. Teams need to be aware of their purpose and reasons for gathering. When overall goals are clear to all team members and immediate goals are prioritized and narrowed through consensus to a workable size, teams have both purpose and motivation to work. However, when overall and immediate goals are vague or undefined, several indicators of potential trouble will arise (Senge et al., 1994). Members will notice one or more of the following problems:

- Repeated changes in direction during a meeting

- Recurrent disagreement about team action

- Concerns about the size or appropriateness of the goals or team's focus

- Inaction and frustration

- Extreme lack of confidence regarding team decisions and actions

When these problems arise, forging ahead with the agenda often simply results in more frustration. Instead, it helps to refocus on the team goals. Refocusing at the broad level can be facilitated by a question such as, *"What are we about in this school"* (e.g., team mission, shared values, or roles)? At the immediate level, it might help to ask, *"What are we doing now to move things forward for students"* (e.g., clarify the boundaries of our immediate goals, reach consensus on their priority for the student and team, simplify or combine goals to workable size and complexity)?

GIVE AND RECEIVE INFORMATION

Team plans for action and those actions that are ultimately put into place are an integrated meld of known practices, ideas, "best guesses,"

and revisions from various members. The process for developing team plans requires team members to frequently turn to each other for information. Information needs to be shared in ways that allow it to be understood and used by all of the team members. Consistent with the concept of role release, defined in Chapter 1, team members take turns stepping into the role of teacher when their knowledge and skills are required by other team members. As one team member fills a "teaching" role, others step into "learning" roles. Team members who fill teaching roles may be from the core team or the whole team. Therapists (occupational therapists, physical therapists, and speech-language pathologists) often function as teachers or consultants to other team members. Sometimes, the student may be put in the role of teaching team members. Less often, individuals from outside the team consult with the team and teach them methods or information they need to address student or team concerns.

Rick's special education teacher and the school psychologist have shared important information with team members on functional assessment of his problem behavior and methods to redirect Rick.

The occupational therapist has frequently provided demonstrations to staff members and to Daniel's mom on lifting and positioning in ways that encourage Daniel's active movement.

Quincey's team called on the regional autism specialist twice last year as a team consultant.

The following six guidelines from Rainforth and York-Barr strengthen the teaching role of team members. The staff member in the teaching role should adhere to these strategies:

1. "Work as an equal, not an authority": Remembering the cardinal rule of parity among team members will make it easier for team members to learn from their fellow team member's instruction.

2. "Participate in school routines": The information taught to team members must be integrated into school routines in order to benefit the student(s). The more familiar "teachers" are with students' routines, the more likely their knowledge will be applicable.

3. Nurture relationships with fellow team members. Learners who feel comfortable with their teachers have increased motivation to learn and are more at ease asking for assistance or clarification. Adults are not an exception to the general rule.

4. "Expect to learn from others and acknowledge when you do": When team members who teach are also willing to learn, all team members will gain.

5. Use an experiential learning approach that allows learners to be successful. Presenting general information or holding in-service sessions are generally less helpful to adult learners than providing actual demonstrations, opportunities to practice, and feedback. Teachers need to observe the performance of the teammates whom they teach and adjust their instruction to build success. Shaping (reinforcing improved approximation over time) and positive encouragement are the best ways to build skills in other team members.

6. "Ask for feedback about your consultation" or teaching of others. Team members can usually improve their teaching by asking for feedback from learners. (1997, p. 287)

MAKE DECISIONS BY CONSENSUS

Making decisions by consensus means that team members agree on a solution; the group's collective opinion is determined after sharing and hearing each team member's respective viewpoints during an open discussion (Rainforth & York-Barr, 1997). Although it is best to reach consensus on important deci-

sions, it is not always possible. Decisions can also be made in ways other than by consensus:

- Poll the group, or take a majority vote.
- Average the opinions of team members.
- A minority subset of the group makes the decision (e.g., the therapists combine to decide a therapy issue).
- A person who has authority over the group makes the decision (building administrator).
- A person viewed as an expert in a discipline of central concern (who may or may not be a member of the team) makes the decision.

None of these nonconsensus options for reaching a decision are without problems. The problem they all potentially share is a lack of commitment to implementation (Rainforth & York-Barr, 1997). Another potential problem might be the erosion of team values (e.g., all opinions are valued, we have equity with each other). If combined with open discussion, some of the previous methods can lead to consensus; listening to an expert or a minority composition of the team and then batting around team reactions and viewpoints will often lead to agreement on an issue. Most experts on teaming agree that making decisions through consensus, although time-consuming and likely to elicit some conflict, has more benefits than other decision-making approaches for several reasons: 1) team members share a commitment to resolve the issue and implement a solution and 2) decisions made by consensus usually benefit the student because they reflect a broader set of perspectives and talents.

Deciding How Consensus Is Reached

Teams need to determine how they will make decisions, when they should reach a decision by consensus, and when they should rely on one of the other methods of decision making. For example, important issues can be *explored* by taking a vote verbally or in writing; important issues should, however, be *decided* by consensus (Senge et al., 1994).

There are several ways that teams can test for consensus. First, they can use data as the basis for decisions:

When team members use their approach for offering Daniel a choice of activities or objects, do they agree on which one he wants and which one he does not want?

Do Jennifer's tutorials show that she is making progress and, therefore, support continuing what we are doing?

Are Rick's outbursts in between classes on the decline?

Second, the meeting facilitator can ask whether the entire team consents when several members appear to be in agreement. ("Millie and Johnna have made a case for involving Rick in the Activity Club; does anyone feel uncertain about this decision?"). Third, the facilitator can let the meeting time determine whether discussion should be shifted to consensus building. During team building sessions, discussion should be directed to these options for collaborative decision-making and teams should identify their preference. If teams reflect on the pros and cons of using noncollaborative decision-making options, they are more likely to decide in favor of using one or more of the collaborative approaches.

Signs of Trouble

Senge et al. (1994) listed several indicators of potential trouble in reaching decisions:

- Team members cave in to others' opinions when no supporting data exists or is presented.
- Decisions are made by default; members don't respond and silence is interpreted as agreement.
- One or several team members "strong-arm" the others into agreeing.
- One or several team members make the decision despite a lack of team agreement.

• Hasty reversion to "the majority rules" in order to avoid open disagreement.

When any of these indicators are present, a team discussion on decision-making is necessary. Some team facilitators might preface an open discussion with data on the team's behavior; an outsider would be asked to observe how the group makes decisions and give the team feedback.

TEAM EFFECTIVELY "ON-THE-FLY"

Remember that teaming interactions occur within two basic formats: planned, "sit-down" meetings and "on-the-fly" interactions between team members. Figure 3.14 compares and contrasts the characteristics of each of these two formats. Because productive communication is the desired outcome during both planned meetings and hurried, "on-the-fly" exchanges, person-to-person sensitivity must occur regardless of the format. Sensitivity encompasses mutual respect, positive interdependence, face-to-face exchange, and trust.

Planning Team Communication Between Meetings

Team members should plan how they will communicate with one another and with the student's family members between meetings. Strategies for communicating with family members often differ from those strategies used by team members and usually require input on what approaches would best suit that particular family. It is important that each student's parents be given the opportunity to determine how they want to be involved with their son or daughter's program and to what degree (Salisbury & Dunst, 1997). The type and amount of involvement is likely to change over time in response to family and child circumstances. The communication ideas listed in Figure 3.15 can be used to guide a conversation with families or can be sent home and completed by the parents.

Two general methods of communication exist: written and person to person. Types of

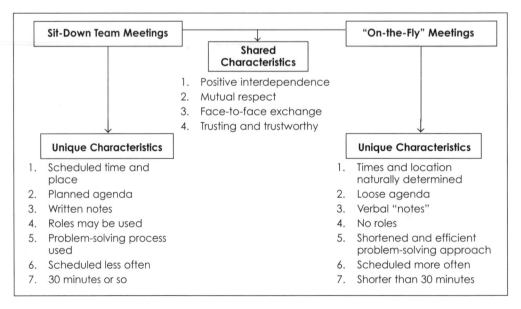

Figure 3.14.   Shared and unique characteristics of teaming formats.

```
┌─────────────────────────────────────────────────────────────────────────────┐
│ Family Member : _____  Teacher: _____  Date: _____  │
│ _____ I'd like to come to the school to meet with you. Days and times that  │
│         work best are:                                                        │
│ _____ Monday  _____ Tuesday  _____ Wednesday  _____ Thursday  _____ Friday │
│ Times:  _____   _____   _____   _____   _____             │
│ _____ I'd like you to come visit at our house.                              │
│ _____ I'd like to write in and read a notebook that travels in my child's backpack. │
│ _____ I'd like to write notes back and forth.                               │
│ _____ I'd like phone calls at home between the hours of _____ and _____ (Tel:_____) │
│ _____ I'd like phone calls at work between the hours of _____ and _____. (Tel:_____) │
│ _____ I'd like to use email; my address is: _____  │
│ _____ I'd like to talk when I drop off or pick up my child on M T W Tr F (circle one) at _____. │
│ _____ I'd like to meet _____ before _____ after PTA meetings.           │
│ _____ I'd like to have a school/class open house and meet there.            │
│ _____ I'd like to observe in the classroom and talk afterward.              │
│ _____ I'd like to receive school and classroom newsletters.                 │
│ _____ I'd like to participate in my child's IEP meeting.                    │
│ _____ I'd like to bring a friend or other family members to meetings with you. │
│ _____ I'd like to talk and plan before the IEP meeting.                     │
│ _____ Another way: _____ │
└─────────────────────────────────────────────────────────────────────────────┘
```

Figure 3.15.   How can we stay in touch?

written communication from which team members can select include

- Informal notes in mailboxes

- Rotating notebook (notebook between home and school)

- Stationary notebook (notebook that remains in a safe, designated place in the classroom in which team members who come and go may leave comments if conversation is difficult)

- Team consultation logs (related services staff record their presence and general activity)

- Individual student progress notebooks or specific forms to record student progress (Refer to another book in this series for more guidance: *Modifying Schoolwork* [Janney & Snell, 2000b]).

- Specific forms that reflect/preserve team decisions or describe team plans for modifying school work or supporting students'

problem behavior (Refer to two other books in this series for guidance: *Modifying Schoolwork* [Janney & Snell, 2000b] and *Behavioral Support* [Janney & Snell, 2000a]).

- Beyond scheduled "sit-down" meeting times, team members need to find time to talk in person regarding student progress or team efforts to implement team plans. Options for face-to-face interactions include obvious or creative times that may be 1) prearranged before or after school, 2) highly probable because work schedules place team members in the same location during school (e.g., lunchroom, planning time, naps), or 3) spontaneous during or after school (Doyle, York-Barr, & Kronberg, 1996).

Obviously, team members need to devise their own plans for keeping communication current in between meetings; although these communication plans must be taken seriously, they also need to be kept flexible and revised if they are inadequate (see Figure 3.16).

Voices from the Classroom

"I try to [talk to team members] individually. I grab a few minutes with the speech teacher, grab a few minutes with this person, and grab a few minutes with that person."

"[On days I'm scheduled in a class] the first thing I think I do is to talk with Jane [the classroom teacher] and Tina [the nurse who supports Michael] about whether what I'm seeing is real representative of what they see, [whether] it may be a good day or it may be a bad day . . ."

"For all of us who come and go [from the classroom, the OT, PT, speech therapist], I try in passing to say 'well this is what he did when I was there and this is what he's doing,' so we can compare—those of us who come and go—can compare notes a little bit."

Figure 3.16. Teacher on communication between meetings. (From Snell, M.E. & Janney, R.E. [in press]. Teachers' problem solving about young children with moderate and severe disabilities in elementary classrooms. *Exceptional Children.*)

Implementing Team Recommendations and Meeting "On-the-Fly"

"On-the-fly" teaming between team members in inclusive schools takes place frequently throughout the school day; the focus of these interactions typically relates to implementation of team decisions. A study of collaboration among teachers (Snell & Janney, in press) illustrated that these informal exchanges

1. Are described by teachers as "checking back," "comparing notes," or "touching base" and entail ongoing communication about students' progress with (or without) an adaptation or accommodation

2. Involve validating the intermittent view of the special education teacher who comes and goes with the ongoing view of the general education teacher who stays with the class

3. Are meant to adapt or refine solutions emanating from meetings, not to design new solutions

4. Have a dynamic focus: "You just keep trying until you hit on something that looks right" (Snell & Janney, in press).

Regardless of the intensity of a student's needs, team members will communicate between team "sit-down" meetings during the school day regarding the implementation of their plans. For students who need extensive support, such as Rick, regular informal interchange between teachers (and Rick) is an essential supplement to weekly team meetings. These exchanges allow teachers to refine their plans by reducing, strengthening, or changing instructional and behavioral supports depending on Rick, the day's conditions, and team goals. For students whose instructional support program, once in place, is easily maintained and successful, meeting "on-the-fly" may become the primary collaboration strategy to keep the student's instruction working well.

During "on-the-fly" collaboration, special education teachers must operate in tandem with classroom teachers; they must perceive the situation from the perspective of the general education teacher, while also having a global view of what is required of the student. "On-the-fly" meetings are usually hurried, as opposed to sit-down meetings, which act as an organized balance to the hurried pace of teaming "on the go."

If teaching assistants are part of the support plan for a student, they usually confer with classroom teachers about the student's progress during the day. Teaching assistants also often have regular, planned opportunities to interact with the special education teacher to whom they report, making the teaching as-

sistant an important link in keeping the special education teacher current and in facilitating communication between members of the core team. If trust is lacking, this link will be weak; however, when team trust and consensus exist, this arrangement is very beneficial. Part of the special education teacher's role and daily routine is to obtain a global view of things by "touching base" with the target students (in addition to providing direct services, if necessary) and with team members regarding the target students, comparing staff perspectives, and working to understand any discrepancies. Teaching assistants' views of a student's progress or problems may lack the sophistication of those of the professional team members; however, the views of the assistant are usually rich in valuable detail. Paraprofessionals may be asked to supplement their verbal descriptions of a student's progress or problems with clarifying demonstrations, (*"Show me what Jennifer did when you had her add"*) or may be directly observed (*"Just continue and I'll watch"*). In fact, this approach to clarifying, if necessary, the teaching assistants' perspective offers not only the opportunity to "compare notes" among team members who work with the student during the day but also the opportunity to build the skills of paraprofessionals in a meaningful context.

REFLECT ON TEAM PROCESS

When teams are in full motion, members should be both involved in discussing and resolving agenda items and tuned into group process (teamwork). The importance of building time into meeting agendas to assess how the team is functioning as a group was mentioned earlier in this chapter. Sometimes, teams resist devoting a few minutes to team processing; many team members have found, however, that this time is critical to the maintenance of collaborative interactions (Johnson & Johnson, 1997; Rainforth & York-Barr, 1997; Thousand & Villa, 1992).

Processing often consists of posing simple questions about team functioning and progress:

1. Questions about prior team achievements and student progress should be asked at the beginning of meetings: *What have we accomplished since our last meeting? Let's celebrate the successes! Let's reconsider the areas of little progress.*

2. Questions regarding individual team member accountability may be asked when team members give and receive information and report back to each other: *Is each team member held accountable for completing his/her work? Would more assistance or encouragement help?*

3. Questions about ongoing interpersonal relationships and their effect on teamwork may be asked at any time during or near the end of a meeting: *How are the relationships among us as team members? Let's discuss our teamwork skills.*

4. Questions regarding progress being made in the current meeting may be asked anytime during or near the end of a meeting: *Are we making progress on our tasks for this meeting? Do we need to make agenda adjustments? Is each team member held accountable for his/her participation?*

5. Questions about accomplishments made in the current meeting should be asked at the end of the meeting: *How well did we do as a team? As problem-solvers? In pulling together an action plan?*

As seems obvious from the name, the processor plays a key role in helping the team members reflect on their interpersonal interactions and their actual work progress. When problems are identified in either area, the team should determine their course of action (e.g., set aside, discuss, collect observation data on group, problem-solve, develop an action plan). Chapter 6 describes team processing in more depth.

Chapter 4

Taking Team Action

Student Snapshot

Walter, who is enrolled in all general classes, has a label of "mild mental retardation." He has good verbal skills and is talented in art. Walter has learned a lot of general information and basic skills in his secondary classes, so his team modified his IEP objectives to reflect this emphasis: 1) in basic English, he will "compose brief journal entries" and 2) in Math, he will "measure lines and angles." Walter blends in well socially with his peers. In his Informal Geometry class, where students are used to giving each other help, his peers seem to know to help Walter a little more.

Walter's teachers say that "the wonderful surprise has been how much of the vocabulary and geometry concepts he is getting. We no longer adapt his guided practice or homework assignments until we see what he does with them." His classroom teacher uses repeated concrete and visual demonstrations during class, which are the best way to enhance Walter's understanding.

Walter's ongoing challenges are to maintain attention to the teacher or group leader and to understand directions and task instruction, although he responds to reminders and praise. This is a concern with his future employability. When he attends, he understands better; therefore, the team is using a self-management point system to get him to look up at teachers when they talk and to put notes down in his planner when they give instructions.

Planning for Walter rests with his IEP team and is uncomplicated. His special education teacher describes it as follows: "I communicate daily to his academic lab teacher, keeping her up on assignments that he needs to work on." Academic lab is a study hall/resource arrangement that Walter attends for one period daily.

Chris Burton, a special education consulting teacher who serves middle and high school students, met with Walter's Informal Geometry teacher, Arlene Brown, for their weekly 20-minute lunch meeting. Chris is scheduled daily in Informal Geometry class, where she lends support to five students with IEPs (of the five, Walter has the most support needs). Chris and Arlene compare notes regularly; today, they take some time to catch up on some of Walter's issues. First, they review how Walter might complete his 6-week project on famous mathematicians. Second, Arlene shows Chris the problems for the upcoming week, and they determine how to modify Walter's work based on his adapted objectives for the class. Finally, they quickly discuss Walter's second week of using a five-point behavior checklist to self-monitor his attending and talk-out behavior during class.

In 20 minutes, Chris and Arlene, two members of Walter's core team, have efficiently and quickly found solutions to several of their concerns regarding Walter's work and behavior in his tenth-grade geometry class. Although pretty amazing, this achievement is not miraculous. First, Chris and Arlene's teaming "habit" can be traced to the value base developed several years earlier when their school prepared structurally and philosophically for a move to inclusion under the strong support of their administration. Second, Chris, Arlene, and other staff members who formed teams learned basic teaming skills and developed a teaming process and a process for interacting with each other around students. In addition to these teaming skills, Chris and Arlene also knew how to problem solve. This chapter describes some of the strategies the two teachers used to plan their actions and to deliver a coordinated program for Walter. By focusing on the actions teams take, three broad teaming questions will be addressed:

1. How do teams translate solutions to student concerns into action plans?

2. How do teams collaborate to design programs?

3. How do teams deliver coordinated programs?

The overall function of team meetings is to develop students' school programs and schedules in ways that address their educational priorities, to ensure some consistency in program implementation, and to problem-solve specific issues that arise. *In the beginning of year, core teams should focus on the student's daily schedule and how the student participates across the day.* The team should ask and answer questions such as,

1. What parts of the schedule can the student participate in with no adaptations?

2. What parts of the day will require adaptations? What kinds of adaptations will be needed (curricular, instructional, ecological)?

3. Do we need to plan routines or other activities that must be completed apart from peers (e.g., self-care, intensive instruction)? If so, when, where, and with what support?

In elementary schools, the team could begin developing the student's program by creating a matrix of IEP objectives plotted against the classroom schedule of activities, times, and locations (see Figure 4.1): Objectives that can be addressed during each particular time block are checked; any needed support may also be indicated in each block. For example, fourth-grader Quincey's learning needs are clustered in communication, independence building, math, and language arts. By constructing a matrix of Quincey's class schedule with his IEP objectives, his team could plan ways to integrate Quincey's general classes with his IEP objectives. When Quincey goes to lunch with his class, he works on objectives in two areas: communication and independence building. The communication objectives on which he works include the following:

- Respond to greetings from others by saying "hi."

- When in the cafeteria line, use pointing to indicate food choices.

- Tap peer to get attention; then use his communication book.

- Raise hand to get teacher's attention; then use communication book.

The following are the independence-building objectives on which Quincey works during lunch:

- Review photos of lunch routine before lunch.

- Follow lunch line routine; watch peers.

- Give cafeteria staff lunch ticket to be punched.

A detailed matrix allows team members to plan when a student's priority objectives can be embedded within ongoing class activities and routines. Team discussions then may shift to

- *How do we mesh instruction of these goals with the classroom schedule and curriculum?*

- *Do we need to make adaptations (e.g., curricular, instructional, or ecological)?*

- *When do we need an extra pair of hands?*

- *When do we need other kinds of supports?*

Daily schedule → IEP Objective	Arrival	Share time	Journals	Reading, LA activities	Other
Communication					
Independence					
Math					
Language Arts					

Figure 4.1. Matrix of IEP objectives plotted against the classroom schedule of activities, times, and locations.

The team then works to problem-solve any needed adaptations and to schedule support to match the student's needs. (The adaptation planning process is addressed in detail in another booklet in this series, *Modifying Schoolwork* [Janney & Snell, 2000b].) In secondary schools, students' grade-level class schedules are planned in coordination with their IEP in the spring, then firmed up over the summer; initial team meetings typically involve several classroom teachers and are focused on designing supports, scheduling needed staff, and addressing issues as they arise.

Following the initial teaming meetings, the team's focus shifts to other tasks:

1. Assessing student progress, resolving difficulties that arise

2. Improving the program

3. Planning for the end-of-the-year transition

USE
PROBLEM-SOLVING METHODS

As stated in Chapter 3, part of a team's strength lies in its basic teamwork skills. However, teams also need to develop specific strategies to resolve problems and to plan their course of action. Only when teamwork skills are combined with these strategies is the power of collaborative teams realized: "None of us is as good as all of us." This section reviews several problem-solving approaches that can be particularly helpful when teams are initially learning to work together. Once team members have become acquainted with one another, they often develop problem-solving shortcuts that are tailored to their ways of working together.

Many groups, including teachers, agree on the same basic problem-solving steps. (Giangreco, 1993; Parnes, 1992; Porter, Wilson, Kelly, & den Otter, 1991; Pugach & Johnson, 1995; Snell & Janney, in press). Figure 4.2, fashioned from the contributions of Cook and Friend (1993), lists these rather traditional problem-solving steps and displays the

interpersonal and the procedural considerations that are associated with each step.

When collaborative teams in elementary schools were observed, it was discovered that teachers' thinking processes actually followed a cycle of steps similar to those of the problem-solving process in Figure 4.2. However, teachers cycled repeatedly through the steps as they fashioned, tried out, and refined solutions to each student difficulty (Snell & Janney, in press). The basic process involved repeating a multiple-step cycle to reach and refine a solution:

- Identify concerns (define the problem).
- Watch and talk (gather and share information pertinent to the problem).
- Throw out ideas (brainstorm).
- Say whether it sounds good OR it won't work (evaluating the ideas and finding the best).
- Give it a shot (trying out the solution).
- More watch and talk (evaluating the solution, refining it, and beginning the cycle again).

To problem-solve a solution, teachers would focus on a problem, observe, talk, brainstorm, decide what to try, and try it out. To reach "real" solutions, they repeated this process, restating the problem as the solution was refined or as the problem changed. The process was not "cut and dried."

Using the five generic steps of problem solving in Figure 4.2 as a framework, the following sections provide guidelines for solving concerns teams have about students.

Step 1
Identify the Problem

 The agenda items that teams select for their meetings are usually a reflection of the concerns of one or more team members regarding the student(s) they support. However, before teams begin to address concerns or

Interpersonal Considerations		Procedural Considerations
• Establish a climate of trust • Share relevant information.	**Step 1. Identify the Problem**	• Focus on the problem, not the solution. • Reach agreement on the problem.
• Encourage input from all parties. • Defer judgment about the solutions.	**Step 2. Brainstorm Possible Solutions**	• Generate as many alternative solutions as possible.
• Be supportive rather than attacking. • Evaluate the solutions, not people.	**Step 3. Evaluate the Possible Solutions**	• Identify criteria by which the solutions are judged. • Modify and combine the solutions as needed.
• Elicit input from all parties. • Be accepting of differences.	**Step 4. Choose a Solution**	• Select a trial solution.
• Ascertain that all participants feel some ownership of the trial solution. • Reach a decision by consensus.	**Step 5. Write an Action Plan**	• Determine what materials will be needed (if any). • Assign responsibility for the specific steps. • Set a timeline. • Establish measurement procedures. • Schedule a follow-up meeting

Figure 4.2. Elements of problem solving: Interpersonal and procedural considerations. (Reprinted with permission from Beck, R. [Ed.]. [1997]. *PROJECT RIDE: Responding to individualized differences in education.* Longmont, CO: Sopris West. All rights reserved.)

find solutions, they need to take time to define and explore the problem. Most experts on problem-solving methods agree with Dewey's observation that "when a problem is well defined it is half solved" (as cited in Giangreco, Cloninger, Dennis, & Edelman, 1994, p. 328).

Many of the student-focused problems in inclusive elementary schools fall into one of three groups: 1) goals and abilities, 2) participation in class, or 3) classroom belonging (Snell & Janney, in press) (Figure 4.3). These same categories of problems may exist at middle- and high-school levels; however, more research is needed to determine whether additional categories arise with older students or with students who have fewer support needs

1. *Student goals and abilities:* These problems center on questions such as, "What is the target student capable of learning?" "What is reasonable, functional, and important to teach this student?" and, "Where shall we begin instruction?"
2. *Participation in instructional activities and routines:* These problems not only address issues such as the ways in which students might take part in class activities and school routines with classmates, but also how they might learn their IEP objectives in these inclusive contexts.
3. *Classroom community and belonging:* Problems in this category involve the target child's membership in the class, ways to lend unobtrusive support to his or her interactions with peers, ways to reduce "special treatment," and ways to address the differences that exist between the target student and his or her peers (e.g., following class rules, work load, adaptations provided).

Figure 4.3. Student-focused problems. (Source: Snell & Janney, in press)

than those in the study. Consider the concerns of Walter's teachers:

Operating from the directions Walter's whole team set at his IEP meeting last spring, his core team spends much of its time focusing on meaningful participation in the classes in which he is enrolled. During their lunch meeting, Walter's geometry and special education teachers had identified several participation *issues (e.g., adapting an assignment, simplifying instructional worksheets, keeping Walter's attention focused). However, Walter's team delineates and confronts its concerns regarding his goals and abilities every year when the IEP is addressed, his classes are selected, and transition plans made. Despite Walter's many needs for academic support, he blends in well with peers, has friends, and behaves in socially appropriate ways; his team is not concerned about his* membership or belonging in classes. *(Figure 4.4 shows Walter's Program-at-a-Glance.)*

Reaching consensus on an issue or problem before the team focuses on a solution can be accomplished in several ways:

- Take a divergent/convergent approach: First, list all of the visible problems and challenges team members have seen the student perform in the class or activity of concern. Then, converge on one problem or a combination of behaviors that defines or restates the problem to reflect the teams' view.

- Examine the problem; avoid discussing solutions.

- Write out the problem, then seek additions, deletions, and alternate ideas.

- Determine the type of problem (e.g., goal/ability, participation, membership) and decide whether other types of problems exist; add these to the problem statement to fully define the concern.

- Apply consensus-reaching methods to reach team agreement on the problem (compare with student data; when there seems to be some agreement, ask the team

"Does everyone feel comfortable with addressing this problem?" Or, set a time limit for discussion, then ask for consensus).

The step of clarifying the problem on which to focus is referred to as "problem-finding" by Giangreco (1993) and Isaksen and Parnes (1992). Problem-finding is identified as the third step in the Osborne-Parnes Creative Problem-Solving (CPS) Process that teachers have used on collaborative teams in inclusive programs (Figure 4.5). Isaksen, Parnes, and Giangreco view problem-finding as a two-phase, divergent/convergent process that involves expanding the problem list prior to defining or limiting it. The expanded list of related problem behaviors can serve as a worksheet for the team and may help shift the focus from the original problem to one that is more relevant to the student or situation, is of higher priority, is more comprehensive or encompasses earlier problems, or needs to be resolved first.

Step 2
Brainstorm Possible Solutions

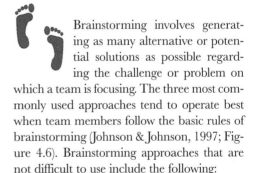 Brainstorming involves generating as many alternative or potential solutions as possible regarding the challenge or problem on which a team is focusing. The three most commonly used approaches tend to operate best when team members follow the basic rules of brainstorming (Johnson & Johnson, 1997; Figure 4.6). Brainstorming approaches that are not difficult to use include the following:

Freewheeling Team members state their ideas as quickly as possible without taking turns. (This method promotes the most spontaneity and enthusiasm and is the easiest to use; however, it may become too lively for the recorder to write down all of the ideas.)

Round Robin Team members take turns stating their ideas in an around-the-circle fashion. If a team member cannot contribute an idea within a few seconds, that member passes and the next person in the circle takes a turn. Brainstorming concludes once each consecutive participant has passed. (This method is

Program-at-a-Glance

Student: _Walter_   **Date:** _9/3/99_

IEP objectives (briefly)	**Accommodations**

IEP objectives (briefly)

All classes

- Bring materials.
- Take notes.
- Participate in class discussions.
- Complete adapted assignments and tests.
- Follow oral directions of teacher.
- Use self-management checks.

Math

- Practice basic operations.
- Read and understand graphs.
- Understand basic geometry terms.
- Complete measurement of lines and angles.

English

- Locate information in reference source.
- Listen to literature selections and answer factual comprehension questions.
- Compose brief journal entries and essays.
- Keep organized notebook and assignment planner.

Transition Plan & Work-Study

- Complete job exploration experiences.
- Identify job interests.

Accommodations

- Walter is exempt from midterm and final exams.
- Extend time on tests and projects as needed.
- Work toward an IEP diploma.

Academic/ social management needs

- Walter needs prompting and positive feedback in order to maintain attention to task.
- Monitor assignment planner notes and self-management checks.

Comments/special needs

Figure 4.4.   Walter's Program-at-a-Glance. (Contributed by Christine Burton.)

most useful when some team members dominate and others are hesitant to participate.)

Slip Method Team members write out each of their ideas on separate slips of paper and pass them in to the recorder. They are then mixed and written on newsprint for the entire team to see. (Although this method is

useful when the problem is controversial, the process is slower than the other two methods.)

Giangreco and his colleagues (1994) described additional approaches for generating ideas during brainstorming. These approaches are used within the structure provided by freewheeling, round robin, or the

Stage 1: Objective-finding ("Mess" finding)

Divergent: List broad objectives or goals of a program; imagine potential challenges (without judgment, explanation, or discussion).

Convergent: Converge on the best way to state the objective; select the best way to state the challenge.

Stage 2: Fact-finding

Divergent:

- List as many facts as possible regarding the objective/challenge: facts might concern the student's needs or the class or activity.
- Present facts without explanation, judgment, or discussion in a short time period (5–8 minutes):
  - Facts can include team members' feelings.
  - Facts include what people believe to be true about the challenge situation.
  - Facts are recorded and saved for later use (during idea finding).

Convergent: Select a subset of relevant facts to assist problem-finding in the next stage.

Stage 3: Problem-finding

Divergent: Clarify the challenge or problem by considering different ways of viewing it: "In what ways might we . . .?" Repeat the question until the team feels confident that it has teased out the real issue.

Convergent: Select one of the new challenge statements that the team agrees it most wants to solve. Prompt consensus by asking team members questions such as

- Which of these challenges do we most desperately want to accomplish or solve?
- If we could help this student or could resolve one problem right now, what would that be?

Stage 4: Idea-finding

Divergent:

- Ideas are potential solutions to the challenge statements from stage 3.
- Ideas emerge through brainstorming (i.e., a divergent process to stretch beyond the obvious): short time periods; people speak quickly in short phrases, not sentences; ideas are recorded quickly; aim for quantity; use free-wheeling or round robin.
- Use techniques and "idea joggers" to jar ideas loose:
  - Forced relationships/ rearrange: Combine two ideas/objects with little apparent relationship in some way to generate a new idea to solve a problem.
  - Synectics: Make the strange familiar and the familiar strange so things can be seen in new ways (facts about student and challenges).
  - Incubation: Move away from the challenge for a time to engage in different activities; return to it later.
  - Idea joggers:
    - Make some fact about the situation smaller or bigger, rearrange it, eliminate it, reverse or turn it upside down or inside out.
    - Hitch-hiking effect: Build new ideas on ideas of another.

Convergent: Separate out the ideas with the most promise and appeal.

Stage 5: Solution-finding

Divergent: List criteria or ways to evaluate the ideas generated.

Convergent: Focus on each idea and evaluate it by each criterion; asking whether it meets or fails the criterion. Eliminate all but those judged as acceptable to the team. Combine those ideas to create the solution(s).

Stage 6: Acceptance-finding

Divergent: Find ways to implement the ideas by asking the following questions: who, what, where, when, why, and how?

Convergent: Develop a plan of action that delineates actions to be taken, by whom, and when.

Figure 4.5.   Stages of the Osborn-Parnes Creative Problem-Solving Process. (From Giangreco, M.F., Cloninger, C.J., Dennis, R.E., & Edelman, S.W. [1994]. Problem-solving methods to facilitate inclusive education. In J.S. Thousand, R.A. Villa, & A.I. Nevin [Eds.], *Creativity and collaborative learning: A practical guide to empowering students and teachers* (pp. 321–346). Baltimore: Paul H. Brookes Publishing Co.; adapted with permission.)

---

1. No negative reactions or comments are allowed.
2. Freewheeling is welcomed, save criticism for later.
3. Withhold discussion and judgment.
4. Focus on quantity, not quality.
5. Set a short time limit; generate ideas quickly.
6. Assign a recorder who writes fast and translates ideas into phrases or key words.

Figure 4.6. Rules for brainstorming. (From David W. Johnson & Frank P. Johnson, JOINING TOGETHER: GROUP THEORY AND GROUP SKILLS 6/E © 1997 by Allyn & Bacon. Adapted by permission.)

slip method to help teams lengthen their list of ideas (diverge) and separate out those that are most promising (converge).

1. *Diverge to generate direct ideas: Direct ideas* are those that result from comparing the two displays of facts that a team may have generated earlier regarding a given problem (e.g., facts about the student and the student's need and facts about the class/activity). Team members can seek connections between the two lists through a comparison of facts (see Figure 4.7). (This approach reveals "naturally occurring opportunities for meaningful inclusion" that can be taken advantage of without making major changes in routine [Giangreco et al., 1994].)

2. *Diverge to generate indirect ideas: Indirect ideas* result from the team's use of "idea-stimulators." Individuals who have studied the creative aspects of problem-solving have found ways to stimulate a group's creativity to facilitate the discovery or innovation

of additional potential solutions by "jogging ideas loose," seeing things differently, building on ideas, and combining ideas (Giangreco et al., 1994; Parnes, 1992). Sometimes the wildest ideas lead to the discovery of another unique but practical idea that would have otherwise not been found.

3. *Converge to find the most promising ideas:* The divergent-convergent approach to brainstorming has teams follow their idea-finding session by culling out or converging upon the most interesting, promising, or intriguing ideas (Isaksen & Parnes, 1992). The recorder might "move" the group through each generated idea and ask, "Keep for now or toss?" This activity is not the same as comparing ideas against team criteria; it simply helps narrow the list. Team members may need to offer brief explanations of ideas that were not fully explained during the divergent brainstorming. The ideas that are circled for further exploration are

---

Facts about Walter and his needs (partial list)	**Facts about the class/activity** (partial list)
• He is talented in art.	• Assignment is to learn and tell about a famous mathematician.
• His English objective is to compose brief journal entries and essays.	• Assignment is due in 2 weeks.
• He needs practice locating information in reference sources.	• Assignment should be on paper.

Q: What about Walter's art skills and his English needs (from the list of facts about Walter) relate to the assignment on a mathematician biography?

A: Walter could complete drawings for his report about the selected mathematician and supplement the drawings with shorter written remarks.

Figure 4.7. Comparison of facts.

considered during the evaluation of possible solutions.

Step 3
Evaluate the Possible Solutions

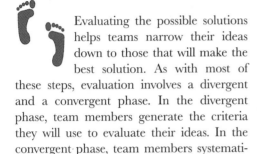

Evaluating the possible solutions helps teams narrow their ideas down to those that will make the best solution. As with most of these steps, evaluation involves a divergent and a convergent phase. In the divergent phase, team members generate the criteria they will use to evaluate their ideas. In the convergent phase, team members systematically compare each idea against the criteria and judge its acceptability; then, they pull the "winning" ideas together into a solution.

What criteria should a team use? Initially, teams might start from scratch and "generate all conceivable consequences, repercussions, or implications of the ideas" (Isaken & Parnes, 1992, p. 439). This list is then edited to eliminate redundant criteria and to improve clarity. Teams who work together for a while often develop some standard criteria that match their shared values and the student(s) they support (Figure 4.8). However, even these teams can benefit from reviewing their criteria list for possible omissions before evaluating potential solutions. Using a criteria worksheet can help teams be more systematic at this stage of problem solving. Figure 4.9 shows a form Giangreco and his colleagues have found useful.

Step 4
Choose a Solution

Although team members select the "best bet" when they choose a solution, the solution should be viewed as only a trial until it proves workable. Also, teams may find several "winning" solutions that can be combined into a more comprehensive answer to the problem. When teams have time to address several problems in a session, multiple solutions will be chosen. The agenda needs to allot enough time for team members to fully examine the solutions to each problem. Attaining team consensus on the choice of solutions also should not be sacrificed due to a

---

Applying Criteria to Potential Solutions:
How will we judge if an idea or a potential accommodation is a good one?

_____ 1. Is it "doable" and reasonable?
_____ 2. Is it time-effective?
_____ 3. Does it promote school/community access?
_____ 4. Does it provide opportunities to interact with peers?
_____ 5. Does it provide opportunities to communicate?
_____ 6. Is it cost effective?
_____ 7. Is it safe?
_____ 8. Is it team generated?
_____ 9. Is it related to specific classroom demands?
_____ 10. Does it empower, rather than humiliate, the student?
_____ 11. Is it student-validated or generated?
_____ 12. Does it meet class requirements?
_____ 13. Does it incorporate best practices?
_____ 14. Other:
_____ 15. Other:

Figure 4.8. Criteria for deciding if an idea is a good one. (From Giangreco, M.F., Cloninger, C.J., Dennis, R.E., & Edelman, S.W. [1994]. Problem-solving methods to facilitate inclusive education. In J.S. Thousand, R.A. Villa, & A.I. Nevin [Eds.], *Creativity and collaborative learning: A practical guide to empowering students and teachers* [pp. 321–346]. Baltimore: Paul H. Brookes Publishing Co.; adapted by permission.)

Solution finding	Criteria				
Potential solutions	Addresses student need	Neutral or positive for students without disabilities	Likely to support valued life outcomes	Perceived as usable by users (e.g., teacher, student, parent)	Other
1.					
2.					
3.					
4.					
5.					
6.					
7.					
8.					
9.					
10.					
11.					
12.					

Figure 4.9. Solution-finding worksheet: Evaluating ideas and finding solutions. (From Giangreco, M.F., Cloninger, C.J., Dennis, R.E., & Edelman, S.W. [1994]. Problem-solving methods to facilitate inclusive education. In J.S. Thousand, R.A. Villa, & A.I. Nevin [Eds.], *Creativity and collaborative learning: A practical guide to empowering students and teachers* [pp. 321–346]. Baltimore: Paul H. Brookes Publishing Co.; adapted by permission.)

lack of time, particularly if the team members not in agreement with the solution are those who will be the primary implementers of it. Sometimes, it may be better for teams to move forward with some solutions and delay others until agreement can be reached.

Step 5
Write an Action Plan

 Teams need to build enough time into their agendas to complete action plans or even the best solutions may never be realized. The primary elements of an action plan are

- *Issue:* What is the issue(s) on which we need to take action?

- *Action:* What action(s) do we agree to take to resolve this issue?

- *Who Is Responsible:* Who will help develop or implement this action(s)?

- *By When:* When will the planned action(s) be implemented?

Teams are usually motivated by their results at this point in a session, and, if everyone has been participating, it usually is easy to reach consensus on each element planned for the issues addressed. Consensus at this point of problem-solving is just as important as at any other point because team members are

Issue/Action Planning Form

Student/Team/Group: _Walter_   **Date:** _11/16/99_

Team Members Present: _Chris Burton, Arlene Brown_

Issue	Planned action	Person(s) responsible	By when
Assignment on famous mathematicians	Walter will listen to the teacher assistant (TA) read biographical information about the mathematician, then he'll tell aloud what he's gotten out of the information while the TA writes it down. Then he'll type it into the computer and print it. Finally, he'll use his art skills to illustrate the one-paragraph report.	Chris will write out, review with Joan, and monitor; Joan (TA) will implement.	11/18
Next week's lessons	Chris will prepare his worksheets by eliminating all the algebraic equation problems.	Chris	11/17
Behavior checklist to self-monitor attending and talk-out behavior in class	Continue as is; teachers will examine at end of each class and comment to Walter.	All	11/17 to 11/23

Figure 4.10. Issue/Action Planing Form for Walter in Geometry.

deciding how their ideas or solutions will be implemented.

Walter's teachers used a simple Issue/Action Planning Form to record their plans (Figure 4.10):

First, they reviewed how Walter might complete his 6-week project on famous mathematicians and agreed to the following adaptations: Walter will listen to the teacher assistant (TA) read biographical information; then, he'll state aloud what he's grasped from the information while the TA (Joan) writes it down. Walter will then type the TA's notes into the computer and print them. Finally, he'll use his art skills to illustrate the one-paragraph report. Second, the classroom teacher showed Chris, the special education teacher, the problems for the upcoming week; and, based on Walter's adapted objectives for the class, Chris agreed to prepare Walter's work by eliminating all the algebraic

equation problems. Finally, the classroom teacher and Chris hurriedly reviewed Walter's second week of using a five-point behavior checklist to self-monitor his attending and talking-out behavior during class. Following the meeting, Chris shared the adapted biography assignment with the TA. Throughout the week, there were frequent "on-the-fly" interactions between the two teachers and the TA in order to implement, evaluate, and improve the ideas that evolved from the lunch-time meeting.

Sometimes, teams will identify preparatory steps that need to be undertaken before an action plan can be fully developed or implemented (e.g., checking with student, peers, or parents; assessment; preparation of materials). This step includes checking with team members or outsiders who were absent when the plan was discussed—but are nonetheless critical participants—so the plan reflects team consensus. Implementation usually works

only when team members continue their collaboration but do it "on-the-fly" while coordinating their efforts. Thus, during the development of the action plan, the team should schedule a follow-up meeting, unless regular core team meetings are already in place. Often, the special education teacher and the general education teacher will repeatedly "touch base" with each other as they implement the plan and observe its effects, sometimes even making quick refinements without drawing the team back together again. Team trust, along with ongoing communication, allows core team members to make these adjustments in the team's plan and shortens the implementation time. Face-to-face discussion allows teams to develop excellent plans, but it is only through actual "field-tests" that solutions can be found and resolution achieved.

Specific Problem-Solving Approaches

This next section presents brief overviews of several problem-solving approaches.

Creative Problem-Solving Approach The Osborn-Parnes Creative Problem-Solving Process in Figure 4.5, when used by a highly experienced team, is designed to take 30 minutes. Initial team exchange considers what the "mess" is and what problems constitute the mess (Stage 1 [objective finding]: e.g., The Famous Mathematicians assignment requires many skills that Walter has not demonstrated on his own). Next, the team lists and describes relevant information about the student, the task, and the class and then circles the facts that relate most to Walter and the mess (Stage 2 [fact finding]: e.g., Walter's IEP objectives in writing or language arts, due date, assignment requirements, Walter's interests, available support). Third, the team returns to the mess and generates a listing of the many related challenges or problems that are relevant (Stage 3 [problem finding]): then, they decide on a single problem to address (e.g., *"The assignment needs be adapted so that Walter can actively participate in all steps and learn some things that are relevant to his IEP."*). This problem is then rephrased as a question to be answered (e.g., *"In what ways might we modify the history assignment so Walter can actively participate in all steps and learn some things relevant to his IEP?"*).

Once a concern has been identified and information has been shared that is pertinent to the concern, teams shift to the task of creating a solution. This task requires several tools, the first of which is brainstorming (Stage 4 [idea finding]). Giangreco and co-workers in Vermont have emphasized the importance of rapid, nonjudgmental, uninhibited, "freewheeling" brainstorming. Stage 5, which addresses solution finding, has team members create, review, or revise a list of criteria against which they judge each generated idea (Stage 5 [solution finding]). Teams that have time limitations might shorten the attention they give to Step 5 by using previously set criteria. Teams will use both sit-down meetings and "on-the-fly" meetings to problem-solve and may need to truncate the "on-the-fly" process due to time limitations and the pressure to "do something" (Snell & Janney, in press).

During sit-down meetings, teams may spend additional time fashioning the solution as they discuss strategies for gaining team consensus (from absent team members and the student) on the solution and plan the actions that need to be taken, by whom, and when (Stage 6 [acceptance finding]).

A specific form is not used with this approach, except for during the last stage; instead, large pieces of paper, each with the step number and title at the top in large letters, are taped to the wall or the blackboard is used instead of the paper. One recorder writes the team contributions on these large pieces of paper for all team members to see (teams often need to refer back to their comments as they move through the steps), while a second recorder documents the details of the action plan on an $8^{1}/_{2}'' \times 11''$ Issue/Action Planning Form (see Blank Forms in the back of this book for a copy).

Get Some Help from SAM This approach is a shorter version of the six-stage CPS method previously described. Very experienced teams can apply this method in 15 minutes, but it is easier to use when a team has 20–30 minutes. SAM frames the problem-

solving around the target student's IEP objectives (Giangreco et al. 1994). Giangreco et al. have used this approach both with teams of staff and parents and teams of students. When peers are very familiar with the target student, this approach can work well. The teacher directs peers to a cluster of relevant goals for the target student and then asks them to consider these goals while seeking solutions to a problem.

Teams *begin* with a problem stated as follows: "*In what ways might we address the educational needs of (student) in (class/activity)?*" Next, they move through the four steps in the SAM process:

- *Fact-Finding:* List facts about the student and the student's needs; list facts about the class or activity.

- *Idea-Finding:* Generate direct and indirect ideas through brainstorming.

- *Solution-Finding:* Evaluate each idea against the team's criteria.

- *Acceptance-Finding:* Write actions plans that address the what, who, where, how, and when.

When teams use the SAM approach to problem-solve, it is particularly helpful to write notes on large newsprint organized to match the form originated by Giangreco and his coworkers (1994, pp. 336–337) in addition to recording written notes on a smaller form to preserve meeting deliberation and results. (Refer to the end of this book for a blank copy of the SAM form.)

Simpler Problem-Solving Approaches Used by Peers

Peer problem-solving is a valuable tool; however, teaching and monitoring is required. Problem-solving skills can be applied to class meetings to resolve problems presented by any student (not just focus students), to work through class conflicts (provided that the methods are used in a respectful manner), and to resolve issues that develop in the school community (Giangreco et al., 1994;

Nelson, 1987). When peers are the problem-solvers, the focus student is often included in the problem-solving sessions; however, teachers, along with the student's parents, friends, and the student him- or herself, should make this decision. (Refer to *Social Relationships and Peer Support,* another booklet in this series, for additional information on peer problem-solving [Snell & Janney, 2000].)

There are several advantages to involving peers in problem-solving. Peers will typically apply peer norms to the problem and avoid ideas that might be stigmatizing to their classmates. They often are more sensitive than adults to the student's chronological age and to what is or is not "cool." Classmates are typically aware of natural supports that students will find agreeable and that may lead to positive peer connections. Finally, peers often think on a different plane than adults. Just when adults are ready to give up, peers offer ideas of which adults never dreamed.

Although including peers in the problem-solving process can prove quite beneficial, opening team issues to peers requires that certain precautions be heeded to maintain the dignity of target students and to protect their rights. Before peers are involved, the focus student should be asked in private whether he or she objects to peer involvement in lending support and in seeking solutions of benefit to him or her. Even if communication with the student is difficult, this step should not be skipped. These plans, if not developed along with the student's parents, are then shared with them. It has been our experience that most parents like the idea of involving their child's peers, but they want the involvement of their child's classmates to be "empowering" and not stigmatizing. Although information relevant to a particular problem is frequently shared among the student's team members, information regarding the student's disability is private and confidential; sharing any aspect of this information with peers must only be done with permission and with sensitivity, and the information should be pertinent to the problem the team is addressing.

Elementary and middle school students are less likely to be involved in team meetings

with professionals and more likely to contribute ideas during small-group or class problem-solving activities. The processes for involving peers are as varied as the teacher's imagination. Giangreco and his co-workers (1994) described several strategies for getting kids to problem-solve:

1-Minute Idea Finding This process (which can last longer than 1 minute) consists of on-the-spot brainstorming by students regarding a situation that needs immediate resolution. The student may be present or absent depending on the situation and the student. For example, a kindergarten teacher might ask her students, *"How can we get Nate to play more with us?"* or, an eighth-grade homeroom teacher might say to his students, *"Erica needs to get things out of her backpack and put things into it every class period, but the pack hangs on her chair behind her and is difficult for her to reach and move. How can we help Erica with this?"*

There are limitations to this approach; time may not allow enough creativity beyond "standard" answers, and students may need additional information in order to provide higher quality ideas.

1-Minute Idea Finding With a Fact-Finding Back-Up With this approach, the teacher assesses whether additional information is needed to focus or to stimulate more effective brain-storming. The teacher might ask idea-jogging questions (*"What would happen if Erica was tired of asking you guys for help every time?"*) or provide needed information (*"It takes longer for Erica to pick things up because she has cerebral palsy, and that means that the muscles in her arms and hands don't do what she tells them to do; they work slower than she wants them to."*). This approach often helps students get "unstuck" from ideas that will not work.

Problem-Solvers Club Salisbury and her colleagues (Salisbury, Evans, & Palombaro, 1997; Salisbury & Palombaro, 1993) described an approach that was developed in an elementary school called the "Problem-Solvers Club." The second, third, and fourth graders in the club learned to use *collaborative problem-solving* steps, which they applied in cooperative groups to problems that arose in their inclusive school. The five steps were not unlike those that teachers use to identify solutions (Salisbury & Palombaro, 1993):

1. *What's happening here?* Deciding on what the problem is when you know something is not right.

2. *What can we do?* Brainstorming solutions and figuring out what should be tried first (the "fun part").

3. *What would really work?* Asking questions for every possible solution: For example *"Will it be good for all kids?"* or, *"Will you or your group really be able to do this? Do you have the materials and the time?"*

4. *Take action!* Getting everyone to agree on the best solution, then trying it out.

5. *How did we do? (Did we change things?)* Figuring out if the solution worked like you wanted it to or if further action is necessary.

The team tackled problems such as 1) getting people with injuries or disabilities out of the school safely during fires or fire drills, 2) name calling in school, and 3) kids in class who are bullies or bothersome. The club's solutions often worked partially, and the evaluation step allowed them to revisit their ideas and improve them. The Problem-Solvers Club proved that students often simply need a little structure and guidance and the permission to apply their creativity to problems they are interested in resolving. Adults do not control these groups; rather, they facilitate them, listen to students, and show respect for their voices and ideas (even if they may not always agree).

No matter who does the problem-solving—core teams, whole teams, or peers with adult facilitators—its central importance to collaborative teams cannot be underestimated.

COLLABORATE TO DESIGN PROGRAMS

Collaboration among team members is required by law (the Individuals with Disabilities Education Act [IDEA] of 1990, PL 101-476) during assessment, IEP development,

and program design because it enhances the efforts of educational teams and benefits students. This section of the chapter provides a brief overview of how teams design their action plans to encompass staff support. (For coverage of collaboration specific to assessment, IEP development, and program design, consult the following resources: two books in this series, *Modifying Schoolwork* and *Behavioral Support* by Janney and Snell, 2000a, 2000b; DeBoer & Fister, 1995–1996; Rainforth & York-Barr, 1997.)

Organizing Support Options with Staff Schedules and Training

Inclusive schools often organize the support for included students according to the needs of the students (McLaughlin & Warren, 1992; Roach, 1995). Support levels differ depending on who is involved, the extent of the student's needs, and the numbers and types of adaptations and accommodations a team recommends in their plan of action.

A primary goal of the IEP committee (i.e., the whole or extended team) in inclusive programs is to determine how they will collaborate as a team in order to facilitate the student's success. In many inclusive schools, IEP committees define support in part by matching the type of collaborative relationship with the amount or intensity of support needed by a target student. Student and staffing schedules are then coordinated so the supports can be delivered. The organization of supports seems to be more formalized in secondary schools than in elementary schools. Figure 4.11 shows one way in which a high school has organized its support options for students with disabilities. The supports for Rick, the ninth grader described previously, are fairly

---

1. **General education instruction with consultation and accommodation**

   Student is enrolled only in general education classes. The special education teacher informs teachers of student's needs and monitors progress in all classes. When accommodations are required (having tests read aloud) or instruction is needed (assistance with organizing a paper), the class teacher or the student makes arrangements with the special educator to provide these services. The special education teacher regularly communicates in person with the classroom teacher.

2. **Support from an instructional aide in one or more general education classes**

   Student may need an aide for assistance with accommodations (e.g., help in reading or note-taking). Classroom teacher and aide consult with special education teacher to monitor student progress.

3. **Special education instruction in context of one or more general education classes and/or a general education tutorial**

   General and special education teachers collaborate within the regular classroom to ensure that student is successful in content classes. The nature of these collaborative relationships vary depending on staff involved but are more intense than the first two levels. These students may be working on adapted curricula (e.g., different goals, materials) or on an unmodified class curricula with accommodations as needed.

4. **Special education instruction in a pull-out setting**

   A few students request instruction in a small class or in a one-to-one setting. This service also may be provided as it is needed throughout the day. One or more places in the building are designated for this level of service including the study hall, library, or another quiet area. Students who have emotional or behavioral problems often use this setting as a "safe zone."

5. **Special education instruction in the community**

   Students with more significant disabilities receive community-based and vocational instruction in the local area.

Figure 4.11. Levels of team support provided in a high school setting. (Contributed by Johnna Elliott.)

intense due to his need for ongoing behavioral and social support; Rick has supports at Level 3 in English and math and at Level 2 in his other classes and tutorials. Walter's support needs are for intermittent assistance to monitor homework completion, to assist with completion of in-class assignments, or to provide accommodations. Walter needs support at Levels 2 and 3. Both the source of support and its intensity are individually determined by the team and re-evaluated over time.

Other practices within school districts (or within particular states) might dictate or influence how special education teachers are assigned to students, which, in turn, may influence how collaborative teams design education programs. For example, experienced special education teachers might be designated as *consulting teachers* in middle schools and high schools or across several elementary schools. Consulting teachers coordinate the efforts of other special education teachers, oversee procedures (e.g., eligibility and IEP meetings), troubleshoot, and serve as the liaison between administration and students. Though consulting teachers often have a slightly smaller caseload of students, the school district's support structure allows them the flexibility to handle any crises that arise (e.g., mediate a conflict that arises between ninth grader Rick and several peers; fill in as the substitute for fourth-grader Quincey when the substitute fails to show up; make a home visit when tenth grader Walter misses a week of classes). In other schools, the principal and teachers use their experience and shared decision-making authority to devise their own procedures for organizing special education support for different grades and students. School districts also may seek waivers from state guidelines when regulations conflict with a district's innovative organization. Waiver options, with some safeguards for abuse, can positively influence change in school districts and improvement in state policy. Thus, school organization and local and state policy may influence team formation and the ways in which special education teachers are assigned to support students; this in turn affects how

collaborative teams design support for the students they serve.

Organizing Paperwork

Consistent with what planning teams do and with the programs and support schedules they design, teams will need to develop ways to organize information about students and to keep records of the students' schedules and staff schedules. (Another booklet in this series, *Modifying Schoolwork* [Janney & Snell, 2000b] provides further detail regarding the organization of information.)

Student Information Often, consulting special education teachers who oversee middle and secondary special education programs find that it is essential to keep, in a safe place, a large notebook containing student information and support schedules readily available to team members. In one section of the notebook, *materials are arranged by student;* the information is kept current and tells at a glance where each student who requires special services is during each period of the day (i.e., student schedule), their grades and personal information (i.e., Student Profile and Information Sheet) and a listing of their objectives and accommodations (i.e., Program-at-a-Glance).

A Program Planning Matrix, when used, is another piece of useful planning information that may be kept in the student section of the notebook. An example of a Student Profile and Information Sheet for ninth-grader Rick appears in Figure 4.12.

Modifying Schoolwork and *Behavioral Support,* two other booklets in this series (Janney and Snell, 2000), describe several other student informational documents that may be more useful for some students than others. For example, with Daniel, the second grader who receives both occupational and physical therapy, a Related Services Schedule would be especially helpful in documenting the actual provision of these services each week. Additional informational forms that pertain to planning that is specific to a particular student's modifications might be designed by teams and kept in a team or grade-level notebook (e.g., minutes of team meetings, Assess-

Student Profile
and Information Sheet

Name: _Rick_

Address: _____

Parent/Guardian: _____

Phone Number: _____

Emergency Contact Person: _Parents_

  Name: _____

  Phone: _____

Date of Birth: _6/2/85_

Grade: _9_

Team: _____

Support Person: _Elliott_

IEP Date: _5/14/98_

Eligibility Date: _12/14/97_

Service %: _100_

Exceptionality: _OHI_

Literacy Passport Test Areas left to take:

Reading ✔   Writing ✔   Math ___

Period/Room Subject/Teacher		1st 6 wk		2nd 6 wk		3rd 6 wk		4th 6 wk		5th 6 wk		6th 6 wk	
		1a	1b	2a	2b	3a	3b	4a	4b	5a	5b	6a	6b
1. Geography Little Warren			B		B		B B						
2. Algebra 1 Dane Talley		complete assign- ment	A	94	A	A	A A A						
3. Health/PE Morris Warren		47	B		A	A	A B B						
4. Art Smith-Ansler Warren		D	B		B		B C B						
5. English 9 Elliot Wilson		80	B	80	B		B D C						
6. Food Occupations Turner Andrews		B+	B	A	B	B	B A B						
7. Study Hall Elliot													

(a) = interim progress report   (b) = 6-weeks grade

Comments:

Figure 4.12.   Student Profile and Information Sheet for Rick. (Contributed by Johnna Elliott.)

ment of Classroom Procedures, Adaptations Plan, Unit Plans, Weekly Plan for Specific Adaptations, Adaptations Instructional Program Plans, Behavioral Support Plan, Lists of Supplementary or Alternative Activities, or tests and worksheets that need to be adapted). Teams will select ways to summarize their plans for a student's modifications that both suit their need for information and match the student's educational program and supports. Often, standard forms are more useful to a team when they are adapted to correspond to the team's own style and organization.

Teacher and Class Paperwork In the second section of large notebook, *materials are arranged by teacher and class.* This section contains copies of forms that pertain to class support and teacher support, such as the Classroom Support Plan for Inclusion and the Teacher Assistance Guide. The Classroom Support Plan summarizes each student's general support needs, when the classroom teacher meets with the special education teacher, peer support used, if any, type(s) of support from special education staff, and a plan to follow if difficulties arise. Whenever a student is scheduled to be included in a class, a Support Plan is completed for that particular class period (Figure 4.13 shows the Support Plan for Inclusion for English 9). A Teacher Assistance Guide (Figure 4.14) is completed for each inclusive classroom that describes class tasks and test characteristics and details the ways in which special education staff will assist. Rick's English teacher, Ms. Wilson, has copies of each of these two forms, which were completed with Rick's core team at the beginning of the school year.

Support Plan for Inclusion

General Ed. Teacher: *Ms. Wilson*   **Special Ed. Teacher:** *Elliott*

Class: *English 9*   **Period:** *5*   **Room:** *V-1* **Date:** *10-2-99*

1. **Students who require special support in this class (attach Program-at-a-Glance for each student):**

   Rick: Social & behavioral support

   Ted: ADHD—attention/focus difficulties

   Ed: Learning disabilities—written language

2. **Schedule for Consultation with Special Education Teacher:**

   Fridays—6th period

3. **Plan for adapting materials:**

   Rick has study hall during which he will try to complete some homework.

   Elliott will modify assignments if necessary.

4. **Peer support plan within this class:**

   Most students know Rick and support him.

   If problems arise, Elliott will talk to students individually—may do a whole class or peer planning.

5. **Amount and type of assistance needed from special education staff:**

   Ongoing daily support, co-teach when possible

6. **Intervention plan if difficulties arise:**

   Elliott will deal with Rick and pull him out if he becomes too disruptive.

Figure 4.13.   Support Plan for Inclusion for Rick and others in English. (Contributed by Johnna Elliott.)

Teacher Assistance Guide

Teacher: _Ms. Wilson_   **Class:** _English 9_   **Semester/Year:** _9/99_

Typical classroom tasks:

- *Take notes from overhead*
- *Participate in discussion*
- *Turn in grammar worksheets*
- *Use reference material in library*

Homework tasks:

- *Write book reports*
- *Write paragraphs on assigned topics*
- *Write research paper*

Testing:

- *Format: multiple choice and short answer*
- *Test types:*
  Literature: short answer
  Grammar: proof and correct sentences for mechanics and usage
- *Sources of information:*
  Class notes (most of literature test taken from notes), literature selections, grammar book
- *Recommended study guide format:*
  Literature: flashcard method; make cards from class notes
  Grammar: none recommended; class practices on grammar worksheets daily

General teacher assistance requested:

Ms. Wilson would like help with the following tasks as time permits:

1. *Duplicate grammar worksheets a few days in advance*
2. *Take small group to library to help using reference materials (may include non-identified students as indicated by teacher)*
3. *Check off those turning in homework as they come into class*

Additional notes:

During grammar lesson on Fridays, pull specified students to study for tests or help them in library with their research

Figure 4.14. Teacher Assistance Guide. (Contributed by Christine Burton and Johnna Elliott.)

It is important to remember that the information on written schedules of special education support is confidential and should not be openly displayed or discussed; use of student initials or codes rather than actual names is preferable.

DELIVER COORDINATED PROGRAMS

Once programs have been designed, a team's focus shifts to implementation. The primary work of implementation is done by the class-

room and special education teachers; the primary tool is communication between team members who implement and those who support. For some students, paraprofessionals may play a critical part in putting action plans into place. However, paraprofessionals do not write programs; they carry them out with instruction and supervision from teachers. When students require services from related services staff (e.g., occupational and physical therapists, speech-language pathologists, vision and mobility specialists, nurses), the program design should reflect the input of

these staff members; program implementation may need their monitoring "to iron out the wrinkles." Again, teachers are critical in the implementation of programs; therefore, they need to maintain communication with therapists so their efforts in realizing the team's recommendations are successful. Coordinating the efforts of team members to ensure smooth delivery of students' programs is challenging. This section addresses several aspects of program delivery in inclusive schools: coordinating with paraprofessionals and related services team members and utilizing administrative support.

Coordinating with Paraprofessionals

Strategies to Build Skills Skill development is often an issue when teaching assistants are involved in the implementation of a student's program. Both teachers and related services professionals are in excellent positions to build the skills of the paraprofessional as they work together to implement teaching programs. Written summaries of instructional modifications for each student (e.g., Program-at-a-Glance, Figure 4.4, and Support Plan for Inclusion, Figure 4.13) are particularly important when paraprofessionals must implement many different adaptations and accommodations for students in various classrooms. These guides serve as reminders to all team members of the team-generated modifications. Photos of teaching approaches can also help promote consistency among teachers, related services staff, and paraprofessionals (who may not know the theory behind the approach or have had training in using the approach). For example, the two paraprofessionals who serve Daniel check photos showing how to lift, move, and position Daniel in his new floor seat before attempting it themselves. In other cases, either the materials, the simple task analysis data sheets, or both will help prompt paraprofessionals and other teaching staff to consistently implement programs in areas such as:

1. Communication: *Daniel uses a switch to activate a taped message; Quincey uses picture symbols to request items.*

2. Daily functional routines: *Jennifer follows the steps to go through the cafeteria line and cleans up when she has finished eating.*

3. Academics: *Quincey uses a number line; Jennifer rounds up to the nearest dollar when making purchases during school-based instruction.*

None of these visuals (e.g., written instructions, materials, photos, or task analyses) should replace direct instruction and monitoring by a teacher or other professional team member. The entire team and the student benefit when students' action plans specify who is responsible for developing the skills of paraprofessionals who deliver team-generated programs and professional staff who might need assistance in using a new or unfamiliar procedure with the focus student.

As is the case with any learner, the skill needs of paraprofessional staff members are highly individual and may be more variable than the skill needs of most team members. In university towns, many paraprofessionals are actually professional teachers waiting for a position to open. By contrast, in rural environments, paraprofessionals may have little experience teaching and learning and may need some sensitization toward children with disabilities.

Supervision From an administrative standpoint, paraprofessionals who support students with special education needs are often considered "special education staff"; therefore, direct supervision is the responsibility of special education teachers. Teaching assistants, however, spend most of their time apart from special education teachers in general education classrooms. Consequently, the process for teaching, monitoring, and supervising paraprofessionals' skills needs to be shared between the classroom and the special education teachers. The classroom teacher and the special education teacher should confer with each other (and with the teaching assistant) regarding the way in which the teaching assistant will be supervised, the skills that the teaching assistant already possesses, those skills that need strengthening, and how these needs will be met. Core teachers are often in the best position to compare notes on the skill

needs and progress of paraprofessionals and to take advantage of the naturalistic opportunities to teach and to reinforce learning in paraprofessionals. When team members practice *role release* and share their talents by demonstrating procedures and methods (either role played or naturalistically), thus adding to team-developed programs, the result often is that paraprofessionals get more instructional time from more team members than do any others on the team.

Coordinating with Related Services Team Members

If related services personnel are members of a team, the typical practices are often molded by time pressures and professional turf instead of by collaborative principles. For example, a survey of professionals and parents regarding team practices (Giangreco, Edelman, & Dennis, 1991) illustrated that

1. Many related services personnel make independent decisions regarding the amount and types of services a student needs prior to fully understanding the student's IEP objectives; thus, related services may not be integrated with IEP objectives.

2. It is not unusual to have separate pages of IEP objectives, written by therapists, that are not integrated with the rest of a student's IEP; this practice often means that the program is fragmented and related services may not be educationally relevant to the student.

3. Often, professionals from related disciplines prefer having control over decisions relating to their own services (e.g., amount, delivery model) rather than sharing these decisions with the team.

When any of the previous practices are operating, teamwork becomes a "tug-of-war." One elementary school teacher, while reflecting on the 10-member team supporting one of her students, simply expressed the threats to teamwork:

There is no time, and everybody has their own tunnel vision. I'm thinking about Nate and Erin and Bobby (my students with special needs) and my other children, and Mary (the OT) is thinking about Nate and the other children she follows here at Brookfield and at the other schools she serves, and June's (PT) mind is occupied by Danielle! So, what's uppermost in my mind may not be Mary's top concern, or June's, or Linda's (the special education teacher), or whoever's! (Snell & Janney, in press)

Teams, not individuals, should make decisions regarding the amount and types of related services, such as therapy, that are needed by a child and the way in which these services will be delivered within the student's daily routine. *Therapy should be integrated instructionally and contextually* into daily, class, school, and home activities and routines (Rainforth & York-Barr, 1997). An integrated approach to therapy requires team members to share their priorities and explain their rationale as well as express their different viewpoints. Ideally, this process leads to "opportunities for reaching agreement."

During times such as these, team members need to remind each other that their unifying goal is to help the student and then refocus the meeting on the current student concerns: *"What can we do to help Jennifer become more independent on the computer?" "In what ways can we redesign the lunchroom routine so Daniel can get his lunch like his classmates?"* To help teams maintain a student-centered focus, one special educator suggested placing a photo of the target student on the meeting table.

Related services team members are more likely to participate periodically at team meetings rather than at every meeting. A related services team member is more likely to attend the team meetings when he or she is based in the same building as the target students than when he or she has to travel between schools (often true for occupational and physical therapists due to low demand and broad distribution of students requiring

their services). Sometimes, special education teachers will address the unavoidable absences of related services staff at team meetings by simply meeting separately with them when they have time. Although time consuming for the special education teacher, this solution enables related services professionals to provide input, keeping both them and the team informed of the student's progress and team deliberations. Rainforth and York-Barr (1997) described another alternative: block scheduling of related services. Staff schedule themselves to be present in particular schools for longer blocks of time, either weekly or biweekly; when in the building, the professional has the flexibility to work with multiple classrooms, staff members, and students providing consultation, collaborating with team members, or providing direct services to students. Keeping related services staff current and involved with the implementation of team action plans is a priority.

When elementary teachers were asked to describe the roles of related service providers in delivering coordinated programs in inclusive classrooms (Snell et al., 1995), they provided some guidelines:

1. Reduce pull-out services and use opportunities to work in the context of the class activities. *Quincey needed to gain fluency with turn-taking during conversations with his peers. His speech therapist prompted Quincey's participation during the many back-and-forth exchanges that occurred during structured partner activities in science.*

2. Provide equipment that helps the child participate in class and school activities. *Daniel's physical therapist helped resolve the team-identified problem of proximity to peers during art activities by suggesting he be moved from his chair to a chair she had adapted; the new chair scooted under the table surface in the art room.*

3. Have flexible schedules that allow therapy to be provided during the most relevant times. *Daniel has his physical therapy on a daily basis during physical education; therapy includes range of motion and other exercises which Daniel completes (with the therapist or a paraprofessional who has learned the techniques) as his peers do their "warm-ups." Daniel's speech therapist observed the second grade PE routine and, with team members, devised ways to take advantage of the options that existed for Daniel's involvement during scheduled games and activities. For example, during team games, Daniel now uses his switch-operated communication device to announce which team gets the point ("Spartan's point" "Cavalier's point").*

4. Based on the teacher's unit topics or lesson plans, weave therapy into planned class activities. *Daniel's PE teacher gives the physical therapist a monthly schedule of target sports, games, and fitness goals; Daniel's second-grade teacher shares the weekly unit plans with the physical therapist and the speech-language therapist.*

5. Come prepared with adaptations and be able to jump in and do whatever the class is doing while facilitating the student's active participation. *The speech-language therapist continues Pete's picture exchange training program even during free play. She follows him to activities in which he is interested, selects the matching picture symbol, places it between Pete and the desired activity, and waits for him to take the symbol and hand it to her before allowing him to have the activity materials. She also observes as his assistant uses the same procedure with him during recess and later involves several of Pete's peers in a few of the request opportunities.*

6. Be sensitive enough to know when to stay in the classroom and when to leave. *Jennifer's occupational therapist worked with her in the tutoring room to teach her some simple relaxation exercises (e.g., tense and relax arms and legs while sitting, take several deep breaths, squeeze a "Happy Sac"). Once Jennifer mastered the exercises as a means to self-manage her extra energy, she and the occupational therapist invited Jennifer's peers to learn the exercises, too. Later, when Jennifer used these exercises in class, her peers understood what she was doing and why; one friend reminded Jennifer to try the exercises when it was hard for her to be still.*

Role of School Administration in Delivering Coordinated Programs

During the implementation and maintenance phase of inclusion, when teams take action to support students in general education, building administrators must lend meaningful support to teams and teamwork. Several examples include

- *Caseload:* The caseload responsibility of special education teachers and related services professionals is planned to facilitate collaborative teaming; care is taken regarding the assignment of students (numbers and intensity of support needs), schools (balanced with rest of caseload and traveling distances), and classrooms (numbers and range). These staff members may be given access to consultants to learn more about innovative scheduling (e.g., block scheduling) and embedding or integrating instruction into daily routines and class activities.

- *Shared decision-making:* The administrator models shared decision-making by relinquishing some of his or her control and involving teachers in making decisions (e.g., asking teachers to assist in the process of assigning students to classrooms, interviewing new teachers and teaching assistants, and organizing the levels of support a school provides).

- *School leader:* The building administrator, as the school leader, is willing to be part of the team-generated educational or behavioral support plans for some students (e.g., one principal learned how to redirect a third grader who had frequent "blow-ups" and, along with other staff, was able to say things that calmed the student and helped him refocus; another principal agreed to be one of the reinforcing options for Jennifer when she was attentive in class and completed her work).

- *Use of problem-solving:* The principal uses a collaborative problem-solving process at faculty meetings to resolve issues related to inclusion and collaborative teaming; the structure involves an initial sharing of successes across classrooms, followed by quick group problem-solving using the issue/action/person responsible planning process to tackle issues raised by individual teachers.

- *Spokesperson for the school:* The principal knows enough about the school's day-to-day successes and challenges with inclusion and collaborative teaming to report meaningful and positive examples to parents (e.g., at PTA meetings and on an individual basis), to personnel in central office, and to members of the school board and community. When supports need to be provided in innovative ways, building administrators appeal to the district level for assistance.

- *Plan ways to monitor team functioning:* Building administrators will work with teams to monitor team functioning and outcomes for students. These methods might include regular reading of teams' minutes, responding appropriately to teams regarding administrative concerns, attending meetings periodically, and reviewing the decisions being implemented with the teams.

Building administrators are a key element in collaborative teams' ability to design and deliver coordinated support programs to included students with disabilities.

ASSESS STUDENT PROGRESS

Periodically, student progress needs to be assessed to determine if team-generated teaching or support plans to address IEP objectives are working. Under current federal special education requirements, teachers are required to report on student progress to parents as least as often as they do for typical peers; they also must report whether the student's rate of progress is sufficient to achieve the annual goal (Bateman & Linden, 1998). Students who are included are typically evaluated on the same grading schedule as their peers, though test content and testing methods may need to be individualized as recommended by the student's team. The methods

team members use to assess progress will vary depending on the student and the skill.

For many students receiving special education supports, the *same general assessment methods* used with other students are also applied to the focus student:

Quincey's (fourth-grade) spelling words, while fewer in number and more functional than his classmates, are tested and checked weekly.

Adapted testing methods (like adapted teaching methods) are needed when students have sensory, motor, communication, or behavioral limitations around which teachers need to work. These methods must be individualized by the team and often require some problem solving and on-the-spot field testing to refine them so the student's learning progress can be assessed without interference from the sensory or motor limitation (Rainforth & York-Barr, 1997).

To assess Daniel's progress on taking turns with peers on interesting games (e.g., computer games, electronic toys), his team members are careful to check his positioning and his hand or head switch and to allow enough time for him to initiate his switch response following the peer's signal: "It's your turn, Daniel," while touching his left hand.

Some students require *accommodations for learning* (i.e., changes made by others to assist the student) such as extra time, instructions in Spanish and English, sitting close to the chalkboard, having a quiet place to study, or using a calculator to perform math calculations. When this is true, the testing process also reflects those accommodations.

Both Walter and Rick are allowed extended time to take their tests; Rick may take them in another location.

Behavioral objectives often require different assessment approaches than those used to keep track of academic skill progress (Janney & Snell, 2000b; Snell & Janney, 2000). Observations of the student will be made during times when appropriate behavior is of concern; often records are made of the frequency of the target skill or the amount of time a student spends engaged in appropriate (or inappropriate) behavior. Sometimes, simple impressions of peers, family members, or staff are used to supplement actual behavior counts.

In English, during which class interruptions have been a problem, Rick and a friend of his keep track of the number of times Rick raises his hand and gets called on before he speaks out loud. His teacher also keeps a running tally of this behavior and of Rick's interruptions.

The *criteria used to grade* many students who receive special education supports may be different from their peers and, like assessment and teaching methods, should be team-generated. Adapted grading criteria can influence a student's eligibility for earning a general high school diploma, so school staff team members should discuss with each student and his or her family the advantages, disadvantages, and requirements for each of these choices. When states require students to pass additional, standardized tests in order to advance from one level to the next or to graduate, teams will need to decide the appropriateness of these content tests, the supports needed for students to prepare for and pass them, and the consequences of taking suitable alternative competency tests when students do not have an extensive knowledge base and functional, not academic, outcomes are appropriate.

The methods teams use to assess student progress closely reflect their decisions about how students are taught. Thus, the curricular, instructional, and ecological adaptations teams plan for students are implemented (as during instruction), and the student is asked to complete the task (e.g., worksheet, math problem job routine, social interaction skill,

task step, activity) without the benefits of extra assistance. Assessment information lets teams know if students can accomplish the targeted IEP skills under criterion conditions. Because of the close connection between teaching modifications and assessment methods, readers might want to consult additional sources that address these issues in detail (Janney & Snell, 2000a; Rainforth & York-Barr, 1996).

REVIEW AND REVISE TEAM ACTION PLANS

Team members regularly report the assessment results on student progress at their meetings. Having access to accurate, current, and relevant information on student learning is essential to teams as they review and revise their action plans for students. Earlier in this chapter, some of the relevant paperwork that should be kept on students and organized so that teams can easily access and use it was discussed. Included in these "big notebooks" for focus students are IEPs, class schedules, test data, grades, personal information, meeting minutes, and action plans. Teams are under more pressure than ever before to regularly assess and report on student progress and to make predictions about the rate of progress made toward IEP goals (Bateman & Linden, 1998). While this is often a demanding task, it is crucial that teams know the effects of their recommendations on students. Assessment data, teaching observations, peer and family comments, and observations from the student all constitute useful information as teams work to make improvements in their programs and action plans for students. (Refer to Janney & Snell, 2000a, for more information.)

Making changes and improving a student's instructional program require exactly the same team methods as we have already described: identify the problem, brainstorm possible solutions, evaluate possible solutions, choose a solution, write an action plan, collaborate to design the teaching program and needed services, deliver the program in a team-coordinated manner, assess student progress, and review and revise team action plans. Revisions made in a team's action plans are assessment-based and team-generated. The process, which is ongoing and dynamic, depends upon the cooperative capability of the collaborative team.

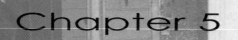

Chapter 5

Teaching Collaboratively

Student Snapshot

Helena is an 11-year-old girl who attends sixth grade in a rural middle school. Her cognitive disability affects her understanding, speaking, and ability to attend and concentrate. She often requires cues to look as teachers give directions, and she benefits from repetition and demonstrations and from being expected to restate directions. In comparison to her peers, her ability to make decisions and interact socially are delayed. She does not readily interpret social feedback. Helena is often paired with peers who can model appropriate behavior.

Andrea Greene, the special education teacher, uses several approaches to provide support to half of the sixth graders with special needs, including Helena. In English, while Ms. Hill leads whole-class activities and discussions, Andrea circulates among the students, paying particular attention to several students who have IEPs. For instance, she helps Helena get started on an in-class writing assignment by asking her to organize her thoughts: "Think about the spring break you had last week. What did you do that you'd like to write about? I'll be back." Then, Andrea moves across the room to check the work of two other students. While she is helping the students with IEPs, she provides assistance to any other students who seek it. From a distance, she monitors a student who has a notetaker to whom he dictates his sentences and checks on a student with multiple disabilities who uses a switch-operated computer. She then returns to Helena and asks for her thoughts on the writing topic. Once Helena verbalizes the incident about which she has chosen to write, Andrea works with her to complete a story map, then prompts her to start writing. Andrea checks back and provides assistance as needed. Soon, students move into small groups to edit their writing; Andrea works with Helena, another student with special needs, and two classmates to address the same activity other groups are engaged in independently.

Helena also receives pull-in support in math and pull-out support in the academic lab in which Andrea works with a small group of sixth graders. In science, she receives the needed support from Andrea Greene, who co-teaches with Ms. Washington, the science teacher.

This chapter addresses how teachers work together in the general education classroom to meet the educational needs of a diverse group of students. *Collaborative teaching* (also called co-teaching or team teaching) is a broad, "umbrella" term, which means *two or more team members teaching together in a classroom to provide effective instruction to a group of students with a range of learning abilities and disabilities.* This chapter describes what collaborative teaching looks like and how teachers can use it effectively.

Collaborative teaching involves

- Special education and general education teachers working together to plan and provide instruction

- Designing teaching roles to reflect the expertise and interests of each of the teachers who are working together

- Expanding teacher roles and skills to enhance student outcomes

- Assessing and considering student and teacher outcomes of the collaborative partnership and exploring improvements

- Communicating and resolving conflicts together

- Using *peer coaching,* a structured process for pairs of teachers who work together to improve their teaching practices (Hargreaves, 1994)

- Using *role release,* a process whereby team members, often of different disciplines, teach and learn from each other

Chapter 1 discusses two terms that are related to collaborative teaching: pull-in and pull-out services. *Pull-in* involves team members (e.g., special education teacher, paraprofessional, related services staff) bringing special education supports that are consistent

Pull-in with collaboration means	**. . . but does NOT mean**
• Planning for the needed support (e.g., what, when, how) • Synchronizing support with class routines • Making instruction part of class activities or making it thematically related • Special education teacher or staff implementing individualized instruction to focus student(s) alongside or with peers • Team evaluating outcomes, resolving difficulties, and making improvements • Teaching to facilitate learning on IEP objectives	• Special education teacher designing supports and schedule by him- or herself • Misaligning activities • Making student feel stigmatized because pull-in activities differ from class • Only using pull-out services in which students with special needs are always taught apart from peers • Teaching without assessing student progress and ignoring problems that arise • Continuing instructional support that "works" for staff but not for students

Figure 5.1. Pull-in with collaboration. (Adapted with permission from DeBoer, A., & Fister, S. [1994]. *Strategies and tools for collaborative teaching.* Longmont, CO: Sopris West. All rights reserved.)

with team planning into the classroom for one or more students. (Special education teachers who provide pull-in service also have been referred to as *consulting special education teachers.*) *Pull-out* (also referred to as *alternative activities*) involves the same team members providing special education support to the target students (or within a small group of students with mixed abilities) but in an environment apart from the general education classroom (e.g., in another school location, in a community training site) and in ways that are consistent with team planning and involve ongoing collaboration. (Figures 5.1 and 5.2

set forth more details of what pull-in and pull-out should and should not be.)

Technically, collaborative teaching is also "the pulling in of special education." In both approaches, special education staff members provide support to identified students at scheduled times in the same location as their peers. There are, however, several differences. First, pull-in services are primarily limited to special education staff or related services personnel who work with the target student in the same room, area, or group alongside peers without disabilities. Pull-in does not include a shared responsibility for teaching other class

Pull-out with collaboration means	**. . . but does NOT mean**
• Students having team-planned, scheduled learning, or flexible break time outside of class, apart from classmates or with a classmate(s) • Team setting guidelines and goals for this time • Focusing learning on personalized objectives, intense skill instruction, and school or community-based instruction • Using flexible break time as part of a crisis management or self-management plan • Team evaluating student's progress made during pull-out and planning for reintegration into more typical settings	• Replacing inclusion with a self-contained program • Always pulling out a particular student, even when classmates may be involved to lend support and/or learn • Removing student for convenience • Teaching skills better learned in an inclusive context • TA needs a break or runs errands while taking student along • Removing and forgetting student • Pulling out has more supports than pulling in

Figure 5.2. Pull-out with collaboration. (Adapted with permission from DeBoer, A., & Fister, S. [1994]. *Strategies and tools for collaborative teaching, Participant's handbook.* Longmont, CO: Sopris West. All rights reserved.)

members. Therefore, although pull-in does involve collaborative planning with the classroom teacher, the planning only addresses the student(s) with special needs, not the whole class. Second, pull-in arrangements involve a more traditional separation of roles between the special educator and the classroom teacher and the students they serve. Third, the two strategies differ in the amount of collaboration they require. Collaborative teaching requires significant planning between the special education and the general education teachers and results in a softening of role boundaries, as the special education and general education teachers teach *both* identified and nonidentified students cooperatively. A collaborative teaching approach is not for all teachers and classrooms; some general education teachers will prefer to have special education services pulled into the classroom according to team planning but not involve the special education teacher in whole- or small-group instruction on a routine, scheduled basis.

The benefits of collaborative teaching have been described and studied by a number of researchers (Nowacek, 1992; Pugach & Wesson, 1995; Walther-Thomas, 1997). Figure 5.3 provides one general education teacher's views on the benefits of collaborative teaching. In addition to the potential advantages for both students and teachers, some challenges do exist, many of which are identical to the challenges of collaborative teams: having adequate planning time and administrative support, helping teachers get accustomed to working together, and providing appropriate training and mentoring. Figure 5.4 summa-rizes the potential benefits and challenges of collaborative teaching.

PLAN AT THE SCHOOL LEVEL

The primary purpose of pull-in services and collaborative teaching is to provide instructional support to students with special needs in the general education classroom (Bauwens & Hourcade, 1991; Walther-Thomas, Bryant, & Land, 1996). Adequate time, cooperation from others, and workload have been listed as three primary obstacles to collaborative teaching (Bauwens, Hourcade, & Friend, 1989; Karge, McClure, & Patton, 1995). Because many solutions have schoolwide influence and are dependent on administrative action (e.g., schedules, school atmosphere and mission, student assignment and load, and in-service training), administrators need to be involved in creating ways to overcome these obstacles.

Some classrooms just "jump" into collaborative teaching; however, others have found that advance preparation for collaborative teaching, beyond the general preparatory steps for collaborative teaming described in Chapters 2, 3, and 4, helps. The first actions that teachers and administrators often take to prepare the way for collaborative teaching include some or many of the following (Walther-Thomas et al., 1996):

1. Designs of the purposes and characteristics of collaborative teaching have been discussed, and potential participants have been identified.

Voices from the Classroom

"Before we started co-teaching, I basically didn't know what my children were doing outside my room; they just went somewhere and did something. They would miss whatever was going on in my class. I wouldn't schedule a test at that time, but they missed the lesson that hour or sometimes they even missed story time, the fun part. They had to miss something. Now [with co-teaching] I'm able to expand on what the children have learned. . . ."

Figure 5.3.   A general education teacher on co-teaching. (From Nowacek, J.E. [1992]. Professionals talk about teaching together: Interviews with five collaborating teachers [p. 263]. *Intervention in School and Clinic, 27,* 262–276.)

Benefits that may come with collaborative teaching	Problems that may arise from collaborative teaching
• Students develop better attitudes about themselves; they are less critical, more motivated, and able to recognize abilities.	• Lack of success may arise if co-teaching skills are lacking.
• Students show academic improvements.	• Learning new roles requires extra support and is difficult without it (e.g., in-service training, staff available to "coach," time).
• Few students are removed from general education because of social or learning failures.	• Teachers may be incompatible or unwilling to work together; not all teachers can co-teach.
• Students' social skills may improve.	• Scheduling is difficult (especially for special educators). This includes planning, evaluating, and having time to schedule students in collaborative classes.
• Students report academic benefits, including those students without IEPs.	
• Positive peer relationships develop.	• Resource classes, if used, may be larger because of fewer resource periods.
• Pupil-teacher ratio is reduced, leading to better teaching conditions.	
• A greater sense of community exists in classroom.	• Staff may be tempted to cluster students with special needs into certain classes, diminishing inclusion.
• Core team is strengthened.	
• Co-teachers report professional growth, personal support, and enhanced motivation.	

Figure 5.4.   Potential benefits and problems that may come with collaborative teaching. (Sources: Nowacek, 1992; Pugach & Wesson, 1995; Walther-Thomas, Bryant, & Land, 1996; Walther-Thomas, 1997.)

2. Administrative support for collaborative teaching exists, and realistic professional caseloads have been assigned.

3. Classroom rosters reflect heterogeneous groups, and students with special needs are hand-scheduled into classes; they are not scheduled by test scores alone (more easily accomplished in elementary and middle schools) (Dawson, 1987).

4. Parents are provided with information regarding the planned changes; their input is obtained and their concerns are addressed.

5. Teachers define their roles and responsibilities.

6. Because classroom teachers have provided input, IEPs reflect skills that are needed in general education classrooms.

7. In some schools, one or several classrooms may pilot the model for pull-in services and co-teaching and then make improve-ments to the program based on the initial attempts; pull-in services and collaborative teaching can then be extended to other classrooms.

Teacher Compatibility

Collaborative teaching partnerships must be entered into with some caution. Many researchers strongly recommend involving teachers in the decision to convert a pull-in arrangement into a co-teaching relationship (DeBoer & Fister, 1995–1996; Trent, 1998; Walther-Thomas, Bryant, & Land, 1996). Potential teaching partners must first determine whether they are compatible enough to teach together (e.g., personality, teaching styles, knowledge) and what their purposes would be in doing so. Arbitrary pairing of teachers may result in too many incompatibilities for the collaborative teaching arrangement to be successful. For example, some of the teacher in-

compatibilities that Trent (1998) observed in a high school environment included differences in teaching styles, communication patterns, organization and operational methods, the amount of planning and preparation, and reliability or follow-through (e.g., following through with planned modifications).

Do teaching partners take on equal parts? Do they start and continue their co-teaching on "equal footing"? Trent (1998), who closely studied several pairs of collaborative teachers in a high school, suggested that equity between teachers is unsubstantiated. What he found instead is that both teachers in a strong co-teaching partnership take turns stepping into the roles of "expert" and "help-seeker" throughout any given day or week. In agreement with Bauwens and Hourcade (1995), Trent found that "although partners may expect an equal split in terms of commitment and sharing of responsibility, roles may vary constantly from day to day, week to week, and so forth, and there may be one collaborator whose skills and knowledge dictate that he or she take the lead in incorporating interventions that best meet the needs of students in general education settings—particularly if this arrangement is desired by the other partner" (1998, p. 511).

Preparatory Steps

Classroom quality must not be threatened by a poor relationship between two collaborative teachers. Preparation for collaborative teaching must include time to identify strong potential partnerships. Teachers should not be *required* to co-teach. Pull-in services can provide adequate support for students in the general education classroom where co-teaching is not advised or desired.

When an interest exists among teachers to learn about and apply a co-teaching approach and to extend or supplement pull-in services with co-teaching, teachers need to take several preparatory steps. Based in part on DeBoer & Fister (1994) and Trent (1998), Figure 5.5 sets forth some guidelines that teachers may use to determine whether co-teaching will work for them (in addition to recommendations for im-

plementing co-teaching and assessing its success at the end of a semester or school year).

Co-teaching arrangements need not be exclusive or extend across the whole day or year. Teachers typically limit their collaborative teaching in several ways (DeBoer & Fister, 1995–1996; Walther-Thomas, Bryant, & Land, 1996):

- *Limited to part of a day:* Co-teaching is used during one or several teaching periods (in secondary schools) or for certain subject areas or activities (in elementary schools).

- *Limited to part of the year:* Co-teaching is limited to a particular grading period, a special unit, a semester, or a series of grading periods.

Often, special education teachers (and sometimes related services staff) will establish limited co-teaching arrangements with several general education teachers. Multiple co-teaching plans can mesh nicely with the schedule of a special educator or related services staff member for lending team-planned support to several classrooms. It has been determined that:

- Limited collaborative teaching arrangements (i.e., one or several periods or activities a day) are more common than co-teaching arrangements that take place all day, every day.

- Because special education teachers often support students in several general education classrooms, they work with multiple classrooms and teachers; this often makes it necessary to limit the co-teaching arrangement with any given teacher to part of the day.

- Special education teachers often use a combination of teaching arrangements because teams decide on a variety of supports for the students whom they serve: collaborative teaching, pull-in, and, depending on student needs and team decisions, *perhaps* some pull-out with collaborative teaming.

- If two teachers do not think co-teaching will work, they can always plan, as a team,

---

Before you start:

- Identify who wants to teach collaboratively and with whom you might be compatible.
- Determine your rationale and objectives for co-teaching.
- Identify the resources/talents you both bring.
- Describe the supports/resources you may need.
- Discuss the content areas that will be co-taught.
- Decide on the time frame for planning and starting.
- Determine the formal approvals/support you will need from school administration.
- Study the class makeup and analyze the students' needs.
- Decide how student outcomes will be monitored.
- Decide how teaching outcomes will be monitored.
- Identify the daily/weekly time period that will be reserved for planning.
- Determine your roles and responsibilities in collaborative teaching.
- Decide how you will explain this arrangement to parents.
- Identify a coach/mentor who can provide you with critical feedback and guidance.
- Formalize your agreement between yourselves and with your administrator/supervisor.

As you implement:

- Explain co-teaching to your students.
- Use planning times; re-evaluate length of time needed.
- Get in the habit of dynamically communicating with each other; check perceptions, ask questions, reinforce each other, and provide feedback regularly.
- Extend your dynamic communication to administrators and facilitators/mentors.
- Monitor student and teacher outcomes, compare with goals, and ask if progress is adequate or if improvements are needed.
- Confer with coach.
- If improvements are needed, identify improvements, develop a plan to make the improvements, and implement the plan.
- If additional training/support is needed identify what this is and generate ways to obtain it.

At the end of the semester/year:

- Continue communication and coaching.
- Monitor student and teacher outcomes, compare with goals, and ask if progress is adequate or if improvements are needed.
- Confer with coach.
- Share student/teacher outcome data with colleagues and administrators.
- Celebrate accomplishments.
- If improvements are needed, confer with coach, identify improvements, develop a plan to make the improvements, and implement the plan.
- Determine your collaborative teaching arrangements for the next year.

Figure 5.5. Guidelines for making collaborative teaching work. (Adapted with permission from DeBoer, A. & Fister, S. [1994]. *Strategies and tools for collaborative teaching, Participant's handbook.* Longmont, CO: Sopris West. All rights reserved.)

for special education supports to be pulled into the classroom.

In Ms. Hill's English class, Andrea Greene (special education teacher) provides daily pull-in support for three students and oversees two teaching assistants who carry out team-generated support plans for two other students; however, because she teaches an instruction group of students during English, Andrea also co-teaches with Ms. Hill. She is an active team member on the sixth-grade team and on the individual student teams. During social studies, she also provides pull-in support. Andrea, who has a special interest in nature and ecology, co-

teaches regularly during two periods of science. Andrea also operates a reading/writing lab for a small group of students, most of whom have IEPs (pull-out with collaborative teaming). She frequently touches base with Ms. Hill so her pull-out tutoring efforts are coordinated with Ms. Hill's English class content and objectives.

Transition to Collaborative Teaching

When schools have made the decision to add collaborative teaching to their options for serving all students in the mainstream, it probably is wise to *begin slowly;* new skills are often required for success. It is often effective for teachers who have experience with collaborative teaching to volunteer first as teaching partners for others who have an interest but no experience. Other teachers who have experience might serve as coaches for these co-teaching partners. During the transition away from pull-out services, DeBoer and Fister (1995–1996) suggested that special education teachers initially design their schedules to use pull-in services one third of the time or more, collaborative teaching one third of the time or more, and pull-out with collaboration one third of the time or less. This may require support staff to schedule multiple arrangements for lending support (like Andrea Greene did). However, it also might mean that some support staff who prefer one type of arrangement will use that arrangement exclusively or primarily. Therefore, in the same school one special educator might teach collaboratively on a full-time basis across grades and classrooms if and when it is suitable, another special educator might only provide pull-in services (consulting teacher role) across grades, and a third teacher, more experienced with resource or self-contained instruction models, might be responsible for any student needing a period of pull-out services with collaboration (e.g., community-based instruction, tutoring, writing labs, study hall support). Ultimately, team decisions regarding individual students should determine the way in which special education supports will be provided and also the way in which special education and related services staff will schedule their times to provide supports.

The person who fills the *mentor or coach role* usually is someone who has co-taught before, although not necessarily in an inclusive environment. In the 1980s, many schools used team teaching models, whereby general education teachers combined classes for certain subject areas. Teachers who have experience with team teaching are aware of the importance of compatibility between teaching partners and the ongoing need for communication; coordination in planning; and collaboration on teaching content, evaluation methods, and schedules. Consulting special education teachers often can be effective coaches or teaching partnerships if and when a school system uses them (described in Chapter 4) to coordinate other special education teachers, oversee procedures (eligibility and IEP meetings), troubleshoot, and serve as the liaison between administration and students.

UNDERSTAND TESTED ORGANIZATIONAL MODELS AND INSTRUCTIONAL STRATEGIES

The previously described organizational approaches to provide support to students with disabilities in general education classrooms (supplementary pull-out with collaboration, pull-in, and collaborative teaching) are typically variations or combinations of tested models but also may be novel or untested approaches. Some current tested organizational models that have been used to address the diverse needs of students placed in general education can be found in Figure 5.6. The cited research has been implemented *primarily* in elementary schools, however, these collaborative approaches to serving students in general education have been found to be effective with students who have a range of disabilities (particularly students with learning disabilities, mental retardation requiring intermittent support, and behavioral disorders).

Organizational Models Effective with Students Who Have Fewer Support Needs
(Quantitative Research)

1. Consultation and Paraprofessional Pull-In System (CAPPS; Welch, Richards, Okada, Richards, and Prescott, 1995): some pull-out
2. Cooperative Integrated Reading and Composition (CIRC; Jenkins, Jewell, Leichester, O'Connor, Jenkins, and Troutner, 1994): some pull-out
3. The Integrated Classroom Model (ICM; Affleck, Madge, Adams, and Lowenbraun, 1988; Madge, Affleck, and Lowenbraun, 1990): no pull-out
4. Mainstreaming Experiences for Learning Disabled (MELD; Zigmond, 1995; Zigmond and Baker, 1990): no pull-out
5. The Team Approach to Mastery (TAM; Bear, Cleaver, and Proctor, 1991; Bear and Proctor, 1990; Juvonen and Bear, 1992): no pull-out

Organizational Models Applied to a Broader Range of Students
(Qualitative Research)

1. Collaborative Problem-Solving (Salisbury, Evans, and Palombaro, 1997)
2. Pull-In Supports with Collaborative Teaming (Giangreco, Dennis, Cloninger, Edelman, and Schattman, 1993; Snell and Janney, in press; York, Vandercook, MacDonald, Heise-Neff, and Caughey, 1992)
3. Collaborative Teaching (Trent, 1998)

Instructional Strategies
(Descriptive)

1. Janney and Snell (2000a); Janney and Snell (2000b)
2. Kronberg, Jackson, Sheets, and Rogers-Connolly (1995)
3. Rainforth and York-Barr (1997)
4. S. Stainback, W. Stainback, and Slavin (1989)
5. W. Stainback, Stainback, and Stefanich (1996)
6. Thousand and Villa (1991)
7. Villa and Thousand (1988)

Figure 5.6. Organizational models and instructional strategies for meeting the needs of heterogeneous groups in general education classrooms. (Source: Deno, Foegen, Robinson, & Espin [1996].)

As indicated in Figure 5.6, two of the five collaboration models found to be effective with students who have fewer support needs involved some pull-out services; *all models depended on both specialist teachers* (e.g., special education, Title I, English as a Second Language, speech and language) *and paraprofessionals, who collaborated with general education teachers, to support instruction in the typical classroom.* A wide range of specific collaborative teaching approaches, varying in their nature and intensity, were used. Indirect collaborative approaches included the provision of special education consultation to the general education teacher for an included student, but not direct instruction of the student him- or her-

self. Other collaborative approaches were direct in that they involved student instruction; the special education teacher either pulled aside some students to provide instruction or co-taught with the classroom teacher. Collaborative intensity varied from being less intensive (e.g., pull-in support several hours a week) to being more intensive (e.g., co-teaching in several classes).

The middle section of Figure 5.6 cites several qualitative research studies in which organizational models for lending pull-in support were applied to a wide range of students with disabilities, including students with severe disabilities and extensive support needs. Although qualitative researchers do not re-

port statistical effects of treatments, they do identify and describe themes or characteristics that are observed directly or that are viewed from teachers' or students' perspectives. Therefore, qualitative research findings enable us to understand the impact of inclusion in "broad strokes." The qualitative researchers listed in Figure 5.6 have studied a wide range of approaches for supporting students in all school-age groups and in a variety of school environments.

Finally, references for descriptions of instructional strategies that have been found effective in inclusive classrooms are listed in the last section of Figure 5.6. Many approaches, alone or in combination, have been identified by educators as being responsible for academic and social gains: Such approaches include cooperative group learning, peer tutoring, systematic evaluation of student progress, curriculum-based assessment, curriculum and activity adaptations, peer support, and advocacy networks. This listing can be helpful for schools that are considering various organizational models for supporting students in the mainstream and as teachers design and supplement their instructional plans for collaborative teaching.

CONSIDER COLLABORATIVE TEACHING STRATEGIES SUITED TO GRADE LEVEL

After schools have planned general strategies for instructing students with special needs in general education, teachers, with the assistance of collaborative teams, should explore the various collaborative teaching strategies they will use and identify methods that are suited to the age and grade level of the target students.

Collaborative Teaching Strategies

Teachers often use several strategies when they teach collaboratively. Several of these strategies will be reviewed in order to provide a more vivid picture of co-teaching: role exchange strategy, complementary instruction,

team teaching, and supportive learning activities.

Role Exchange Strategy Kenna Colley, a special education consultant, describes role exchange as a strategy that enables teachers to coach or model for each other while they develop new routines that all staff will implement with one or several target students. First, the team member who has the most experience with the developing teaching procedure models the teaching routine in an actual classroom situation while other team members observe. Team members give their input during or after the demonstration and then adjust the procedure. Then, during the next natural opportunity to use the teaching routine, the teaching role shifts to another team member (e.g., classroom teacher, paraprofessional, related services staff) who tries it out in front of other team members who can coach or provide input as appropriate. Once team members discuss the success or lack of success of the procedure, needed improvements are added to the teaching routine. The routine continues to rotate to other team members who will be using the procedure, and the same coaching, teaming, and refinement process is applied.

In January, Quincey's team wanted to expand his schedule to include the fourth-grade writing-to-read computer lab; however, they knew they would need consistency across team members in implementing this schedule change. Quincey, a fourth grader with autism, posed significant behavioral challenges whenever his schedule was changed to include new routines. His teachers started the change by planning the routine with the computer teacher. Next, the teaching assistant and special education teacher accompanied Quincey and his classmates to computer lab for the first week. The special education teacher modeled the targeted routine by walking Quincey through the steps (e.g., sitting down at the computer that displayed his name card, typing in his name and date, and redirecting him back to the computer when he got up

and left). Following the suggestions of the special education teacher, the teaching assistant tried taking Quincey through the routine the next day. The special education teacher tried it again the following day with suggestions from the assistant. The general education teacher observed all week as she supervised Quincey's classmates in computer lab and offered ideas. Finally, after 5 days of this process, a set routine was written down at the team meeting with the input of the two teachers and the assistant. The following week, the general education teacher implemented the procedure in the presence of either the special education or the assistant. In this example, role exchange and coaching allowed team members to both try out their ideas as they developed them and to model them for each other during collaborative teaching.

Complementary Instruction Several authors have used the term *complementary instruction* in reference to the division of labor used by collaborative teachers to teach a classroom of diverse students efficiently and effectively. For example, the special education teacher (or a teaching assistant) might prepare study guides; keep a notebook of class notes; organize students into working pairs and facilitate their active teamwork to review facts or complete application activities and worksheets; teach half of the class part of a lesson and then rotate groups; teach a smaller group that requires more adaptations; teach organizational skills to the whole class; take notes on the board while the teacher lectures or leads a class discussion regarding assigned reading; modify the class worksheets for some or all students; or read exam questions to some students. These teaching duties, however, need to complement the classroom teacher's role; therefore, co-teachers need to think through their complementary roles for every lesson.

To determine the complementary roles a team of two teachers used in a high school English class, the following example mimics the example of Walter-Thomas et al. (1996), who observed teachers participating in *comple-*

mentary instruction in a middle school classroom. Johnna Elliott, who is a high school consulting teacher, spent time observing in a ninth-grade English class where a team of a general education and a special education teacher co-taught 29 students, 6 of whom received special education services. Figure 5.7 depicts the first 30 minutes of this class. Note from this "script" that the classroom teacher maintained primary responsibility for teaching the subject matter and the special education teacher filled a complementary role: She assumed "primary responsibility for students' mastery of the academic survival skills necessary to acquire the subject content" at the time they were needed (Bauwens, Hourcade, & Friend, 1989, p. 19).

Team Teaching In addition to complementary instruction between two teachers, another variation of co-teaching is *team teaching.* During team teaching, the teachers involved in collaborative teaching plan and teach academic content to all students, including those with special needs and those without. Who teaches what depends on the teachers' preferences, training, and strengths.

Supportive Learning Activities *Supportive learning activities* is a version of co-teaching (Bauwens, et al., 1989) that is very similar to complementary instruction. The classroom teacher introduces the primary academic content of a lesson while the special educator plans and teaches activities that supplement and enhance the primary academic content. These activities might include teacher-led group discussions; cooperative learning groups, labs, or experiments; or drill and practice using a classwide peer tutoring method.

During a fourth-grade unit on plant life in Quincey's class, the classroom teacher addressed photosynthesis using explanation, overhead pictures, and a filmstrip. Afterward, the special education teacher conducted a lab designed to enrich the content on photosynthesis. Students organized into cooperative groups examined plants that had been growing under different amounts of light and measured their growth.

The English Teacher:	**The Special Education Teacher:**
• Reviews the past 2 days	• Takes roll silently
• Introduces discussion of questions completed on homework	• Gives student locker pass
• Locates materials for a student	• Assists student in locating materials
• Leads discussion of each question, including reading the question, calling on students for the answers, probing for more in-depth responses, reinforcing students for their comments, and writing responses on the board	• Walks around room to check for completed homework; makes record in grade book
	• Restates several questions for clarification while checking work
	• Takes over duty of recording answers on board
• Moves around room continuing to question	• Prompts student to lift head
• Questions a detail that requires students to locate an answer in book	• Locates passage in student's book
	• Prompts student to read aloud
• Calls on student to reread for clarification	• Prompts student to attend to discussion
	• Adds details to discussion
• Continues to lead discussion of questions, reinforcing students for their answers	• Walks around room with eyes on students' books to be sure all are on correct page
	• Helps a student find the correct page
• Prompts a student to behave	• Continues board note-taking; verbally reinforces student
• Tells students when to expect a turn to answer when several students want to answer a question	• Quietly prompts student to behave
	• Checks student's notes for clarity
• Continues to lead class discussion	• Restates point from a different perspective
• Wraps up discussion, reinforces everyone's effort	• Writes assignment on board
• Announces the reading of "Old Demon" for homework	• Prompts student to write down assignment
• Announces quiz on this story	• Writes "QUIZ" on board
• Provides alternative assignments for students who need them	• Reminds teacher that two students need alternate assignments to replace missed assignments
	• Records alternative assignments

Figure 5.7.   Co-teaching complementary roles in a high school English class. (Contributed by Johnna Elliott.)

Variations for
Teaming Across Grade Levels

There are numerous possibilities for applying co-teaching with or without pull-in services across different age groups. The following three sections provide several examples.

Elementary Schools   June, a special education teacher, teaches a reading group two times a week in a first-grade classroom. There are five students in this group (also on her caseload), one of whom has a disability. The first-grade teacher, Amanda, knows that June is working on the same skills with this group

that she teaches to the rest of the class; however, each lesson is not co-planned in detail. When the two teachers meet weekly and touch–base "on-the-fly" during the day, they relate their progress. In kindergarten, June teaches small groups and plans her own reading readiness activities, all of which overlap with kindergarten or pre-kindergarten objectives; the small groups rotate through June's "teaching station" just as they rotate through the other adult-directed activities. June's teaching assistants are scheduled in three classrooms to support several students who require fairly intense assistance. They like to

follow a process whereby two assistants rotate to support a single child while maintaining close communication with the special education teacher, the classroom teacher, and each other. Having teaching assistants rotate in this manner appears to prevent "burnout" and promotes flexibility in teaching approaches. The teaching assistants implement team-developed plans rather than initiating adaptations on their own. June's schedule allows her to both observe the paraprofessionals as they work with the children who require intensive support and to work directly with students herself.

Secondary Schools   As in elementary and middle schools, variations of pull-in services and co-teaching (as well as some pull-out with collaboration) are used at the high school level. One high school that practices inclusion has approximately 1,100 students enrolled, 11% (120 students) of whom qualify for special education services. This caseload is divided among seven special education teachers, most of whom are responsible during the day for managing their caseload of students and for teaching by means of pull-in and co-teaching approaches. Four of the seven special education teachers work in partnership with general education teachers for four or five periods out of the seven-period day. Each teacher provides direct instruction in a resource environment for one or two periods and has a planning period.

Ann, one of the previously mentioned special education teachers, begins her day with a planning period. During second period, she provides pull-in services to Rick in Algebra 1 while monitoring several other students in the class. During third period, she goes to the study hall and checks on four students who often require assistance with studying or may need to complete tests for other classes. During fourth and sixth periods, Ann provides pull-in support in two tenth-grade English classes. During fifth and seventh periods, she co-teaches in English 9. Therefore, Ann's day consists of

providing pull-in support during general education classes and study hall and co-teaching for two of the seven periods.

At the same high school, one special education teacher (the consulting teacher) provides resource support and maintains a pull-out option for students who require or request one-to-one instruction in adapted content, direct instruction in reading, or intensive short-term behavioral support. Another special education teacher coordinates and supervises several alternative, noninclusive options for one or more periods of the day for students who, along with their parents, have elected these activities. These options include 1) community-based instruction, 2) supported employment, and 3) self-contained academic instruction. The consulting special education teacher, who manages a smaller caseload, oversees the entire program; she coordinates the teaching assistants and teachers, reviews all paperwork, provides emergency support to students and teachers, and chairs eligibility and child study committees. Finally, five teaching aides lend support by attending scheduled classes and assisting identified students with their accommodations (e.g., one teaching aide serves as a notetaker for Kaye in earth science). Assistants monitor each student's progress and then consult with the student's case manager.

PLANNING BETWEEN COLLABORATIVE TEACHERS

The obvious foundation for collaborative teaching is collaboration within the core team for each student with special needs who is enrolled in the classroom. *Collaborative teachers implement team-generated plans for individual students.* Extended team members, including occupational therapists, physical therapists, speech-language pathologists, and guidance counselors, may also pair up with a classroom teacher, though they are more likely to provide pull-in services in the classroom for specific students. Other collaborative teams

What the Research Says

Pugach and Wesson interviewed teachers and students regarding their year in two team-taught fifth grade classrooms. The teachers (general and special educators) and students (with and without learning disabilities) reported

- A positive climate existed.
- Students felt good about themselves.
- Giving and receiving help was "the accepted norm."
- Teacher help came more quickly with teaming.
- Cooperative groups and hands-on activities were commonplace.
- A variety of instructional activities were used.
- Flexible groups of students and sites were used.
- The special education teacher was seen as a "helping" or "relief" teacher.
- Teachers planned jointly and were viewed by students as being "good workers."

Figure 5.8.   Teachers' views on collaborative teaching. (From Pugach, M.C., & Wesson, C.L. [1995]. Teachers' and students' views of team teaching and general education and learning-disabled students in two fifth-grade classes. *The Elementary School Journal, 95,* 279–295. © 1995 University of Chicago. All rights reserved; adapted with permission.)

that address the needs of groups of students (e.g., grade-level or department teams) can contribute support to teachers who pair together to teach, particularly in middle school where students rotate among a team of teachers. Figure 5.8 presents teachers' views on collaborative teaming.

Collaborative Planning of Classroom Practices

Using pull-in arrangements for support often means that the special education teacher is more like a visitor to a number of classrooms rather than part of an actual teaching team. Special education teachers often need to work hard to "fit into" existing classroom practices, implementing team-designed modifications or adding supplementary instructional practices to the existing programs for students who have special needs. Under pull-in support arrangements, the classroom teacher may initially regard the target student as the "special education teacher's student" and yield to that teacher on what is "best." This viewpoint usually changes once the classroom teacher becomes familiar with the student and his or her needs, gains confidence, and uses methods modeled by the special education teacher.

Teachers' efforts are more fully integrated when they follow the planning steps for co-

teaching than when they follow the steps for a pull-in approach. Both teachers must learn about each others' practices and probably will influence each other a great deal as they blend their teaching ideas. Although both pull-in services and collaborative teaching require the contributing team members (e.g., special education teacher, related services staff) to understand the classroom teacher's practices, collaborative teaching goes a step further than pull-in: Teachers need to actually reach consensus on classroom practices, as both will actively use them. These practices include class rules and consequences, homework procedures and policy, in-class participation, grouping, teaching methods (e.g., lecture, discussions), practice options (e.g., independent work, cooperative groups, labs), approaches for monitoring and evaluating progress, and approaches for communicating with families. Collaborative teaching requires that both teachers share their ideas and philosophies regarding these practices with one another and, through teaming, learn new approaches from each other as they design the shared portions of the day.

Collaborative Planning of Instruction

Once teachers and administrators have successfully navigated the steps leading to col-

laborative teaching, the team of teachers jointly addresses two broad questions about instruction:

1. *What should we teach?*

2. *How should we teach this content so all students learn what they need to learn?*

Another booklet in this series, *Modifying Schoolwork* (Janney & Snell, 2000b), describes in detail the collaborative planning of instruction within the framework of designing modifications to school work. This section will briefly overview the process teachers take to plan instruction for co-teaching.

Daily during third period, Andrea co-teaches with Nancy Washington in sixth-grade general science class. Five students with IEPs are enrolled in science: Three students have learning disabilities, one student has multiple disabilities, and the fifth student, Helena, has cognitive disabilities (Figure 5.9 shows a Program-at-a-Glance for Helena). Along with their principal, the two teachers arranged for three days of planning time during the summer. First, they identified the roles and responsibilities each teacher would fill in science class. (See Figure 3.7 for an example of this planning step.) Then, they set about to plan their instruction. First, they identified who might need curricular adaptations and of what general kind. Second, using a Unit Plan form (Figure 5.10), they outlined the units they would use during the school year. Third, they designed activity-based lessons for each unit to provide active learning for all students. Finally, they determined how cooperative learning would allow them to make use of peer support in heterogeneous groups of students. After these 3 days of planning, they felt ready to start a year of collaborative teaching for the general science class; their weekly planning period, along with regular communication before school on an "as needed" basis, would provide them with the time they would need to adjust this planned structure over time.

MultiLevel Curriculum and Curriculum Overlap Students who are included in general education may have curriculum objectives that do not differ from their typical classmates. However, their IEPs may also specify objectives that differ in complexity from their classmates or that are drawn from different subject or skill areas. The term *multilevel curriculum* refers to lessons involving objectives of varying degrees of difficulty for various students; *curriculum overlap* refers to lessons for which students' objectives are drawn from different subject or skill areas (Giangreco & Putnam, 1991). Both types of objectives involve the provision of individualized adaptations to enable students with IEPs to participate in learning activities with their classmates. Multilevel instruction (instruction at different levels of difficulty) is regarded by most teachers as simpler, more ordinary, and less special than curriculum overlap. Therefore, multilevel curriculum objectives are preferred if they enable social and instructional participation for the target students. If improved participation can be obtained for a given student through the use of curriculum overlap, then teachers should use this type of curriculum adaptation for that particular student.

Collaborative Planning of Instructional Units Thematic units that integrate several curriculum areas (e.g., reading, writing, science) under an organizing topic, can be easily applied for a class of students who have a wide range of abilities and interests. Teachers work to identify the unit's "Big Ideas" (i.e., concepts, principles, and issues that it will address) and minimal competencies (i.e., facts, skills, and processes that are regarded as essential for all students to learn). Then, considering the range of students in the class, the teachers identify extended or advanced learning objectives (for those whose capabilities exceed the minimal competencies) and simplified or adapted objectives for those students who need them. Next, teachers identify the tasks and the activities for the unit, making sure to use as many input modes (i.e., ways to present material) and output modes (i.e., ways for students to respond) as possible. The major

Program-at-a-Glance

Student: _____Helena_____ Date: _4-28-99_ Grade: _6_ _____Middle School_____

IEP Objectives (briefly)	Accommodations

• *Written Language: Write name, address, days, month, mother's name; learn weekly spelling words; complete forms with simple sentences; write paragraph and personal letter; use story map or outline to write.*
 	
• *Reading: Read Dolch Word List in context, use decoding strategies, identify main story elements, summarize stories, make predictions, make sound/symbol correspondence; use Cloze procedure.*
 	
• *Math: Correctly count money, give equal values for dime, nickel, quarter, and dollar, make change, tell time to half hour; measure lengths.*
 	
• *Content/Survival Skills: Bring materials to class, participate in classroom projects and discussions, master three to five vocabulary concepts per week; recite months, seasons, locate dates.*
 	
• *Social/Language*
  • *Appropriately initiate conversations with peers.*
  • *Appropriately respond to peers in conversations.*
  • *Reduce off-target responses.*
  • *Maintain conversations with peers and adults.*
	• *Use visual with auditory input to introduce instructions and directions.*
	• *Helena will need prompts of initial sounds to help her recall words or symbols.*
	• *Helena will need to observe modeling of sounds.*
	• *Give Helena help generalizing information.*
	• *Let Helena use word books to recall words.*
	• *Read or modify tests/assignments.*
	• *Provide close supervision on field trips; pair her with "her" network of girls.*
	• *As needed, redirect Helena to students who can model appropriate behavior; support those students with peer planning group.*

Academic/ Social Management Needs	**Comments/Special Needs**
• *Provide close supervision when outside school building.* • *Facilitate her proximity to positive peers.*	• *Medication has been prescribed to improve Helena's attention.*

Figure 5.9. Helena's Program-at-a-Glance. (Contributed by Christine Burton.)

projects and activities planned for the unit are listed, and needed adaptations are noted; a listing or folder of supplementary activities for students to complete as alternatives to the major activities is created for each unit. Teachers plan their methods for evaluating the students, with notes regarding adapted measures for those students who need them. Finally, unit materials are listed, and any needed adaptive materials are noted (see Figure 5.10).

The units that Nancy and Andrea select reflect concepts and issues in sixth-grade

Unit Plan

Unit theme: _____   Teachers: _____

Dates and times: _____

Unit goals: "big ideas" (Concepts, principles, and issues)	Minimal competencies: (Essential facts, skills, and processes)
Extended/advanced objectives	**Adapted objectives**

Tasks/activities

____ Lecture: _____

____ Reading: _____

____ Discussion: _____

____ Library research: _____

____ Writing: _____

____ Building/creating: _____

____ Solving: _____

_____

Major unit projects (Note adaptations)	Supplementary activities
Evaluation measures	**Adapted evaluation measures**
Materials needed	**Adapted materials needed**

Figure 5.10.   Unit Plan form.

standards of learning from the state. They decide to organize the sixth-grade science concepts into units that are relevant to inter-related environmental issues evident in their region of the state.

Activity-Based Lessons Activity-based lessons are those lessons that involve a "hands on" activity through which teachers instruct students or provide them with practice of previously taught skills. Activity-based teaching provides students with an active means for learning; lectures and worksheets are passive learning formats. For example, in place of a worksheet on liquid measurement equivalencies, students might fill the class aquarium using several equivalent measures or make Kool-Aid or concentrated juice for the class.

Activity-based lessons are prevalent in inclusive classrooms because they 1) provide practical meaning to abstract concepts, 2) make it easier to present material in several ways (e.g., visual, kinesthetic, auditory, tactile), and 3) follow a structure that facilitates the use of a variety of curriculum objectives in a single lesson. Activity-based instruction does not and should not replace skill-based instruction; instead, it is often supplemented with direct instruction on specific skills in addition to drill and practice in the use of those skills and the application of the acquired knowledge.

Once the units have been organized to cover the sixth-grade standards of learning and to address regional environmental issues, the two teachers identify related environmental activities that have direct application in their communities (e.g., composting, recycling, logging business and forestry, water pollution) that they can weave into each unit.

Cooperative Learning Groups Teachers should make use of cooperative learning groups because of their proven effectiveness in promoting social and academic learning within mixed ability classrooms. To ensure

success, teachers should identify cooperative learning activities that mesh with the unit being studied and teach their students the cooperative skills required for these groups to be productive. Cooperative learning has five essential components that teachers will need to implement:

- *Positive interdependence among students* (much like that which exists in collaborative teams)
- *Individual accountability* (all group members must do their part in the cooperative learning activity)
- *Heterogeneous grouping* (small base groups of students with differences in abilities, interests, and personal characteristics who work together over a period of time)
- *Direct instruction of necessary social skills,* which are required for the group to function cooperatively
- *Group processing methods* that enable groups to examine their cooperation and learning

(More on cooperative learning groups can be found in another book in this series, *Social Relationships and Peer Supports* [Snell & Janney, 2000].)

After studying the records of the students in the third-period science class, Nancy and Andrea made a preliminary list of cooperative groups. Although the students had worked in cooperative groups before, Nancy and Andrea felt that they should schedule the first 3 weeks to review or teach the concepts of positive interdependency, individual accountability, group processing, and the required social skills. They decided to use cooperative group activities twice a week.

Scheduling

When special education teachers provide pull-in services and co-teach, they usually rotate among classrooms, rather than work with only one classroom. Some researchers recommend

concentrating students with disabilities in a smaller number of classes, thereby reducing the number of classrooms in which the special education teachers must co-teach. Although this approach may make the special education teacher's job easier and more efficient, it is still preferable that the *guideline of natural proportions* be followed: students with special needs should be assigned to classrooms with their peers without disabilities in proportions similar to their natural proportions in a neighborhood school. Therefore, because 11% of students at this particular middle school have special needs, approximately three students in each class of 30 will have identified special needs; however, the proportion may be less in advanced courses. This approach requires the school administrator and consulting teacher to work closely with classroom teachers at each grade level to assess teachers' talent for and interest in having students with disabilities in their classroom and to provide necessary training and support. Over time and with ongoing in-service training and support from the special education teacher, all teachers should have the opportunity to expand their skills in serving students with disabilities.

The schedules of special education teachers and other support staff should reflect the needs of the students on their caseload, which can vary from intensive (e.g., one-to-one teaching for a period) to limited (e.g., monitoring during study hall).

Andrea's schedule as a special education teacher on the sixth-grade middle school team is a good illustration of this balance. Andrea rotates among seven classes using pull-in services for three to five students in social studies, reading, math, and language arts; co-teaches (primarily in a complimentary role) in science; and uses pull-out services for five students in the form of an academic lab geared primarily toward three students with special needs.

Ideally, special education teachers in inclusive schools will have broader training and experience that allows them to adequately serve all or most of the children with identified needs for a single grade level, multiple grade levels (e.g., K–2, eighth-grade team), or high school department (depending on the size of the school). Those students who have more extensive support needs may require services from a special education teacher who rotates across all grade levels to consult with the classroom teachers and to support these students directly. When only a few children with severe disabilities are present in a school and teachers with specialized training in severe disabilities are not on staff, the school's central office might assign a teacher from a nearby school to support these students on a consultative basis (preferred) or may assign the students to a school within the school division where a specialized teacher is employed. Because enrollments at middle schools and high schools are usually larger, these specialized teachers may be assigned to single schools and may work with students in all grades. Regardless of the number of schools they support, special education teachers' schedules will incorporate a variety of methods for pulling in support and for collaborating on the programs and progress of each student on their caseload. Figure 5.11 provides an example of collaborative team teaching under excellent conditions.

The organizing schedules that teachers develop are crucial to the implementation of needed individualized supports. Teams will modify these schedules over time when new students enroll, students move, staff and semesters change, and schedule complications arise. These schedule changes should be generated, or at least approved, by the team(s) involved.

EVALUATE OUTCOMES

Teachers who co-teach will want to evaluate the outcome of their teaching at two levels: their interpersonal effectiveness as a teaching team (e.g., comfort, shared decision-making, compatibility) and their impact on students (e.g., attitudes, knowledge and skills, behavior,

Voices from the Classroom

In an elementary school in a midwestern city, teachers from two fifth-grade classes combined their teaching efforts with a special education teacher for a year. The 55 students students (13 of whom had learning disabilities) were assigned to one of the two classrooms, but students and staff had additional space available (the former resource room on a continuous basis and two small group rooms during part of the day). Both classroom teachers taught reading and math, but elected either *social studies (Hal)* or *science (Dick)* to teach to both classes. *Ann, the SE teacher,* initially moved back and forth between the two classes providing support to students. Later, Hal, Dick, and Ann decided that Ann would select one subject to teach when they teamed; she chose reading and language arts. Ann's teaching method depended on the style of the teacher with whom she was working. With Hal, who used more lecture and a teacher-directed approach, Ann taught related reading and language arts using small groups and individual instruction. With Dick, who used a high activity, hands-on approach in science, Ann gave support during the continuous high activity lessons.

Over the year, Ann's role changed from whole group instruction during the math and reading periods to a flexible range of small group instruction and varied methods of lending assistance to students. Group composition, size, and location were highly flexible, depending on both the purpose of the instruction and student preference.

The three teachers had a daily joint planning period that lasted 35 minutes, and typically made some instructional decisions informally during the day. During one weekly planning period, teachers (with the program support teacher) focused specifically on teaming: how things were going, what they could do to improve, better ways to teach certain concepts, and needed materials or resources.

Interviews with students and staff indicated that "*Giving and receiving help* was an accepted norm" and that students could obtain help easily, from teachers and from each other (pp. 283, 285). One student with disabilities compared last year's resource room approach with this year's team teaching approach: "*I really didn't like it last year because you had to go up to her classroom for reading and stuff like that. And then we probably wouldn't have learned some of their [regular class] stuff, too, I think*" (p. 287). Another said: "*When you're in a bigger class, it's funner. When you're in a little class, it's dumb*" (p. 287).

Figure 5.11.   Collaborative team teaching of fifth graders under excellent conditions. (From Pugach, M.C., & Wesson, C.L. [1995]. Teachers' and students' views of team teaching and general education and learning-disabled students in two fifth-grade classes. *The Elementary School Journal, 95,* 279–295. © 1995 University of Chicago. All rights reserved; adapted with permission.)

friendship and group skills, and referrals). Most researchers of collaborative teaching suggest that evaluations be conducted regularly, not simply at the semester or year's end (e.g., DeBoer & Fister, 1995–1996; Trent, 1998). Teachers should develop a plan and a regular schedule for evaluating their co-teaching, even if this plan is limited to verbal debriefings every week. If problems do arise between teachers or with the success of collaborative teaching, these evaluation plans will provide teachers with a previously determined opportunity to examine data and to make modifications; it is awkward to suggest conducting an evaluation only after problems have already arisen.

Evaluating the Effects of Collaborative Teaching on Students

As shown in Figure 5.12, DeBoer and Fister (1995–1996) suggested five areas from which teachers may collect evaluation information as well as the specific types of information they should gather and review. Although the grid looks overwhelming at first glance, much of the data listed in the three areas is information that is routinely gathered (i.e., knowledge and skills, behaviors, referrals); this information, however, can be used creatively to assess the impact that a shift to collaborative teaching has had on students in terms of achievement (i.e., knowledge and skills), be-

Areas for collecting information	Groups from Whom to Collect Information		
	Students	**Educators**	**Parents**
Attitudes	• Questionnaires • Interviews	• Questionnaires • Interviews	• Questionnaires • Interviews
Knowledge and skills	• <u>Performance assessment</u> • <u>Written tests</u> • <u>Norm-referenced tests</u> • <u>Grades</u>	• Peer coaching • Clinical coaching • Self-reporting	N/A
Behaviors	• <u>Work completion</u> • <u>Attendance records</u> • <u>Behavior referrals</u> • <u>Behavioral data on target skills</u>	• Attendance and absenteeism • Self-reporting	• Attendance at parent teacher interviews, etc.
Friendships/ group skills	• Observation • Interviews • Self-reporting	• Interviews	
Referrals	<u>Counting the number of increases and decreases</u>	N/A	N/A
Note: The types of student information that are underlined are those gathered on a more routine basis in schools.			

Figure 5.12.   Evaluation options for collaborative teachers. (Adapted with permission from DeBoer, A., & Fister, S. [1995–1996]. *Working together: Tools for collaborative teaching.* Longmont, CO: Sopris West. All rights reserved.)

havior, and referrals for special education services. The two remaining areas (attitudes and friendships/group skills) are not typically assessed by teachers; however, they can add valuable information to the database teachers might want to examine when they assess the effects of collaborative teaching on students.

At the end of their first sixth-grade science unit in October, Nancy (science teacher) and Andrea (special education teacher) used a questionnaire to assess the effect that their collaborative teaching had on the class. They read 10 questions aloud and asked students to circle one of five ratings (depicted by smiley face [liked very much], neutral face [was okay], and sad face [didn't like at all] symbols and two in-between ratings) to rate the new teaching methods they had

used. After they collected the questionnaires (without student names on them), they held an open discussion regarding the questions and other issues that came up.

Parental viewpoints on the change to collaborative teaching may also be worth examining. DeBoer and Fister (1995–1996) suggested looking at changes in parents' attitudes toward co-teaching (e.g., from skepticism to enthusiasm or vice versa) and changes in their participation in the school program, which may or may not be related.

Processing Together Between Teachers

Similar to processing within collaborative teams (see Chapters 3 and 6), teachers who are involved in collaborative teaching should take a few minutes after each co-taught lesson

Item	Not at all								Completely
1. I feel that my knowledge and skills are valued.	1	2	3	4	5	6	7	8	9
2. I believe that information and materials are freely shared.	1	2	3	4	5	6	7	8	9
3. I believe that I am an equal partner in the decisions that are made.	1	2	3	4	5	6	7	8	9
4. I am frequently acknowledged and reinforced by my partner.	1	2	3	4	5	6	7	8	9
5. I believe we are using sound instructional practices.	1	2	3	4	5	6	7	8	9
6. I am learning as a result of our roles and responsibilities.	1	2	3	4	5	6	7	8	9
7. My time is used productively when I am in the classroom.	1	2	3	4	5	6	7	8	9
8. I am satisfied with our roles and responsibilities.	1	2	3	4	5	6	7	8	9
9. I am satisfied with the way we communicate with and coach each other.	1	2	3	4	5	6	7	8	9

Figure 5.13. A questionnaire for teachers to reflect on collaborative teaching. (Adapted with permission from De-Boer, A., & Fister, S. [1995–1996]. *Working together: Tools for collaborative teaching*. Longmont, CO: Sopris West. All rights reserved.)

to compare notes regarding their impressions of the session and to explore ways they might improve less successful areas. Figure 5.12 suggests a more comprehensive array of evaluation options for teachers, which span four of the five areas of evaluation that are suggested for students: attitude, knowledge and skills, behaviors, and friendships. One of the several teacher reflection questionnaires to which DeBoer and Fister (1995–1996) refer is provided in Figure 5.13. Teachers should develop their own questionnaires based on the shared values and ground rules they developed with their collaborative team(s); they should also add items regarding the specific roles and responsibilities identified early in co-teaching to their listing of interpersonal skills.

Chapter 6

Improving Communication
and Handling Conflict

John, an eighth-grade special education teacher, just learned that his comments regarding next year's class schedules, offered in confidence to help his team plan their students' eighth-grade support schedules, have been wildly circulating among teachers in the lounge. He is angry and disappointed: "I thought I could trust them . . . after all our time together!"

On another team, Roberta, the earth science teacher, sighs; "His mom is single, works a job and a half, has two other kids . . . she doesn't have time for Bernie and she probably doesn't know the material enough to help Bernie with his homework. It's a shame, really."

On a third team, Millie, the special education teacher, is late once again to the team meeting—this time, by 20 minutes; the meeting was almost over. Rhonda reacted, "How do you expect us to work together if you are never here on time?"

The first four topics discussed in this chapter are characteristics of strong and effective teams: team trust, effective communication, sensitivity to diversity, and positive staff–family interactions. These interrelated characteristics contribute to the interpersonal relationships and communication among team members, both of which are essential for creative and cooperative work conditions. Inevitably, even when these characteristics are in place, most teams periodically experience problem behavior from one or more team members and nonconstructive conflict within the group. The last section of this chapter discusses strategies for addressing these threats to team effectiveness.

KNOW AND TRUST EACH OTHER

Although Chapter 3 described the initial steps that teams take to build trust through basic teamwork skills, this section will elaborate on team trust. Establishing trust among team members is not a simple process; it requires both trusting others and being trust-

worthy (Johnson & Johnson, 1997). When each team member trusts his or her fellow team members, several qualities are realized:

- *Interdependency:* Team outcomes depend on others as well as on oneself.

- *Risk:* Team outcomes can be good or bad and can result in gains or losses for oneself, the student(s), and/or the team.

- *Confidence:* Team outcomes will be good and will yield benefits (Deutsch, 1962).

Interdependency, for example, involves a willingness on the part of each team member to contribute to the achievement of team goals by 1) sharing their resources for group gain (e.g., talents, materials, ideas, time, energy), 2) giving help to others (e.g., modeling skills, volunteering for tasks in team action plans), 3) receiving help from each other (e.g., learning from one another's demonstrations, seeking and listening to the viewpoints, advice, or information of other team members), and 4) dividing the team's work. These interdependent behaviors are associated with team members' open expression of ideas, feelings, reactions, opinions, and information (Johnson & Johnson, 1997).

An example from Rick's ninth-grade English teacher, Carrie Wilson, helps clarify both the risk element of trust and the consequences (harmful or beneficial) dilemma:

As Rick's teacher in English 9, I am a member of Rick's team (a ninth grader whose behavior requires close and ongoing positive support). I contributed some to the design of his support plans, which were drawn up in August. However, after 2 months of using these plans, I'm very frustrated by the way in which other students seem to "push his buttons," which almost always causes him to get upset; then I get upset and off task. Co-teaching with Ann (Rick's special education teacher) is working well; however, she seems much more able to ignore these interactions, to let them just go, or to prompt him (like we agreed in

the action plan) to say things such as, "get off my back" or, "lay off." I get tense and fearful that Rick will explode, I won't know what to do, and the whole class will fall apart. I've decided to say something, even though I'm concerned that the problem might really be my problem, but I worry: "If I openly express myself, will my team members use it against me? Will they think I'm less capable or that I'm not trying or that I'm just a baby?"

The way in which Ms. Wilson's teammates respond to her trusting and open expression will have a lasting influence on her comfort with the team as well as on her ability to be successful in supporting Rick.

How Team Members Gain Trust

Team member's build trust through their actions and communication with one another. Trust can be increased or decreased depending on what individual team members say and do; trust is an indicator of current team health (Johnson & Johnson, 1997). DeBoer (1995) identified three basic strategies for facilitating trust among co-workers and team members:

1. *Empathy* toward other team members occurs when one team member is able to take the perspective of others, to "stand in their shoes," and to understand their feelings, concerns, and priorities.

   "You know Carrie, I feel the same way sometimes," says another teacher.

   "I see Rick a lot every day, and he's not the first challenging student I have had; however, I remember that same fearful feeling when I first met Rick!" Ann, his special education teacher adds.

2. *Acceptance of the other team members for what they are* means showing genuine positive regard for another person; this includes his or her capacity, experiences, talents, and unique viewpoints. Acceptance, however, does not encompass agreeing (or disagreeing) with that individual or granting your approval (or disapproval). Acceptance in-

volves taking people for who they really are, not who one wishes them to be. Acceptance of others "communicates an acceptance of their attitudes [beliefs, feelings, and behavior] from their frame of reference" (DeBoer, 1995, p. 176).

   "I can understand how scary it can be—you've seen one of his worst explosions, says a counselor, who remembers Rick's anger in English during the first week of classes. That was the time he forgot his medication; school had just started, high school was brand new for him, and he was confused about his schedule. He has not fallen apart like that since, thank goodness—and I think it's because of our supports!" the counselor adds.

3. *Credibility* means that team members perceive each other as compatible or similar and competent (i.e., having some talents to bring to the team that others value) and as someone who openly speaks his/her mind and takes the group's interest to heart.

   Carrie and her teammates have many years of high school teaching experience among them. They have strong respect for each other's talents. Each team member interacts with Rick regularly, and, for the most part, their team-generated action plan for supporting him has been highly successful.

Trust building between two individuals can be analyzed in several ways, and each way involves risk and confirmation (Johnson & Johnson, 1997). Trust is built when an individual takes a risk in initiating an interaction with another person and is affirmed; trust is destroyed with an individual takes a risk in initiating an interaction with another person and is disaffirmed by that individual. In both examples in Table 6.1, the initiators take a risk and trust that the respondent will listen and confirm their remarks. In the first example, Soo is trusting when she risks disclosing her viewpoints to James, and James is trustworthy because he responds to her disclosure in a supportive way and then reciprocates by disclosing his own personal viewpoints. Furthermore, James' confirming reaction ensures that Soo will experience the beneficial consequences of feeling like a valued team member.

Table 6.1.   The dynamics of interpersonal trust

Initiation	Response
1. Soo *takes a risk* and discloses her thoughts, information, conclusions, feelings, and reactions to the immediate situation.	James responds to Soo in an accepting, supportive, cooperative way and reciprocates her openness by disclosing his own thoughts, information, conclusions, feelings, and reactions to the immediate situation and to her.
2. Carla *takes a risk* and communicates acceptance, support, and cooperativeness toward Sarah.	Sarah responds by disclosing her thoughts, information, conclusions, feelings, and reactions to the immediate situation and to Carla.

Adapted from Johnson & Johnson, 1997.

In the second example, Carla is trusting when she takes a risk (though perhaps less of a risk than Soo takes in the first example) and communicates her support for Sarah (something Sarah has said or done); Sarah responds by disclosing her viewpoints and confirming Carla's trust.

Trust is built and maintained through trustworthiness (Johnson & Johnson, 1997) and leads to team members' open sharing (disclosure). Therefore, in each example, open sharing and trust are reinforced by more open sharing and trust, which in turn builds a cooperative cycle of interaction among team members. The reactions of Carrie Wilson's teammates to her confessions of fear about defusing interactions between Rick and his peers were highly confirming to Carrie:

- *"We understand your fears; we feel or have felt them ourselves."*

- *"We have generally been very successful with Rick over the past 2 months; our plans are working."*

Although trust is still strong, the team should explore ways that they can lend meaningful support to Carrie through the use of one or several methods that Carrie feels might prove helpful (e.g., role play, classroom observation, additional attention to the "defusing" procedure, talking separately to Rick's peers, or modeling by another team member).

There are limits to trust, however. For example, it is not advisable *to always trust* or *to never trust*. Trust in another team member is appropriate when risk exists but only when

there also is confidence that the potential for benefit is greater than the potential for harm. This requires "sizing up" the situation and initiating or reacting accordingly.

COMMUNICATE ACCURATELY AND UNAMBIGUOUSLY

Communicating includes both listening to and speaking with others. This section of the chapter elaborates on team trust and the use of accurate and unambiguous communication within teams. Guidelines on effective interpersonal communication from several authors (DeBoer & Fister, 1995–1996; Johnson & Johnson, 1997) is shared.

Sending Messages

If interpersonal communication among team members is to be effective, attention needs to be paid to the ways that members send and receive messages. Senders who want their messages to be understood have to meet three rudimentary requirements (Johnson & Johnson, 1997):

1. *Phrase the message in a way that listeners can understand:* Avoid acronyms and technical terminology, use examples, and adjust language to the audience (Figure 6.1).

2. *Be a credible message sender:* Receivers must regard your messages as trustworthy.

3. *Ask others for feedback regarding their understanding of and reaction to what was communicated.*

Sending messages effectively	Receiving messages effectively
• Own your messages by using first person (i.e., "I" and "My").	• Check your understanding of the message by paraphrasing as accurately as possible, without any judgment of the sender's message or feelings. To do this,
• Use complete and specific messages (as needed, communicate your frame of reference, assumptions, and intentions).	• Restate the message in your own words.
• Be congruent in your verbal and your nonverbal messages.	• Do not communicate any approval or disapproval.
• Repeat your message in more than one way and through another channel to be clear.	• Do not add to or take away from the message.
• Seek feedback from teammates on your message.	• Step into the speaker's "shoes" to understand the meaning of his or her message.
• Match the message to listeners' frame of reference (e.g., student, another teacher, parent, administrator).	• Communicate that you want to fully understand before you make an evaluation.
• Be unambiguous by describing your feelings (e.g., name them, use figurative speech, or state actions): "I feel happy" "I'm down in the dumps!" or, "I want to run away from this."	• Check your perceptions of the sender's feelings by describing them:
	• Describe tentatively; seek confirmation.
• Describe the behavior of others but do not evaluate or interpret it (e.g., "You keep interrupting" not, "You are a horrible listener").	• Do not communicate any approval or disapproval or try to interpret or explain your perceptions (e.g., "It seems like you are worried about Jennifer being in sixth-grade classes. Am I right?").
	• Talk to the sender and negotiate the interpretation of his/her message until you both agree on the meaning.

Figure 6.1. Being effective senders and receivers of messages. (From David W. Johnson & Frank P. Johnson, JOINING TOGETHER; GROUP THEORY AND GROUP SKILLS 6/E © 1997 by Allyn & Bacon. Adapted by permission.)

Of these three requirements, *sender credibility* seems to be the most essential. Communicators have credibility when they are viewed as being knowledgeable about the content under discussion, when their motives are not suspect, when their tone and style is friendly, when listeners regard them as trustworthy, and when they are assertive and emphatic in communicating their messages.

Receiving Messages

The skill of listening to or receiving a message has two fundamental requirements: 1) communicating, primarily through nonverbal behavior, that you want to understand the speaker's message and feelings, and 2) actually understanding the speaker's message and feelings (Johnson & Johnson, 1997). Of these two

requirements, it appears that it is more important for communication to be effective when receivers communicate their intent to understand than when they actually understand a message. The communication of intent is achieved mainly through the receiver's nonverbal behavior (e.g., receiver should face the speaker, establish eye contact, look interested, and not interrupt).

The biggest barricade to effective listening is the evaluation of messages as they are being received. When a receiver makes immediate judgments regarding a speaker's message without first confirming his or her understanding of the message, he or she often stops listening or leaps to conclusions based on a premature or erroneous evaluation of the message. Trust is consequently eroded. Pre-

mature evaluations by receivers also cause senders to be defensive and closed and less able to explain or expand on their message.

When Jennifer's fifth-grade team met with her future team members at the middle school in March, trust had not developed between both groups. Ms. Harris narrated the video her fifth graders had made of class activities that showed off many of Jennifer's talents. She described the various ways the team supported Jennifer (e.g., small group pull-in, co-teaching, peer tutoring) and emphasized that pull-out was rarely needed anymore. Two of the sixth-grade teachers started frowning; one shook her head but said nothing. Ms. Harris, who had been happily sharing Jennifer's successes, felt judged and angry, as if her ideas were being discredited. She abruptly stopped talking; the meeting room became quiet and was filled with tension.

Whenever receivers are not clear about a sender's message, they must take time to clarify their understanding by rephrasing the message without any judgment, seeking feedback from the sender, and then working to settle the differences in understanding between the receivers and the sender (see Figure 6.1). In this case, the sixth-grade teachers needed to clarify their understanding by rephrasing what they heard. Receivers should make an evaluation of a message only once they completely understand it.

After Ms. Harris abruptly stopped, one of the sixth-grade teacher sensed the tension and misunderstanding. She said, "It seems as if you and Ms. Ager (special educator currently serving Jennifer) have experienced a lot of success in teaching Jennifer alongside her fifth-grade classmates. This makes your whole team feel successful."

"That's right," beamed Ms. Harris, happy that one of the listeners understood her message. "It was hard at first, because I had never had someone like Jennifer in my classroom, and it took some creative

team problem-solving to make it work as well as it has. Jennifer, however, has met all her IEP goals, her family is happy with her success, she never misses school anymore, she has friends, and, as you saw in the video, her classmates have positive things to say about having her as a classmate."

The sixth grade teacher who had spoken up added, "We might need your help . . ."

Ms. Ager spoke up: "We'd like to help . . . and we know that middle school is not elementary school. We might have to change our strategies to fit middle school a little better, and you probably will think up lots of new ideas that work better with your class schedules. We'd be very willing, however, to show you all that we have learned about fifth-grade academic work and social issues."

The expressions on the faces of all three sixth-grade teachers brightened.

When the sixth-grade teacher sought clarification from Ms. Harris, she also acted to support and confirm the fifth-grade teacher's report of Jennifer's successes; this response from the sixth-grade teacher reestablished the trust that had been operating in the beginning of the meeting and allowed Ms. Harris to confess to the challenges that the fifth-grade team had worked through. Finally, with trust again operating, the sixth-grade teachers were able to reciprocate and request the assistance they knew they would need.

DeBoer (1995) described the "tough listening" situations in which we all have found ourselves at one time or another. Tough listening times occur when a speaker sends a message that takes a judgmental position; it is often accompanied by highly visible nonverbal behaviors. Often, the message conflicts directly with strongly held beliefs or values of the listener. It is especially important to listen and hear what the speaker is saying during these situations, or it may be impossible to influence him or her later. If the conditions for responding are poor (e.g., others may be present, you may feel embarrassed, surprised, hurt, flustered, or very angry), it may be best

When team members are in tough situations, it is critical that they hear what others are saying. Only then do they have any hope of influencing the beliefs, feelings, or behaviors of their coworkers. The following are examples of tough listening:

- A teammate who was absent from a meeting tears apart the team's carefully developed action plan, which you had a big part in developing; to makes things worse, some of her strongest complaints seem to have some validity. You listen.

- A colleague openly cuts down your values on inclusion, hitting on many things you hold dear. You listen, although only because you know that if you try to defend yourself now, she will not pay attention later.

- In the presence of others in the teachers' lounge, a fellow teacher severely berates a student whom you know well and care for greatly. Several teachers who are listening agree with the complainer and sympathize with her miseries of having him as a student. Your admiration for that student is great; however, given the negative and heated climate, you decide not to say anything now but to listen to her message and plan your response for a less emotional opportunity.

- As the team focuses on several teaching challenges, you are brimming with ideas that you think are brilliant and could resolve all the challenges. You resist jumping in and dominating the discussion and sending messages of your impatience with their contributions. While you think you could outline the entire action plan, you know it would be your plan and not the team's plan. Instead, you take your turn, contributing the best of your ideas, listening to others' ideas, and looking for chances to integrate the team's ideas into a creative plan that is truly team-generated.

All of these tough listening situations involve team members sending clear messages about their feelings and their needs. The nonverbal behaviors that speakers and listeners use—facial expressions, gestures, physical stance, voice volume and tone, and eye contact—are the primary ways such messages are sent. While it is not easy to listen under these tough conditions, it is essential to do so; *"until people feel certain you have heard their message, it is impossible for them to listen to you"* (p. 71).

To gain a complete understanding of other team members' messages, skilled listeners can use *facilitative listening skills:* 1) attending, 2) responding (e.g., by paraphrasing, clarifying, reflecting, and checking perceptions), and 3) using leading strategies (e.g., interpreting, explaining, encouraging, assuring, suggesting, agreeing/disagreeing, challenging, and humoring) (see Chapter 3).

Figure 6.2. "Good listening is tough listening." (Adapted with permission from DeBoer, A. & Fister, S. [1995–1996]. *Working together: Tools for collaborative teaching.* Longmont, CO: Sopris West. All rights reserved.)

to listen and wait until later to make a more reasoned response. Figure 6.2 provides examples of these situations, in addition to guidance on how to listen.

It is clear that effective interpersonal communication requires skill from both message senders and receivers. The best way to resist judging others' messages prematurely is to get in the habit of seeking clarification from speakers regarding their messages. Team members need to feel that it is acceptable to ask each other for clarification. When team members take time to process, it is often a good idea to quiz themselves on their natural comfort with questioning others (Johnson & Johnson, 1997) (Figure 6.3). If a team's comfort level is low in seeking clarification of a

message through questioning each other, they might want to 1) devise interesting exercises to practice the skill (e.g., give incomplete directions; tell a story/joke but leave out a key line; describe a favorite recipe, book, or store but leave out important identifying information), 2) modify their ground rules ("Listen and understand me before you judge my ideas"), and 3) recall examples of their own tough listening situations and discuss alternative ways they might have used effective listening strategies.

Giving and Receiving Feedback Effectively

Some people are talented at giving feedback to others in ways that motivate them to listen, to

---

Checking Out My Communication Behavior

Directions: Complete all the questions by yourself. Review your answers in a round-robin fashion by having each member summarize his/her current communication performance. Discuss any implications for individual and team improvement.

1. If I were to explain something to teammates and they sat quietly with blank faces, I would
   _____ try to explain clearly and then move on
   _____ encourage members to ask questions until I knew everyone understood

2. If our facilitator explained something to the team that I did not understand, I would
   _____ keep silent and find out from someone else later on
   _____ ask the facilitator to repeat the explanation or to answer my questions

3. How often do I let other members know when I like or approve of something they say or do?
   Never 1 - 2 - 3 - 4 - 5 - 6 - 7 - 8 - 9 - 10 Always

4. How often do I let other teammates know when I am irritated or impatient, embarrassed by, or opposed to something they have said or done?
   Never 1 - 2 - 3 - 4 - 5 - 6 - 7 - 8 - 9 - 10 Always

5. How often do I check out teammates' feelings and not just assume that I know what they are?
   Never 1 - 2 - 3 - 4 - 5 - 6 - 7 - 8 - 9 - 10 Always

6. How often do I encourage others to let me know how they feel about what I say?
   Never 1 - 2 - 3 - 4 - 5 - 6 - 7 - 8 - 9 - 10 Always

7. How often do I check to be sure I understand what others are saying before I think judgmentally (e.g., "I don't agree" "She's right!")?
   Never 1 - 2 - 3 - 4 - 5 - 6 - 7 - 8 - 9 - 10 Always

8. How often do I check to be sure I understand what others are saying before I express my judgments *nonverbally* (e.g., head shake, frowning) or *out loud* (e.g., "I don't agree" "She's right!")?
   Never 1 - 2 - 3 - 4 - 5 - 6 - 7 - 8 - 9 - 10 Always

9. How often do I paraphrase or restate what others have said before I respond?
   Never 1 - 2 - 3 - 4 - 5 - 6 - 7 - 8 - 9 - 10 Always

10. How often do I keep my feelings, reactions, thoughts, and ideas to myself during meetings?
    Never 1 - 2 - 3 - 4 - 5 - 6 - 7 - 8 - 9 - 10 Always

11. How often do I make sure that all information I have regarding the topic under discussion is known to the rest of the group?
    Never 1 - 2 - 3 - 4 - 5 - 6 - 7 - 8 - 9 - 10 Always

Question content: Questions address the following aspects of communication: 1 and 2—One-way and two-way communication; 3 and 4—Your willingness to give feedback to others on how you react to their messages; 5 and 6—Your willingness to ask for feedback on your messages; 7–9—Your receiving skills; 10 and 11—Your willingness to contribute (send) relevant messages about the team's work.

Figure 6.3.   A quiz for team members to assess their communication behavior. (From David W. Johnson & Frank P. Johnson, JOINING TOGETHER: GROUP THEORY AND GROUP SKILLS 6/E © 1997 by Allyn & Bacon. Adapted by permission.)

understand, and to be inspired to improve. Those who are good at giving constructive feedback for improvement are usually also good at giving positive feedback (and do so). They usually only provide credible feedback and are sensitive to the receptivity of the recipient, able to tailor their phraseology to suit the individual, and caring in their motives for giving feedback (Johnson & Johnson, 1997; Lundy, 1994). Ultimately, however, any improvement that results from constructive feedback given to a teammate depends equally on the talents of the person receiving the feedback. Receivers must be able to listen, seek

clarification without being defensive, explore suggestions regarding change, take steps to self-improve, and seek feedback from teammates on their behavior. The responsibilities of both the sender and receiver of constructive feedback are pretty hefty (Figure 6.4). Despite this, the process of giving and receiving positive and constructive feedback may be the best way to prevent conflict among team members and to improve effectiveness in collaboration.

BE SENSITIVE TO DIVERSE CULTURES

The students in today's schools are more culturally diverse than ever before; however, the professionals who teach and administer in our schools often do not reflect the same rich array of culture and ethnic background as their students and students' families (Williams, 1992). Cultural diversity, when combined with intercultural knowledge, communication, and positive experiences, is always an asset. However, if these conditions are lacking, misunderstanding, stereotypes, prejudices, and even racism, each having the power to divide team members and students and greatly hinder or prevent teamwork, can result.

Ignorance is probably the best explanation for prejudice toward those who are different from us, whether the differences are in culture, accent, language, religion, personal beliefs, gender, age group, disability, lifestyle, dress, or physical characteristics. The *"us"* is the *dominant culture or group* in a given environment, and the *"others"* are those in the environment's *minority culture/group*. An *environment* includes any existing group of people: a country, a state, a community, a neighborhood, a school, a church, a sports team, a classroom, a reading group, or a collaborative team. *Ignorance* often is due to a lack of experience with the minority culture/group in a particular environment or inadequate knowledge of the practices, beliefs, and characteristics of the members of that culture/group.

Ignorance of other cultures often breeds stereotypes: "a set of cognitive generalizations that summarize, organize, and guide the processing of information about members of a particular group" (Johnson & Johnson, 1997, p. 390). Stereotypes reflect false beliefs about causal connections between two unrelated, and often negative, factors: being poor and lazy, being white and successful, having a disability and being ignorant, being overweight and having a great sense of humor, or having Down syndrome and being stubborn. Stereotypes are dangerous because they guide the ways that we think about groups of people, and they are highly resistant to change. For example, Trent (1997) found that teachers' sociocultural stereotypes regarding students' abilities and their home life were negatively associated with their reduced expectations for students with disabilities and for students' lack of progress.

Johnson and Johnson (1997, pp. 391–392) listed the ways that stereotypes are protected:

- Stereotypes influence what we perceive and remember about the actions of out-group members.

- Stereotypes create an oversimplified picture of out-group members—and the larger the out-group, the more likely oversimplifications are to occur.

- Individuals tend to overestimate the similarity of behavior among out-group members.

- People tend to have a false consensus bias by believing that most other people share their stereotypes.

- Stereotypes tend to be self-fulfilling.

- Stereotypes lead to scapegoating.

- People often develop a rationale and explanation to justify their stereotypes and prejudices.

All of the elements outlined in teamwork skills (e.g., shared decision-making, team consensus, the use of shared values and ground rules to guide team action, regular team processing of interpersonal relationships, good listening and communication skills) can be

Providing Positive Feedback	Providing Constructive Feedback for Improvement	Receiving Feedback
Goal: To help another realize the way that his or her behavior has had a positive influence on a person, group, or issue; to encourage the person to continue or to expand the behavior	*Goal: To help another receive information about improving or changing his/her behavior; reaching this goal depends on the receptivity of the recipient, the capability of the sender at giving feedback, and the credibility of the feedback*	*Goal: To hear what is being offered nondefensively and to consider feedback as an opportunity for self-improvement. Lundy (1994) notes "Those who defend their weaknesses can keep them, and probably will; the greatest weakness is the awareness of none."*
• When you mention specific behaviors, acts, or events, the person will understand more clearly.	• Be perceptive to the recipient's readiness for feedback.	• Keep your mind open and listen; absorb as much as you can.
• Tell why you think the behavior had a positive impact (e.g., your feelings, others reactions).	• Word your feedback in ways that do not hurt or damage.	• Listen for understanding, quell judgments, and focus totally on what is being said.
• Give only sincere praise; undeserved praise can have bad effects and insincere praise can threaten relationships.	• Identify specific behaviors and situations; be unambiguous and do not generalize beyond the specific or exaggerate.	• Do not interrupt to maximize your understanding. Make notes to help clarify your understanding later.
• Sincere praise is easy to give and goes a long way.	• Address behavior and actions, not personality traits.	• Hold your desire to react in check. Take a deep breath, be quiet, and think through your questions.
• Find appropriate opportunities to give public credit that is due—orally or in written reports.	• Tell how you feel, but omit any judgments or speculations on the recipient's motives.	• Confirm your understanding of the message with the sender right away or later if you need time to gain self-control; sooner is better than later because you may misunderstand the feedback.
	• Give feedback promptly; time erodes our memory of events.	• Seek clarification—ask about confusing aspects, and request illustrations. Avoid being defensive in the process.
	• Make your feedback brief and avoid unneeded repetition; this helps minimize defensiveness.	• Size up the situation: what the sender is saying reflects how they feel—their reality.
	• Confirm understanding by listening to the person's reaction or thoughts regarding self-improvement.	• State your appreciation, even if you do not agree; try to regard feedback as a "gift of information" (p. 164).
	• Preface your suggestions with introductory questions: "Have you considered . . . ?" "Do you suppose . . . ?" "Would it help . . . ?"	• Seek more information to clarify whether the viewpoint is shared by other teammates. If so, or if you agree with the criticism, continue the steps below.
	• Suggest, but do not dictate.	
	• "Look forward to opportunity, not backward to blame" (p. 162). Suggest alternatives for the future.	*(continued)*

Figure 6.4.   Giving and receiving feedback from teammates. (Adapted with permission form T.E.A.M.S. Copyright 1994 by Dartnell, 360 Hiatt Drive, FL 33418. All rights reserved. For more information on this or other products published by Dartnell, please call (800) 621-5463, ext. 567.)

Figure 6.4.   *(continued)*

	• Check back with the person on their comfort level with suggestions. • Make the person's needs the focus, not your needs as the helper.	• Discuss ways to improve; those giving feedback may be good sources for ideas. • Focus on changing your behavior; seek the assistance of teammates. • Ask for feedback on progress.

undone by the negative stereotypes one or several team members hold regarding another team member or the student for whom they are collaborating.

Collaborative teams must be vigilant in identifying, discussing, confronting, and eradicating the conditions that breed or protect stereotypes. Simultaneously, teams need to fight ignorance with education. The following paragraphs provide several examples of teams working to eliminate stereotypes toward other team members and students:

• When one or several team members' culture is different from that of the rest of the team, the familiarization phase should involve time to learn first hand, from the team member(s) whose culture is nondominant, information about his or her culture. This might include learning vocabulary from the individual's language, recognizing a holiday, sharing some food from that culture, or learning how many years the individual has been living in the United States and the town and country where his or her family originated.

• When the dominant culture of the professional staff differs from that of the paraprofessional staff and the students in a school, the effort to educate dominant and nondominant groups must be extensive and ongoing. (Figure 6.5 provides an example.)

• Schools should prepare staff and students to understand the background of the nondominant group(s) in ways that *do not overgeneralize* the information.

Consider, as an example, the large range of linguistic and intracultural differences among people often identified as Hispanic, including Cubans, Puerto Ricans, Central and South Americans, Spaniards, and Mexicans (Harry, 1992; Mardinos, 1989). Likewise, individuals who are recent immigrants often differ in their cultural practices and language from first- and second-generation immigrants.

• Religion may also play an important role in the family's or staff members' views of disability and their related beliefs regarding learning and independence of students with disabilities; these views may conflict with the dominant view of a team. Understanding the cultural foundation of the beliefs is a first step toward finding common ground between the nondominant and dominant views. Without common ground, team members' purposes often differ.

• Professionals must recognize their own cultural values prior to developing a sensitivity to the diversity in language, culture, customs, and attitudes of the students and families with whom they work (Harry, 1992; Salisbury & Dunst, 1997).

In the United States, the dominant group often possesses Western values (e.g., independence is best, efficiency is important, parents should be "actively involved"), which may be highly divergent from the values of other nondominant cultures (e.g., interdependence is typical and applauded, it is okay to be late, communication should be indirect and illus-

Situation: In a large, urban school district, the population distribution is 70% Mexican-American, 20% Native American, and 10% Anglo students, but the teachers are primarily Anglo. The assistant principal has concerns regarding the teachers' lack of understanding of the dominant culture and the high rates of referral to special education on the basis of their culturally determined behaviors. The assistant principal is responsible for developing a summer orientation for all new teachers in the system that will familiarize them with the cultural background of their Mexican-American students. Ms. Roledo works with a team of experienced teachers and develops an action plan that she will use to develop the in-service, entitled, "Understanding Mexican-American Students and their Families."

Step 1: Consultation with Mexican-American school personnel	Seek input from Mexican-American faculty on the issues that should be raised in the in-service and the problems they may have encountered with faculty or staff who were insensitive to the Mexican-American population.
Step 2: Consultation with target Mexican-American families	Contact several Mexican-American families who were active in the school last year and ask them to talk openly about 1) what they want teachers to know about the Mexican-American culture, and 2) any problems they encountered with teachers at the school.
Step 3: Consultation with Mexican-American high school students	Meet with several students who have been at the school for one year or longer. Ask them to talk about 1) what they think teachers should know about Mexican-American values and culture, and 2) what problems they have encountered at school that may relate to misunderstandings of their culture.
Step 4: Setting up a panel discussion	Invite three Mexican-Americans (e.g., a faculty member, a parent, and a student) to be part of a panel for the in-service session. Share the topical areas that will be discussed during panel discussion and spend time listening to them practice their responses to the questions she will ask.
Step 5: Compiling the information	Contact the local Mexican-American church and invite the priest to visit. Seek his reactions to the information gathered from the other consultants. Ask him to review in-service session materials.
Step 6: Presentation of the in-service	Mail school staff the materials and information about the Mexican-American students enrolled in their classes a week prior to the in-service. Hold the in-service during the first week of school pre-planning in August. Conduct the panel discussion. Allow time for interaction between panel members and school staff. Gear the inservice to the Mexican-American culture in general, but encompass the particular "lived culture" of the Mexican-Americans in the school community.

Figure 6.5.   A plan to educate Anglo-American school staff on the cultural background of their Mexican-American students. (INTERACTIVE TEAMING: CONSULTATION & COLLABORATION, 2/E by Thomas, © 1991. Reprinted by permission of Prentice-Hall, Inc., Upper Saddle River, NJ.)

trated with personal stories, teachers are the experts, parents receive information) (Sileo, Sileo, & Prater, 1996). When there are wide discrepancies in team members' values as they relate to time, efficiency, independence, and equity, teams should apply practices that are sensitive to those differences. When family members are from a nondominant culture and professional team members are not, several steps should be taken to make members' styles more congruent (Sileo et al., 1996):

- Differences in team members' regard for time might imply that the team needs to allow more time to think aloud together and not just aim for a "quick fix."

- When there are conflicts in beliefs concerning the target student's independence, pro-

fessionals should encourage extended family members to join the team to design programs that reflect their home practices of shared child rearing responsibility.

• When the equity beliefs of team members differ from those of the student's family, professionals should regard the target student's family's view of itself as an expert view in its own right.

FOSTERING STAFF–FAMILY INTERACTION

When 226 teacher team members and 397 parent team members were asked by several researchers to respond to the question, *"What things enhance the ability of your team to collaborate?"* the team trait that was most often cited revolved around the team's ways of working together (Dinnebeil, Hale, & Rule, 1996, pp. 334–335). The trait specifically mentioned by parents and teachers was positive communication conducted in flexible ways, characterized by honesty, positive tone, and tactfulness; this positive communication enables the exchange of information that is both relevant to the child and contributed by all members. How does this happen? Chapter 3 describes ways that teams can develop a teaming process that is suitable to the target student's family members. This section will list and describe methods to foster the interactions between a team's staff members and family members. Experience has shown that teams cannot plan adequately for students without input from the students' families; by contrast, teams that obtain and integrate family opinions into their plans to support students are likely to succeed and to generalize that success from school to home.

The initial meetings that family members attend—evaluation and identification, IEP planning, and placement—are the most critical and often the most difficult for several reasons: 1) Parents and professionals usually do not know each other (especially when a child is first considered for special education); 2) team membership has not yet been estab-

lished because eligibility, program planning, or placement have not yet be determined; and 3) family members are presented with information about their child that is often new, complex, confusing, unpleasant, and scary. Conditions for effective communication are sometimes lacking at this stage of team development, and family members are often at an uncomfortable disadvantage. Much has been written about the essential elements of these complex and critical meetings and the legal, procedural, and communicative processes that should be in place (Bateman & Linden, 1998; Turnbull & Turnbull, 1990). The focus of this section is on fostering family membership on teams once decisions about eligibility, program, and placement have been made. Positive collaborative teaming experiences for a family and for staff members can have clear and positive effects on the tone and quality of these less frequent meetings that focus on special education services.

Attitudes that Welcome

Staff members on collaborative teams can foster family members' involvement in the teaming process through the attitudes they communicate and the teaming procedures they use (Losen & Losen, 1994; Turnbull & Turnbull, 2000). The following set of guidelines concerns the attitudes communicated by staff members to family members. Most staff team members are used to obtaining and utilizing family input on a student; this may not be clearly communicated to the parents. Often, parents do not have confidence about their value to the team. Parents have no equals on the team; they are the "outsiders" even if they are welcomed. The reason the team exists is because of their child. The work and problem solving in which the team engages is for the benefit of their child. Parents often feel guilty about this, and their guilt is intensified when their child has more extensive needs for support. In addition, school staff members, in boosting the value of family members' roles on teams, may unintentionally communicate that "involvement" is never enough or that "appro-

priate family involvement means ____"; team members may inadvertently communicate a one-size-fits-all approach, which no family really fits.

Teams can communicate supportive attitudes to family members in many ways:

- Be cognizant of, sensitive to, and respectful of the family's culture, values, and viewpoints.

- Communicate repeatedly and in various ways the importance of family input to the team; the family's knowledge, information, concerns, hopes, and opinions about their child are very valuable.

- Unless there is clear evidence to the contrary, take parents at their word; question for clarity, not for accuracy. Be sensitive to communicating doubt or superiority.

- There is no standard measurement for family involvement. Instead, the extent to which and ways in which a family is involved in teaming for their child is highly individualized and will vary over time as family demands change and as the child changes. For some families, especially during more stressful points in the family's life cycle, just getting the child dressed, fed, and to school on time is a major undertaking.

- Be vigilant about feeding into any parental guilt over a child's disability or learning or behavioral challenges. Blame, to which parents may be hypersensitive, can be communicated in subtle ways.

- Communicate that the team *shares* the responsibility for designing and implementing programs to support the student's learning and behavior.

Team Procedures that Encourage Family Members

The next set of guidelines concern the procedures that are used by teams. Although family members typically are not present at every team meeting and rarely are present for "on-the-fly" interchanges between staff members during the school day, their role as team members must not be forgotten. Family members are in the minority on the team. Their voices and perspectives may differ in many ways from those of other team members. These differences may be in dialect; language; level of income and education; attitude toward schools and education; knowledge about children, learning, disability, and special education; disciplinary practices; and confidence in themselves and trust in others. The ways that school staff members act toward family members in meetings and in their interactions outside of meetings can be instrumental in fostering the family's participation:

- Develop one or several reliable means for gathering input and keeping current with families. Exercise these channels; revise the communication means when family circumstances change or when necessary.

- When parents have the need for and interest in information, help them find ways to meet those needs. One of the most effective methods for meeting the informational needs of parents is to connect them with other parents who have experience with disability and special education. Most regions have a parent support or information service, which may sponsor parent groups or, at the very least, connect parents with other informed parents. Encourage parents to observe in the classroom and school; however, prepare them for what they will see, and be available to narrate and answer their questions. Examine any forms that will be used during a meeting (e.g., permission to test, IEP, transition plan) and review the procedural steps with the parents rather than just handing them a printed form or a legal notice of their rights. Personalized sources of information can be more helpful to families because they are focused to suit the family and are often "friendlier."

- Guarantee that family members will be able to contribute their input on every issue and every action plan. If family members are unable to attend meetings, seek their ideas beforehand, include them in the meeting process, and check team decisions with them before assuming team consensus.

- Use encouraging and other suitable methods to promote family input (e.g., inviting their input, allowing adequate time for them to process, reinforcing their input even if it is critical of the content being discussed).

Parents rarely bring legal council to team meetings. It is more common for parents to bring advocates or parent advisors with them. Public law encourages parents to invite trusted friends, advisors, or family members to attend team meetings with them to lend support and assist in their understanding and their articulation of concerns. The presence of these individuals, however, can be adversarial for professional staff. Lawyers rarely feel obligated to follow a team's procedure, as their dedication is to their client; therefore, the presence of lawyers may be not only psychologically, but also procedurally, disruptive (Losen & Losen, 1994). Legal council is more often sought by parents because of a dispute with program administrators than a dispute with specific team members; the controversy, however, often seeps into the team as well and may be impossible to ignore. Recognizing the rightful presence of these outsiders and acknowledging their right to interrupt, the team facilitator can appeal to the group for cooperation and request their help in avoiding confrontation:

> We should acknowledge, before we begin, that Mr. Lagiano is here to represent the Clarks as their attorney. He may be helpful to all of us in our proceedings, but since most of us are unaccustomed to working with lawyers present, we will need to be sure that our discomfort does not lead us to be overly cautious in what we say or how we say it. (Losen & Losen, 1994, p. 129)

The team facilitator needs to remind the team members that their focus must remain on the student. The agenda, processing steps (e.g., celebrate, examine team relationships), and team procedures should not be forgotten even though they may be difficult to carry out. Well-established teamwork routines can help overcome a difficult atmosphere and allow the important day-to-day decision making to get done. Although the team facilita-

tors will not want to alienate parents by limiting the guest's participation in the team meeting, facilitators should interrupt when a guest's comments are out of place, premature, or not suited to the team's current task. Facilitators can remind the guest and the other team members to follow the agenda and to focus on their purpose: meeting the student's educational needs.

TAKE TIME TO PROCESS GROUP SKILLS

Even the best collaborative teams run into communication blocks and get side-tracked by conflict. The best prevention for uncooperativeness and competition among team members is routine self-evaluation or *team processing.* It is easier to raise issues about interpersonal barriers and address them so they do not interfere with team outcomes when team and member self-evaluation is an accepted practice. This section describes three elements of team processing: 1) taking time to process, 2) assessing group functioning, and 3) observing the behavior of team members (Thousand & Villa, 1992).

Take Time to Process

Taking time to process means building time into the agenda to reflect on teaming skills. Teams often begin their meetings by celebrating their successes, an activity that contributes to team building. Teams also will often stop halfway through their agenda, and again at the end of the meeting, to process interpersonal dynamics and meeting progress. Processing often consists of posing questions such as the following:

- *How are we doing?*
- *Are we making progress?*
- *Do we need to adjust our agenda to reflect what now seems to be the priority?*
- *Do we have interpersonal problems that are blocking our progress?*
- *If we do, what can we do differently?*

Thousand and Villa (1992) are strong proponents of scheduling processing steps as part of every meeting agenda rather than evaluating the team only periodically. Their meeting worksheet, which appeared in Chapter 3 (see Figure 3.10), includes celebrations and team processing in the agenda listing. When teams learn to schedule and then pose processing questions, they briefly shift their attention to themselves during the meeting, thereby increasing the probability that interpersonal channels will operate more smoothly (Johnson & Johnson, 1997).

Assess Group Functioning

Regular self-assessment of team health is a good preventative measure for serious conflict; it can often help avoid the unpleasant need to confront members who have problem behaviors. Procedures teams use to process group functioning include effective ways to give feedback to team members (Thousand & Villa, 1992, p. 97). One member is designated to be the group observer; this person not only contributes to work on agenda items but also watches interactions among members. Group observers, in addition to other members, help the team self-examine in a number of ways:

- Team members self-evaluate against a checklist of teaming skills and then reflect as a group (Figure 6.6).

- Teams target one or several areas on which to focus in the next meeting.

- At the next meeting, the team observer reminds team members of the targeted areas, observes these areas, and then shares the observations with other members while giving feedback to each member.

- Team members comment on the observations.

- The observer shares incidents of positive teamwork and encourages others to contribute their observations.

- Team members discuss the observations and then identify or refine goals for improvement at individual and group levels.

Feedback can be better absorbed by team members if observers are positive and direct in their reports. Observers should establish eye contact with team members, present them with objective data and not judgmental statements, and be honest and avoid "false compliments" (Thousand & Villa, 1992, p. 97). Refer to Figure 6.4, which provides suggestions for giving constructive feedback, for more guidance.

Teams often report that rating themselves using checklists of positive teaming traits can be constructive:

Greg Martin, a member of the "Energizer Team" at a nearby middle school, reports that each member of this team regularly appraises their team, from high to low, on 25 questions concerning how they are operating together. In their first evaluation, one teacher combined the anonymous ratings, and the team reviewed them by celebrating their high scores and discussing their lower scores. They reached consensus on areas of need and created a plan for improvement. The Energizer Team discovered that they needed work in several areas: using their time better, improving communication with parents, and striving to integrate separate subject areas while coordinating major assignments and units. They scheduled time to tackle each area and later reevaluated themselves.

Instead of having team members rate themselves using an entire checklist, a shortened process in which members just indicate the *highest need items* and the *greatest strength items* for themselves and for the team, is often used. Alternately, open-ended checklists that require brief written reflection (Figure 6.7) on broader areas of teaming behavior can be used in place of lengthy behavior-specific checklists.

Teams may wish to process *without* the use of an inside (or outside) observer. For example, during processing time, using round robin turns, each team member shares the skills they used to assist the team. Second, team members *self-evaluate* using team skill

Directions: Circle the points to the left of each item only if all group members answer "yes" to the item. Total the number of points circled. The maximum score is 100 points.

POINTS

2	1.	We meet in a comfortable physical environment.
2	2.	We start our meetings on time.
2	3.	We arrange ourselves in a circle when we meet.
2	4.	The size of our group does not exceed 7 members.
2	5.	Our meetings are structured so that there is ample "air time" for all participants.
	6.	Needed members:
2		• Are invited (Note: members may change from week to week based upon the agenda items).
2		• Attend.
2		• Arrive on time.
2		• Stay until the end of the meeting.
2	7.	We have regularly scheduled meetings which are held at times and locations agreed upon in advance by the team.
2	8.	We do not stop the meeting to update tardy members. Updates occur at a break or following the meeting.
	9.	We have a communication system for:
2		• Absent members.
2		• "Need to know" people, not part of the core team.
	10.	We use a structured agenda format which prescribes that we:
2		• Identify agenda items for the next meeting at the prior meeting
2		• Set time limits for each agenda item.
2		• Rotate roles
2		• Have public minutes.
3		• Process group effectiveness regarding both task accomplishment and social skill performance.
2		• Review and modify the agenda, whenever necessary.
2	11.	We have publicly agreed to the group's overall goals.
2	12.	We have publicly shared our individual professional "agenda": that is, we each stated what we need from the group to be able to work toward the group goals.
2	13.	We coordinate our work to achieve our objectives (as represented by the agenda items).

(continued)

Figure 6.6. "Are we really a team?" quiz. (From Thousand, J.S. & Villa, R.A. [1992]. Collaborative teams: A powerful tool in school restructuring. In R.A. Villa, J.S. Thousand, W. Stainback, & S. Stainback [Eds.], *Restructuring for caring and effective education* [pp. 73–108]. Baltimore: Paul H. Brookes Publishing Co.; adapted by permission.)

Figure 6.6.   *(continued)*

POINTS

3

3

2

3

2

3

3

2

3

2

2

3

2

3

2

2

3

2

2

3

3

2

14.	We have established group social norms (e.g., no "put downs," all members participate) and confront one another on norm violations.
15.	We have a "no scapegoating" norm. When things go wrong, it is not one person's fault, but everyone's job to make a new plan.
16.	We explain the norms of the group to new members.
17.	We feel free to express our feelings (negative and positive).
18.	We call attention to discussions which are off-task or stray from the agenda topics.
19.	We openly discuss problems in social interaction.
20.	We set time aside to process interactions and feelings.
21.	We spend time developing a plan to improve interactions.
22.	We have arranged for training to increase our small group skills (e.g., giving and receiving criticism, perspective taking, creative problem solving, conflict resolution).
23.	We view situations and solutions from various perspectives.
24.	We discuss situations from the perspective of absent members.
25.	We generate and explore multiple solutions before selecting a particular solution.
26.	We consciously identify the decision-making process (e.g., majority vote, consensus, unanimous decision) we will use for making a particular decision.
27.	We distribute leadership functions by rotating roles (e.g., recorder, timekeeper, observer).
28.	We devote time at each meeting for positive comments.
29.	We structure other group rewards and "celebrations."
30.	We have identified ways for "creating" time for meetings.
31.	We summarize the discussion of each topic before moving on to the next agenda item.
32.	We distribute among ourselves the homework/action items.
33.	We generally accomplish the tasks on our agenda.
34.	We have fun at our meetings.
35.	We end on time.

_____ **Total possible points = 100**

Process elements	Positives	Issues and concerns
Informal behaviors: entering the room, seating arrangement, interaction patterns, signs of trust		
Structure of the team meeting: agenda, designated facilitator, sense of purpose, evidence of organization		
Communication: sharing of information, values, perspective-taking, listening, and speaking styles		
Participation by members: shared participation, verbal and nonverbal signs of involvement or withdrawal, invited and encouraged participation		
Problem-solving and decision making processes: clarity of the question, consideration of alternatives, use of consensus, assignments for action, sense of ownership for decision		
Conflict resolution: acknowledgment of differences, open discussion of positions, compromise		
Giving and receiving feedback: by and to individuals, discussion of how team is functioning		
Effectiveness of leadership during meeting: shared leadership, facilitator, timekeeper		
Needs for future team development: current state of development, types of training, experience, and consultation that would help this team achieve the highest stage of development		

Figure 6.7. Observing team process. (From Garner, H.O. [1997]. *Observing team process.* Unpublished document, Virginia Commonwealth University, Richmond; reprinted by permission.)

checklists and then discuss the ratings. Third, teams use a *"strength bombardment"* approach, which is oral or written in nature: Each member comments aloud or in writing on a card that circulates on a given team member's observed strength in teaming. Fourth, teams *view or listen to selections from tapes of the meeting* (video or audio) and react to positive examples of teaming skills.

Observe the Behavior of Team Members

Several observation methods can be useful to teams that need an objective check on specific interpersonal difficulties. When there is clear evidence of problems in listening, communicating, practicing shared values and ground rules, or reaching consensus, teams may select a group member or seek an outsider to observe their interactions. When definitive signs of difficulty have been noted and discussed by team members, it is good to have team members select one or several specific collaborative *skills* to observe that are closely linked to the signs of difficulty. When skills, and not problems, are the focus of observation, then teams are less likely to experience blame, accusations, hurt feelings, and anger.

Once the specific skills of concern have been identified, teams are advised to

- Have the team observer check on members' understanding of the targeted skills.

- Use an observation process that the team agrees on; this process could include a simple grid of team members' skills, as suggested by Thousand & Villa (1992) (Figure 6.8).

- Have the observer record the frequency of team members' skill performance.

- Record positive examples of members using the skill and other relevant teaming interactions that are not related to the target skills.

- Have observer summarize the observations to the team.

- Take time to discuss these observations and to explore ways to improve team skills.

- Use team processing in later meetings to check team progress.

When teams take a short amount of time on a regular basis to directly address the quality of their interactions, members can develop a sensitivity to their own interactions and assume more responsibility for maintaining effective listening and communication. Teams that learn to focus on themselves in this way can expect better results when they shift their focus to students.

RESOLVE CONFLICT CONSTRUCTIVELY

When disagreements or conflicts arise within a team, they must first be identified. Once identified, teams need to decide whether they want to address them. Some conflicts are best handled by being ignored, especially if they are minor or their open recognition is adequate to sensitize members (i.e., *"Gosh, we're really ready for spring break!"*). Other conflicts need to be addressed, either indirectly or "head on." The way that teams choose to handle conflicts depends in part on the particular team members (i.e., their skills and preferences for dealing with conflict) and in part on the particular conflict.

Identify the Conflict

Many interpersonal team conflicts are capable of immobilizing a team to the point that its focus remains centered on team problems and not on student needs. Although some unaddressed conflicts will diminish over time, others have a way of festering quietly until they threaten the health of the team. Several categories of team conflict exist (Snell & Janney, in press):

- *Disagreement about child goals and problem identification:* A lack of consensus on child goals sometimes leads to disagreement regarding what is or is not a problem. As one teacher expressed, "Everybody has their own tunnel vision." The goals or problems that one

Observer: _____ **Date:** _____

Team Meeting: _____

Target Skills	Carla (GE)	Kenna (SE)	Joy (SLP)	Brenda (Parent)	Mary (TA)
Waits for team member to finish speaking before talking					
Follows team ground rules					
Avoids arguing but expresses disagreement by seeking clarification or stating an alternate viewpoint					

✓ indicates an instance of the behavior/skill

– indicates a need for the behavior/skill

Anecdotal record of "good" examples of skill performance (note member)
Other relevant observations that are related to target skills

Figure 6.8. A grid for observing cooperative skills used by team members. (From Thousand, J.S., & Villa, R.A. [1992]. Collaborative teams: A powerful tool in school restructuring. In R.A. Villa, J.S. Thousand, W. Stainback, & S. Stainback [Eds.], *Restructuring for caring and effective education: An administrative guide to creating heterogenous schools* [pp. 73–108]. Baltimore: Paul H. Brookes Publishing Co.; adapted by permission.)

team member views as important for a particular student might differ from another team member's view of the same student.

- *Coordination problems:* Conflict sometimes arises while making or implementing plans that is the result of logistics (e.g., class schedules, available equipment, movement of students) and fragmentation of services and time.

- *Implementation and evaluation problems:* These are team problems that concern the quality with which team solutions are applied or evaluated; they are often related to the skill of the person implementing the solution, the lack of team consensus in developing a solution, inadequate solutions, or a failure to improve and refine solutions over time.

- *Communication problems:* These problems result from communication that is largely due to inadequate time to fully discuss supports; communication problems often lead to secondhand reporting. Another cause might be teammates' lack of familiarity with each other at the beginning of the school year and a lack of trust. A third reason involves the separate nature of many suggestions made to classroom staff by related services people and the unavailability of the related services personnel during team meetings.

Prior to taking any action at all, it is often a good idea for team members to reach consensus on the problem to ensure that, once defined and understood by team members, it doesn't require direct action. The team members involved in these discussions and the way in which the discussions are initiated often depends on one or both of the core teachers. When problems seem to be associated primarily with one team member, a subset of the team (often the core teachers) may discuss the concern separately from the rest of the team. This is usually the best way to address the problem; such discussions are often awkward when the targeted team member is present. Only once the problem has been identified, however, can it be addressed. Once teams reach agreement on the specific problem they

are experiencing, they are in a better position to decide whether to take action and what action to take.

Nonconfrontational Solutions

At times, a simple, indirect intervention will diminish the problem enough for the team to once again function normally. For example, team members might decide not to confront the person directly, but may instead model the desired behavior and shape its growth by giving praise for consistent improvements. If ground rules are being broken (e.g., being late, leaving early, not participating), teams might review these rules and discuss potential changes. In other cases, team members might choose to work around the problem instead of confronting it, a strategy illustrated by a special educator:

> *When Marcie was an itinerant special education teacher working at two different schools, communication was too infrequent, and it was difficult to build trust. For one team in particular, there was a role conflict between the classroom teacher and Marcie, which made it difficult to be a team. A preventive plan was formulated with other team members who recognized the conflict. To avoid conflict, these team members directed their focus to the target child, who had many needs, and tried to accomplish one small but important child-focused task during each weekly meeting. Whenever there was a hint of conflict with the classroom teacher, team members used a mediation strategy to refocus the group and prevent a reaction to that team member. This experience taught Marcie that one of the biggest enemies of team trust is time. The next year, the system Marcie worked in stopped assigning teachers to more than one school, and the problem disappeared.*

For problems such as being late or frequently absent, modeling is not effective because the person is not present to appreciate the examples! In these and other cases, it is critical to explore why the problem has oc-

curred ("Was the meeting time inconvenient for you?" "Should we take another look at the meeting time?"). The identified reasons will often suggest the best approach(es) for resolving the problem.

Confronting Team Problems

Team problems frequently stem from one person's failure to follow team procedures (e.g., always late, often absent, doesn't follow through on team solutions) or from the behavior of a team member during meetings (e.g., overly negative or critical, interruptive, dominating, frequently off-task). When these problems cannot be ignored, do not respond to modeling and shaping, and an exploration of their cause seems unhelpful, there are several types of confrontation that may be pursued: gentle or indirect confrontation and direct confrontation.

The *gentle and indirect confrontation* involves calling attention to the behavior in a meeting, but within one of two possible contexts:

1. *Use humor to call attention to the difficulty:* "How many strong personalities can we fit into one room?"

2. *Suggest an alternative to the problem behavior:*
   a) Turn the unfavorable behavior into a favorable behavior but without confrontation.
      Have the "joker" be responsible for starting each meeting with a funny story; ask the person who always wanders off task to give a signal when others get off task (Thousand & Villa, 1992, p. 94–95).
   b) Make the difficult member an "expert" on certain team needs.
      Clarice, who was viewed as "always critical," was the only faculty member who had taken a specialized reading course during the fall and learned new approaches for grouping and adaptation that the middle school team could use. When Chris, the special education teacher learned that Clarice had taken the course, she asked Clarice to come and offer some of her ideas during the next brain-storming session on Helena, whose reading abilities were a constant challenge to classroom teachers. At the

same time, Chris informed Clarice of the things that might work with Helena in an attempt to influence her success.
   c) As Thousand and Villa suggested, turn the individual's problem into an asset: ". . . assign an 'aggressor' the role of devil's advocate for certain issues . . . assign a 'dominator' the role of 'encourager' or 'equalizer'" (1992, pp. 94–95).

3. *Encourage self-assessment:* By using the procedures discussed under the processing section of this chapter (e.g., answering the question "How are we doing?"), teams can identify problem areas that two or more team members have recently found troublesome. Without identifying who the individuals are, the team facilitator leads the group in discussing several interrelated questions:
      "Why do we engage in _____(the problem behavior)?"
      "In what ways do we behave toward the offender that tend to encourage the problem behavior?"
      "In what ways can we behave toward the offender to help change the problem behavior?"
      "How might our team procedures be changed to help reduce the problem behavior?"

Direct Confrontation

When indirect confrontation strategies do not work, a more direct approach should be considered (Johnson & Johnson, 1997; Thousand & Villa, 1992). A head-on confrontation may mean that one team member decides or is "elected" to confront the dysfunctional member but only if the problem occurs regularly and cannot be ignored. Most of us are very uncomfortable with both being confronted and confronting another; therefore, this approach must be taken with care. Team members may want to plan who should undertake the task; one team member may have better confrontation skills than another. Sometimes it helps to have the "confrontor" be someone who knows the "receiver" well and can relate personally to him or her. Confrontation in private is often preferable to confrontation in

front of the entire team, especially if it is likely that the person will be unhappy, embarrassed, or angered by the feedback. The section on communication, presented previously in this chapter, gave some suggestions for giving and receiving constructive feedback. It may prove beneficial to reread the middle and right columns of this table that address the goals and suggested approaches for giving criticism and taking it from other team members prior to confronting the dysfunctional team member. These suggestions should be combined with the following techniques for using *I* messages.

When confronting a person, it is often best to describe the troublesome behavior to the individual in objective terms in addition to describing its effect on the team. *I* messages are an effective way to confront without attacking (DeBoer, 1995); *You* messages should be avoided; they often sound condescending, abrasive, and judgmental (e.g., *"It sounds as if you are angry . . ." "You need to____." "You did not understand my question"*). *I* messages have four parts and require some practice to use:

- The *first element* of an *I* message is a description of the behavior that is not acceptable or causes stress (e.g., "When someone interrupts, me I cannot think straight . . .").

- The *second element* should be a description of the effect of this behavior (e.g., "I get distracted by my anger, which makes it difficult for me to focus on the complexities of Rick's special needs").

- The *third element* in the *I* message addresses the effect that the behavior has on the confronting person's feelings (e.g., "I feel angry").

- The *fourth and final element* describes the preferred behavior and specifically states what is needed from the dysfunctional member instead of the problem behavior (e.g., "What I need is for you to wait until I finish what I am trying to say").

The following examples involve all four elements:

"When I am not involved in a decision about Daniel's school program, I feel devalued in my role as a professional, and I am hurt and wonder why my opinion was not consulted. I need to be consulted before changes are made to Daniel's program, and I need to have my viewpoints heard before a final decision is made." (This statement was made by a second-grade teacher to a speech-language therapist who, without team consensus, made major changes in a communication system that was previously developed by the team.)

"When I see students we share are primarily on a punishment system, I feel sad because I see the debilitating side effects. I need for us to mutually design a positive system that meets both our needs" (DeBoer, 1995, p. 106). (This statement was made by a special education teacher to a general education teacher regarding the class that they had co-taught the previous semester.)

Although *I* statements are less offensive than *you* statements, they are still very difficult to deliver and somewhat unnatural to construct. The giver should practice confronting the dysfunctional team member ahead of time; he or she may even write out the statement and check for the needed elements. Once an *I* statement has been used to confront a teammate, the giver should shift from the speaker role to the listener role. DeBoer suggested that active listening be conducted "with an attitude of empathy for the person's situation and an acceptance of them as an individual," which does not mean that the person confronting the team member must agree with the troublesome behavior (1995, p. 108). The confronting team member could ask the person what her or his thoughts and feelings are and what might be done. From problem-solving discussion, which may best take place at a second meeting when emotions are lower, should come mutually generated suggestions for reducing the problem during future team sessions. Sometimes, after

listening to the confronted team member's perspective, it may be necessary for the confronting team member to restate the original *I* message or rephrase the message in order to remind the person of his or her viewpoint and move toward a resolution.

Well-Managed Team Conflict

Some team conflict is to be expected; unfortunately, most conflict is poorly managed and actively avoided due to the fear and anxiety it provokes in most team members. In fact, some researchers suggest that controversy within teams is not bad and should even be encouraged *as long as it can be effectively managed* (Johnson & Johnson, 1997; Parker, 1994). Well-managed controversy within teams can stimulate interest, thinking, problem-solving, new ideas, and decision-making; however, there are many societal norms operating against conflict. Many people work hard to avoid conflict. Unlike the decisions that result from collaborative teams, "[g]roup decision making often goes wrong because alternatives are not considered carefully, minority opinions are silenced, and disagreement among members' controversy is suppressed" (Johnson & Johnson, 1997, p. 304). Johnson and Johnson (1995, 1997) maintain that decisions made by groups are often less than optimal when controversy is avoided and/or mismanaged.

When controversy is well-managed, it involves a process that stimulates inquiry and leads to synthesis of information and ideas. Johnson and Johnson (1997) described the series of steps involved in this process:

1. Draw conclusions from what you know.
2. Share your viewpoints with others.
3. Be challenged by opposing viewpoints.
4. Experience conflict and uncertainty.
5. Actively search for additional information to understand opposing ideas.
6. Reconceptualize by taking others' perspectives and integrating ideas.

The outcomes of constructive disagreement are many: increased interest, interpersonal attraction, peer support, enjoyment of topic and controversy, better decisions, and stronger team bonds (Johnson & Johnson, 1997).

For controversies to be productive, teams will benefit from the following guidelines (Johnson & Johnson, 1997, pp. 315–317):

1. Emphasize the team's shared value: *make the best possible decision cooperatively.*
2. Be on the lookout for opportunities to engage in controversy: Identify disagreement, and recognize contrasting viewpoints; seek out diversity in opinion, knowledge, perspective, and background.
3. Plan and present a case to support your view.
4. Argue convincingly for your view, but do so with an open mind.
5. Support others, and listen as they argue for their viewpoint.
6. Identify the areas of disagreement between your view and opposing views; then, challenge the ideas or viewpoints, not the proponents.
7. Listen to others' arguments with your view, but do not personalize them.
8. Repeat cycles of debate that enable differentiation of positions and, then, integration of ideas into a new, creative position.
9. Take the other members' perspectives to see the ideas from a range of viewpoints.
10. Observe the rules of rational argument, and avoid making decisions too early.
11. Combine the most promising ideas from all the viewpoints presented, discussed, and debated.

When coupled with the cardinal rules of collaborative teaming, this process is not unlike the divergent and convergent processes involved in problem solving. It is clear both that constructive controversy is not the same as team conflict and that it can thrive within strong collaborative teams.

References

Affleck, J.Q., Madge, S., Adams, A., & Lowen-braun, S. (1988). Integrated classroom versus resource model: Academic viability and effectiveness. *Exceptional Children, 54,* 339–348.

Almanza, H.P., & Mosley, W.J. (1980). Curriculum adaptations and modifications for culturally diverse handicapped children. *Exceptional Children, 46,* 608–614.

Bateman, B.D., & Linden, M.A. (1998). *Better IEPs: How to develop legally correct and educationally useful programs* (3rd ed.). Longmont, CO: Sopris West.

Bauwens, J., & Hourcade, J.J. (1991). Making co-teaching a mainstreaming strategy. *Preventing School Failure, 35*(4), 19–24.

Bauwens, J., & Hourcade, J. (1995). *Cooperative teaching: Rebuilding the school house for all students.* Austin, TX: PRO-ED.

Bauwens, J., Hourcade, J., & Friend, M. (1989). Cooperative teaching: A model for general and special education integration. *Remedial and Special Education 10*(2), 17–22.

Bear, G.G., & Proctor, W.A. (1990). Impact of a full-time integrated program on the achievement of nonhandicapped and mildly handicapped children. *Exceptionality, 1,* 227–238.

Bear, G.G., Cleaver, A., & Proctor, W.A. (1991). Self-perceptions of nonhandicapped children and children with learning disabilities in integrated classes. *The Journal of Special Education, 24,* 409–426.

Briggs, M.H. (1993). Team talk: Communication skills for early intervention teams. *Journal of Childhood Communication Disorders, 15*(1), 33–40.

Cook, L., & Friend, M. (1993). Interpersonal and procedural considerations of collaborative teams and problem-solving. In R. Beck (Ed.), *Project RIDE: Responding to individual differences in education* (p. 44). Longmont, CO: Sopris West.

Dawson, M.M. (1987). Beyond ability grouping: A review of the effectiveness of ability grouping and its alternatives. *School Psychology Review, 16,* 348–369.

DeBoer, A. (1995). *Working together: The art of consulting and communicating.* Longmont, CO: Sopris West.

DeBoer, A., & Fister, S. (1994). *Strategies and tools for collaborative teaching* (Participant's handbook). Longmont, CO: Sopris West.

DeBoer, A., & Fister, S. (1995–1996). *Working together: Tools for collaborative teaching.* Longmont, CO: Sopris West.

Deno, S., Foegen, A., Robinson, S., & Espin, C. (1996). Commentary: Facing the realities of inclusion for students with mild disabilities. *The Journal of Special Education, 30,* 345–357.

Deutsch, M. (1962). Cooperation and trust: Some theoretical notes. In M.R. Jones (Ed.), *Nebraska symposium on motivation* (pp. 275–320). Lincoln: University of Nebraska Press.

Dinnebeil, L.A., Hale, L.M., & Rule, S. [1996]. A qualitative analysis of parents' and service coordinators' descriptions of variables that influence collaborative relationships. *Topics in Early Childhood Special Education, 16,* 322–347.

Dinnebeil, L.A., & Rule, S. (1994). Variables that influence collaboration between parents and service coordinators. *Journal of Early Intervention, 18,* 349–361.

Doyle, M.B., York-Barr, J., & Kronberg, R.M. (1996). Creating Inclusive School Communities: Module 5. *Collaboration: Providing support in the classroom.*

Dunst, C.J., Johanson, C., Rounds, T., Trivette, C.M., & Hamby, D. (1992). Characteristics of parent-professional partnerships. In S.L. Christenson & J.C. Conoley (Eds.), *Home–school collaboration: Enhancing children's academic and social competence* (pp. 157–174). Silver Spring, MD: National Association of School Psychologists.

Ford, A., Messenheimer-Young, T., Toshner, J., Fitzgerald, M.A., Dyer, C., Glodoski, J., & Laveck, J. (1995, July). *A team planning packet for inclusive education.* Milwaukee: The Wisconsin School Inclusion Project.

Forest, M., & Lusthaus, E. (1989). Promoting educational equality for all students: Circles and maps. In S. Stainback, W. Stainback, & M. Forest (Eds.), *Educating all students in the mainstream of regular education* (pp. 43–57). Baltimore: Paul H. Brookes Publishing Co.

Friend, M., & Cook, L. (1990). Collaboration as a predictor for success in school reform. *Journal of Educational and Psychological Consultation, 1,* 69–86.

Friend, M., & Cook, L. (1992). *Interactions: Collaboration skills for school professionals.* New York: Longman.

Fullen, M.G., (1991). *The new meaning of educational change* (2nd ed.). New York: Teachers College Press.

Garner, H.G. (1997). *Observing team process.* Unpublished document, Virginia Commonwealth University, Richmond.

Garner, H.G., Uhl, M., & Cox, A.W. (1992a). *Interdisciplinary teamwork videotape.* Richmond: Virginia Institute for Developmental Disabilities, Virginia Commonwealth University.

Garner, H.G., Uhl, M., & Cox, A.W. (1992b). *Interdisciplinary teamwork: A guide for trainers and viewers.* Richmond: Virginia Institute for Developmental Disabilities, Virginia Commonwealth University.

Giangreco, M.F. (1993). Using creative problem-solving methods to include students with severe disabilities in general education classroom activities. *Journal of Educational and Psychological Consultation, 4,* 113–135.

Giangreco, M.F. (1996). *Vermont interdependent services team approach (VISTA): A guide to coordinating educational support services.* Baltimore: Paul H. Brookes Publishing Co.

Giangreco, M.F., Cloninger, C.J., Dennis, R.E., & Edelman, S.W. (1994). Problem-solving methods to facilitate inclusive education. In J.S. Thousand, R.A. Villa, & A.I. Nevin (Eds.), *Creativity and collaborative learning: A practical guide to empowering students and teachers* (pp. 321–346). Baltimore: Paul H. Brookes Publishing Co.

Giangreco, M.F., Cloninger, C.J., & Iverson, V.S. (1998). *Choosing options and accommodations for children (COACH): A guide to educational planning for students with disabilities* (2nd ed.). Baltimore: Paul H. Brookes Publishing Co.

Giangreco, M.F., Dennis, R., Cloninger, C.J., Edelman, S., & Schattman, R. (1993). "I've counted Jon": Transformational experiences of teachers educating children with disabilities. *Exceptional Children, 59,* 359–372.

Giangreco, M.F., Dennis, R., Edelman, S., & Cloninger, C. (1994). Dressing your IEPs for the general education climate: Analysis of IEP goals and objectives for students with multiple disabilities. *Remedial and Special Education, 15*(5), 288–296.

Giangreco, M.F., Edelman, S.W., & Dennis, R.E. (1991). Common professional practices that interfere with the integrated delivery of related services. *Remedial and Special Education, 12*(2), 16–24.

Giangreco, M.F., & Putnam, J.W. (1991). Supporting the education of students with severe disabilities in regular education environments. In L.H. Meyer, C.A. Peck, & L. Brown (Eds.), *Critical issues in the lives of people with severe disabilities* (pp. 245–270). Baltimore: Paul H. Brookes Publishing Co.

Hargreaves, A. (1994). *Changing teachers, changing times.* New York: Teachers College Press.

Haring, T.G., & Breen, C.G. (1993). A peer-mediated social network intervention to enhance the social integration of persons with moderate and severe disabilities. *Journal of Applied Behavior Analysis, 25,* 319–333.

Harry, B. (1992a). An ethnographic study of cross-cultural communication with Puerto Rican-American families in the special education system. *American Educational Research Journal, 29,* 471–494.

Harry, B. (1992b). *Cultural diversity, families, and the special education system: Communication and empowerment.* New York: Teachers College Press.

Hennen, L., Hirschy, M., Opatz, K., Perlman, E., & Read, K. (1996). *From vision to practice: Ideas for implementing inclusive education.* Minneapolis: Institute on Community Integration, University of Minnesota.

Idol, L. (1990). The scientific art of classroom consultation. *Journal of Educational and Psychological Consultation, 1,* 3–22.

Isaksen, S.G., & Parnes, S.J. (1992). Curriculum planning for creative thinking and problem solving. In S.J. Parnes (Ed.), *Source book for creative problem-solving* (pp. 422–440). Buffalo, NY: Creative Education Foundation Press.

Janney, R.E., & Snell, M.E. (2000a). *Teachers' guide to inclusive practices: Modifying schoolwork.* Baltimore: Paul H. Brookes Publishing Co.

Janney, R.E., & Snell, M.E. (2000b). *Teachers' guide to inclusive practices: Behavioral support.* Baltimore: Paul H. Brookes Publishing Co.

Janney, R.E., Snell, M.E., Beers, M.K., & Raynes, M. (1995). Integrating students with moderate and severe disabilities into general education classes. *Exceptional Children, 61,* 425–439.

Jenkins, J.R., Jewell, M., Leichester, N., O'Connor, R.E., Jenkins, L., & Troutner, N.M. (1994). Accommodations for individual differences without classroom ability groups: An experiment in school restructuring. *Exceptional Children, 60,* 344–358.

Johnson, D.W., & Johnson, F.W. (1997). *Joining together: Group theory and skills* (6th ed.). Englewood Cliffs, NJ: Prentice-Hall.

Johnson, D.W., & Johnson, R. (1995). *Creative controversy: Intellectual challenge in the classroom* (3rd ed.). Edina, MN: Interaction Book Company.

Johnson, D.W., & Johnson, R.T. (1987). *Learning together and alone: Cooperation, competition, and individualization* (2nd ed.). Englewood Cliffs, NJ: Prentice-Hall.

Juvonen, J., & Bear, G. (1992). Social adjustment of children with and without learning disabilities in integrated classrooms. *Journal of Educational Psychology, 84,* 322–330.

Karge, B.D., McClure. M., & Patton, P.L. (1995). The success of collaboration in resource pro-

grams for students with disabilities in grades 6 through 8. *Remedial and Special Education, 16,* 79–89.

Katzenbach, J., & Smith, D. (1993). *The wisdom of teams.* Cambridge, MA: Harvard Business School Press.

Kincaid, D. (1996). Person-centered planning. In L.K. Koegel, R.L. Koegel, & G. Dunlap (Eds.), *Positive behavioral support* (pp. 439–465). Baltimore: Paul H. Brookes Publishing Co.

Kronberg, R., Jackson, L., Sheets, G., & Rogers-Connolly, T. (1995). A toolbox for supporting integrated education. *Teaching Exceptional Children, 27*(4), 54–58.

Little, J.W. (1990). The persistence of privacy: Autonomy and initiative in teachers' professional relations. *Teachers College Record, 91,* 509–536.

Losen, S.M., & Losen, J.G. (1994). Teamwork and the involvement of parents in special education programming, In H.G. Garner & F.P. Orelove (Eds.), *Teamwork in human services: Models and application across the life span* (pp. 117–141). Newton, MA: Butterworth-Heinemann.

Lundy, J. (1994). *Teams: Together each achieves more success.* Chicago: Dartnell.

Madge, S., Affleck, J., & Lowenbraun, S. (1990). Social effects of integrated classrooms and resource room/regular class placements on elementary students with learning disabilities. *Journal of Learning Disabilities, 23,* 439–445.

Mardinos, M. (1989). Conception of childhood disability among Mexican-American parents. *Medical Anthropology, 12,* 55–68.

McLaughlin, M.J., & Warren, S.H. (1992). *Issues and options in restructuring schools and special education programs.* College Park: University of Maryland and Westat, Inc.

National Association of State Boards of Education (NASBE) (October, 1992). *Winners all: A call for inclusive schools.* Alexandria, VA: NASBE.

National Center for Children and Youth with Disabilities (NICHCY) (July, 1995). Planning for inclusion. *NICHCY News Digest, 5*(1), 1–31.

Nelson, J. (1987). *Positive discipline.* New York: Ballantine Books.

Nowacek, J.E. (1992). Professionals talk about teaching together: Interviews with five collaborating teachers. *Intervention in School and Clinic, 27,* 262–276.

Parker, G. (1994). *Cross-functional teams.* San Francisco: Jossey-Bass.

Parnes, S.J. (1992). Creative problem-solving and visionizing. In S.J. Parnes (Ed.), *Source book for creative problem-solving* (pp. 133–154). Buffalo, NY: Creative Education Foundation Press.

Perske, R. (1988). *Circles of friends.* Nashville, TN: Abingdon Press.

Porter, G.L. (1994). *Teachers helping teachers: Problem-solving teams that work.* North York, Ontario, Canada: The Roeher Institute.

Porter, G.L., Wilson, M., Kelly, B., & den Otter, J. (1991). Problem-solving teams: A thirty-minute peer-helping model. In G.L. Porter & D. Richler (Eds.), *Changing Canadian schools: Perspectives on disability and inclusion* (pp. 219–238). North York, Ontario, Canada: The Roeher Institute.

Pugach, M.C., & Johnson, I.L. (1988). Rethinking the relationship between consultation and collaborative problem solving. *Focus on Exceptional Children, 21*(4), 1–8.

Pugach, M.C., & Johnson, I.L. (1990). Fostering the continued democratization of consultation through action research. *Teacher Education and Special Education, 13,* 240–245.

Pugach, M.C., & Johnson, L.J. (1995). Unlocking expertise among classroom teachers through structured dialogue: Extending research on peer collaboration. *Exceptional Children, 62,* 101–110.

Pugach, M.C., & Wesson, C.L. (1995). Teachers' and students' views of team teaching and general education and learning-disabled students in two fifth-grade classes. *The Elementary School Journal, 95,* 279–295.

Rainforth, B., & York-Barr, J. (1997). *Collaborative teams for students with severe disabilities: Integrating therapy and educational services* (2nd ed.). Baltimore: Paul H. Brookes Publishing Co.

Roach, V. (1995, May). *Winning ways: Creating inclusive schools, classroom, and communities.* Alexandria, VA: National Association of State Boards of Education.

Salisbury, C.L., & Dunst, C.J. (1997). Home, school, and community partnerships: Building inclusive teams. In B. Rainforth & J. York-Barr (Eds.), *Collaborative teams for students with severe disabilities: Integrating therapy and educational services* (2nd ed., pp. 57–87). Baltimore: Paul H. Brookes Publishing Co.

Salisbury, C.L., Evans, I.M., & Palombaro, M.M. (1997). Collaborative problem-solving to promote the inclusion of young children with significant disabilities in primary grades. *Exceptional Children, 63,* 195–209.

Salisbury, C.L., & Palombaro, M.M. (Eds.). (1993). *No problem: Working things out our way.* Pittsburgh, PA: Allegheny Singer Research Institute, Child and Family Studies Program.

Senge, P., Roberts, C., Ross, R., Smith, B., & Kleiner, A. (1994). *Learning to work together: The fifth discipline fieldbook.* New York: Doubleday.

Sileo, T.W., Sileo, A.P., & Prater, M.A. (1996). Parent and professional partnerships in special education: Multicultural considerations. *Intervention in School and Clinic, 31,* 145–153.

Snell, M.E., & Janney, R.J. (in press). Teachers' problem solving about young children with moderate and severe disabilities in elementary classrooms. *Exceptional Children.*

Snell, M.E., Lowman, D.K., & Canady, R.L. (1997). Parallel block scheduling: Accommodating students' diverse needs in elementary schools. *Journal of Early Intervention, 20,* 266–278.

Snell, M.E., Raynes, M., Byrd, J.O., Colley, K.M., Gilley, C., Pitonyak, C., Stallings, M.A., VanDyke, R., William, P.S., & Willis, C.J. (1995). Changing roles in inclusive schools: Staff perspectives at Gilbert Linkous Elementary. *Kappa Delta Pi Record, 31,* 104–109.

Snell, M.E., & Janney, R.E. (2000). *Teachers' guides to inclusive practices: Social relationships and peer support.* Baltimore: Paul H. Brookes Publishing Co.

Soodak, L.C. (in press). Parents and inclusive schooling: Advocating for and participating in the reform of special education. In S.J. Vitello & D. Mithaug (Eds.), *Inclusive schooling: national and international perspectives.* Mahwah, NJ: Lawrence Erlbaum Associates.

Stainback, S., Stainback, W., & Slavin, R. (1989). Classroom organization for diversity among students. In S. Stainback, W. Stainback, & M. Forest (Eds.), *Educating all students in the mainstream of regular education* (pp. 131–142). Baltimore: Paul H. Brookes Publishing Co.

Stainback, W., Stainback, S., & Stefanich, G. (1996). Learning together in inclusive classrooms: What about the curriculum? *Teaching Exceptional Children, 28*(3), 14–19.

Talbert, J.E. (1993). Constructing a schoolwide professional community: The negotiated order of a performing arts school. In J.W. Little & M.W. McLaughlin (Eds.), *Teachers' work: Individuals, colleagues, and contexts* (pp. 164–184). New York: Teachers College Press.

Thomas, C.C., Correa, V.I., & Morsink, C.V. (1995). *Interactive teaming: Consultation and collaboration in special education.* Englewood Cliffs, NJ: Prentice-Hall

Thousand, J.S., & Villa, R.A. (1991). Accommodating for greater student variance. In M. Ainscow (Ed.), *Effective schools for all* (pp. 161–180). Baltimore: Paul H. Brookes Publishing Co.

Thousand, J.S., & Villa, R.A. (1992). Collaborative teams: A powerful tool in school restructuring. In R.A. Villa, J.S. Thousand, W. Stainback, & S. Stainback (Eds.), *Restructuring for caring and effective education* (pp. 73–108). Baltimore: Paul H. Brookes Publishing Co.

Townsend, B.L. (1998). Social friendships and networks among African American children and youth. In L.H. Meyer, H.-S. Park, M. Grenot-Scheyer, I.S. Schwartz, & B. Harry (1998). *Making friends: The influences of culture and development* (pp. 225–241). Baltimore: Paul H. Brookes Publishing Co.

Townsend, B.L., Lee, R.S., Thomas, D.D., & Witty, J.P. (1996). Diversity and school restructuring: Creating partnerships in a world of difference. *Teacher Education and Special Education, 19,* 102–118.

Trent, S. (1998). False starts and other dilemmas of a secondary general education collaborative teacher: A case study. *Journal of Learning Disabilities, 31,* 503–513.

Trent, S.C. (1997). Teaching urban African American students with learning disabilities in inclusive classrooms: Using study groups to facilitate change. *Learning Disabilities Research and Practice, 12*(2), 132–142.

Turnbull, A.P., & Turnbull, H.R. (2000). Fostering family-professional partnerships. In M.E. Snell & F. Brown (Eds.), *Instruction of students with severe disabilities* (5th ed., pp. 31–66). Upper Saddle River, NJ: Merrill/Prentice Hall.

Turnbull, A.P., & Turnbull, H.R.(1990). *Families, professionals, and exceptionalities: A special partnership* (2nd ed.). Columbus, OH: Merrill.

Villa, R.A., & Thousand, J.S. (1988). Enhancing success in heterogeneous classrooms and schools. *Teacher Education and Special Education, 11,* 144–154.

Walther-Thomas, C.S. (1997). Co-teaching experiences: The benefits and problems that teachers and principals report over time. *Journal of Learning Disabilities, 30,* 395–407.

Walther-Thomas, C., Bryant, M., & Land, S. (1996). Planning for effective co-teaching: The key to successful inclusion. *Remedial and Special Education, 17,* 255–265.

Welch, M., Richards, G., Okada, T., Richards, J., & Prescott, S. (1995). A consultation and paraprofessional pull-in system of service delivery. *Remedial and Special Education, 16,* 16–28.

West, J.F. (1990). Educational collaboration in the restructuring of schools. *Journal of Educational and Psychological Consultation, 1*(1), 23–40.

West, J.F., & Cannon, G.S. (1988). Essential collaborative consultation competencies for regular and special educators. *Journal of Learning Disabilities, 21,* 56–63.

West, J.F., & Idol, L. (1990). Collaborative consultation and the education of mildly handicapped and at-risk students. *Remedial and Special Education, 11*(1), 22–31.

Williams, B.F. (1992). Changing demographics: Challenges for educators. *Intervention in School and Clinic, 3,* 157–163.

York, J., Vandercook, T., MacDonald, C., Heise-Neff, C., & Caughey, E. (1992). Feedback about integrating middle school students with severe disabilities in general education classes. *Exceptional Children, 58,* 244–258.

York-Barr, J. (Ed.). (1996). *Creating inclusive school communities.* Baltimore: Paul H. Brookes Publishing Co.

Zigmond, N. (1995). Inclusion in Pennsylvania: Educational experiences of students with learning disabilities in one elementary school. *The Journal of Special Education, 29,* 124–132.

Zigmond, N., & Baker, J. (1990). Mainstreaming experiences for learning disabled students (Project MELD): Preliminary report. *Exceptional Children, 57,* 176–185.

Appendix A

Blank Forms

A Building Administrator's Checklist for Collaborative Teaming

Phase			
P	**I**	**M**	**Actions that may be taken**
X			• Plan times for open dialogue at the district level and the school level about inclusive education and its benefits and challenges.
X	X		• Arrange for staff to view and learn more about inclusive school models (e.g., visits, videos, panels from schools). Participate in these workshop sessions with staff.
X	X	X	• Attend workshops on inclusion and related topics as collaborative teams; process in-service content as teams
X	X		• Recognize that staff have varying levels of comfort, understanding, and values about inclusion; provide time for staff to learn and experience the new philosophy and gain comfort with the changes inclusion brings.
X	X		• With teachers, plan for a schoolwide program on ability awareness or "climate for learning" to emphasize themes of appreciation and understanding of diversity.
X	X		• Be alert to staff morale and use team-building activities during the school year to promote collegiality.
X			• Engage staff in creating a common definition of their school community—one that addresses what it is (or is becoming) and why. Expand this definition into a mission statement to guide school improvement.
X	X	X	• Involve all stakeholders in reaching mutual decisions
X	X	X	• Identify school and grade level inclusion goals, and support taking small steps towards those goals.
X	X	X	• Make use of "round robin" brainstorming at meetings to hear all voices.
X	X	X	• Recognize that listening and being empathic may be more useful than solving a problem.
	X	X	• Recognize and celebrate successes.
	X	X	• Be alert and responsive to staff needs as they change over time.
	X	X	• Make consultative services available to general educators and collaborative teams.
	X	X	• Know that support takes different forms and functions for different classroom teachers; develop a school/district menu of support options.
	X	X	• Encourage staff/teams to share their ideas and resources with others.
	X	X	• Orient new staff to school philosophy and progress; link them with strong teams.
	X	X	• Find ways to record, share, and publicize student success stories.

P = Preparation: As schools are preparing for inclusion
I = Implementation: As teams are being planned and implemented
M = Maintenance: Once teams are in use

(Sources: Hennen, Opatz, Perlman, & Read [n.d.]; NICHCY, 1995; and Roach, 1995.)

Collaborative Teaming, Snell & Janney, © 2000 Paul H. Brookes Publishing Co.

Ideas for Scheduling and Creating Team Meeting Time

Create Time

- Dismiss school early periodically.
- Meet during independent work time, rest (in early grades), recess (while TAs or parents supervise class), or planning periods.
- Involve peers periodically in team meetings, and hold meetings as a class activity.
- Identify and preserve a regularly scheduled time, convenient to all team members, to plan, problem-solve, and discuss topics of concern.
- Ask special education teachers to join grade level team meetings to collaborate on issues of instruction and curriculum for students with support needs.
- Assign teaching assistants to specific grade levels, and have them use their flex time to attend grade level team meetings.
- Use faculty meetings on alternate weeks for team meetings.
- Use part or all of some faculty meetings for sharing or for problem-solving; have the principal facilitate.
- Schedule meeting time on a school-wide basis so common prep time can be scheduled for all members of grade-level teams.
- Plan, schedule, and use Collaboration Days during the school year.
- Create early release days (e.g., create five/year by increasing each school day by 5 minutes; create 1 day weekly by adding 15 minutes to daily students' schedules 4 days each week.
- For one day each week, schedule a common lunch period; ideally this lunch period should be scheduled before or after a common prep period.
- Combine classes for a period to free up a teacher for teaming.
- Plan special events (by grade level or for the entire school) on a monthly basis that are operated by nonschool staff; this frees up staff members for team meetings.

Coordinate Schedules

- Have principals and teachers design a school teaming schedule.
- Designate and coordinate planning times for grade/department planning meetings.
- Re-structure school planning teams (grade level and department) so special education teachers are members.
- Establish common lunch or recess schedules by grades.
- Use parallel block scheduling (Snell, Lowman, & Canady, 1997) to create meeting times.
- Have principals arrange master schedule so a given grade level has back-to-back "specials" twice a week to assist in planning.
- Have PTA/PTO advocate with school board for some compensated team planning time.
- Hire a floating, trained, substitute teacher to rotate among classes and free up 30–45 minute blocks of the classroom teacher's time.
- Use school funds to cover compensatory time.
- Advocate annually with central office when the school calendar is planned to have professional time reserved for teaming.

(Sources: DeBoer & Fister, 1995–1996; Hennen, Hirschy, Opatz, Perlman, & Read, n.d.; Rainforth & York-Barr, 1997.)

Collaborative Teaming, Snell & Janney, © 2000 Paul H. Brookes Publishing Co.

Collaborative Team Meeting Worksheet

Members present:	Date: _____	Others who need to know:
_____	Members absent:	_____
_____	_____	_____
_____	_____	_____
_____	_____	_____
_____	_____	_____

Roles:	This meeting	Next meeting
Timekeeper	_____	_____
Recorder	_____	_____
Facilitator	_____	_____
Jargon Buster	_____	_____
Processor or Observer	_____	_____
Other: _____	_____	_____

Agenda

Items		Time Limit
1.	Celebrations _____	
2.	_____	
3.	_____	
4.	_____	
5.	How are we doing? _____	
6.	_____	
7.	_____	
8.	_____	
9.	How did we do? _____	

Minutes of Outcomes

Action Items	Person(s) Responsible?	By when?
1. How we'll tell others who need to know: _____		
2. _____		
3. _____		
4. _____		
5. _____		

Agenda Building For Next Meeting

Date: _____

Time: _____

Location: _____

Expected agenda items:

1. _____   3. _____

2. _____   4. _____

(From Thousand, J.S., & Villa, R.A. [1992]. Collaborative teams: A powerful tool in school restructuring. In R.A. Villa, J.S. Thousand, W. Stainback, & S. Stainback [Eds.], *Restructuring for caring and effective education: An administrative guide to creating heterogenous schools* [pp. 73–108]. Baltimore: Paul H. Brookes Publishing Co.; adapted by permission.)

Collaborative Teaming, Snell & Janney, © 2000 Paul H. Brookes Publishing Co.

SAM Problem-Solving Form

Objective-finding and Problem-finding: _____

In what ways might we address the educational needs of _____ in _____ ?
                                                    (student's name)   (class/activity)

Fact-finding		Idea-finding	
Facts about student's needs 1	Facts about class/activity 2	Direct Ideas 3	Indirect Ideas 4

(continued)

(From Giangreco, M.F., Cloninger, C.J., Dennis, R.E., & Edelman, S.W. [1994]. Problem-solving methods to facilitate inclusive education. In J.S. Thousand, R.A. Villa, & A.I. Nevin [Eds.], *Creativity and collaborative learning: A practical guide to empowering students and teachers* (pp. 321–346). Baltimore: Paul H. Brookes Publishing Co.; adapted with permission.)

Collaborative Teaming, Snell & Janney, © 2000 Paul H. Brookes Publishing Co.

(continued)

Solution-finding Potential solutions	Criteria				
	Addresses student need	Neutral or positive for students without disabilities	Likely to support valued life outcomes	Perceived as usable by users (e.g., teacher, student, parent)	Other:
1.					
2.					
3.					
4.					
5.					
6.					
7.					
8.					
9.					
10.					
11.					
12.					

Acceptance-Finding: What needs to be done? Who is going to do it? When is it going to be done? How can the ideas be improved? Where will it be done?

Issue	Action	By whom?	When?

Unit Plan

Unit Theme: _____   **Teachers:** _____

Dates and Times: _____

Unit Goals: "Big Ideas" (Concepts, principles, and issues)	**Minimal Competencies:** (Essential facts, skills, and processes)
Extended/Advanced Objectives	**Adapted Objectives**

Tasks/Activities

_____ Lecture _____

_____ Reading _____

_____ Discussion _____

_____ Library research _____

_____ Writing _____

_____ Building/creating _____

_____ Solving _____

_____

Major Unit Projects (Note adaptations)	**Supplementary Activities**
Evaluation Measures	**Adapted Evaluation Measures**
Materials Needed	**Adapted Materials Needed**

Collaborative Teaming, Snell & Janney, © 2000 Paul H. Brookes Publishing Co.

Checking Out My Communication Behavior

Directions: Complete all the questions by yourself. Review your answers in a round-robin fashion by having each member summarize his/her current communication performance. Discuss any implications for individual and team improvement.

1. If I were to explain something to teammates and they sat quietly with blank faces, I would
    _____ try to explain clearly and then move on
    _____ encourage members to ask questions until I knew everyone understood

2. If our facilitator explained something to the team that I did not understand, I would
    _____ keep silent and find out from someone else later on
    _____ ask the facilitator to repeat the explanation or to answer my questions

3. How often do I let other members know when I like or approve of something they say or do?
    Never 1 - 2 - 3 - 4 - 5 - 6 - 7 - 8 - 9 - 10 Always

4. How often do I let other teammates know when I am irritated or impatient, embarrassed by, or opposed to something they have said or done?
    Never 1 - 2 - 3 - 4 - 5 - 6 - 7 - 8 - 9 - 10 Always

5. How often do I check out teammates' feelings and not just assume that I know what they are?
    Never 1 - 2 - 3 - 4 - 5 - 6 - 7 - 8 - 9 - 10 Always

6. How often do I encourage others to let me know how they feel about what I say?
    Never 1 - 2 - 3 - 4 - 5 - 6 - 7 - 8 - 9 - 10 Always

7. How often do I check to be sure I understand what others are saying before I think judgmentally (e.g., "I don't agree" "She's right!")?
    Never 1 - 2 - 3 - 4 - 5 - 6 - 7 - 8 - 9 - 10 Always

8. How often do I check to be sure I understand what others are saying before I express my judgments *nonverbally* (e.g., head shake, frowning) or *out loud* (e.g., "I don't agree" "She's right!")?
    Never 1 - 2 - 3 - 4 - 5 - 6 - 7 - 8 - 9 - 10 Always

9. How often do I paraphrase or restate what other have said before I respond?
    Never 1 - 2 - 3 - 4 - 5 - 6 - 7 - 8 - 9 - 10 Always

10. How often do I keep my feelings, reactions, thoughts, and ideas to myself during meetings?
    Never 1 - 2 - 3 - 4 - 5 - 6 - 7 - 8 - 9 - 10 Always

11. How often do I make sure that all information I have regarding the topic under discussion is known to the rest of the group?
    Never 1 - 2 - 3 - 4 - 5 - 6 - 7 - 8 - 9 - 10 Always

Question content: Questions address the following aspects of communication: 1 and 2—One-way and two-way communication; 3 and 4—Your willingness to give feedback to others on how you react to their messages; 5 and 6—Your willingness to ask for feedback on your messages; 7–9—Your receiving skills; 10 and 11—Your willingness to contribute (send) relevant messages about the team's work.

(From David W. Johnson & Frank P. Johnson, JOINING TOGETHER: GROUP THEORY AND GROUP SKILLS 6/E © 1997 by Allyn & Bacon. Adapted by permission.)

Collaborative Teaming, Snell & Janney, © 2000 Paul H. Brookes Publishing Co.

"Are we really a team?" Quiz

Directions: Circle the points to the left of each item only if all group members answer "yes" to the item. Total the number of points circled. The maximum score is 100 points.

POINTS

2	1.	We meet in a comfortable physical environment.
2	2.	We start our meetings on time.
2	3.	We arrange ourselves in a circle when we meet.
2	4.	The size of our group does not exceed 7 members.
2	5.	Our meetings are structured so that there is ample "air time" for all participants.
	6.	Needed members:
2		• Are invited (Note: members may change from week to week based upon the agenda items).
2		• Attend.
2		• Arrive on time.
2		• Stay until the end of the meeting.
2	7.	We have regularly scheduled meetings which are held at times and locations agreed upon in advance by the team.
2	8.	We do not stop the meeting to update tardy members. Updates occur at a break or following the meeting.
	9.	We have a communication system for:
2		• Absent members.
2		• "Need to know" people, not part of the core team.
	10.	We use a structured agenda format which prescribes that we:
2		• Identify agenda items for the next meeting at the prior meeting
2		• Set time limits for each agenda item.
2		• Rotate roles
2		• Have public minutes.
3		• Process group effectiveness regarding both task accomplishment and social skill performance.
2		• Review and modify the agenda, whenever necessary.
2	11.	We have publicly agreed to the group's overall goals.
2	12.	We have publicly shared our individual professional "agenda": that is, we each stated what we need from the group to be able to work toward the group goals.
2	13.	We coordinate our work to achieve our objectives (as represented by the agenda items).

(continued)

(From Thousand, J.S., & Villa, R.A. [1992]. Collaborative teams: A powerful tool in school restructuring. In R.A. Villa, J.S. Thousand, W. Stainback, & S. Stainback [Eds.], *Restructuring for caring and effective education: An administrative guide to creating heterogenous schools* [pp. 73–108]. Baltimore: Paul H. Brookes Publishing Co.; adapted by permission.)

(continued)

POINTS

3	14.	We have established group social norms (e.g., no "put downs," all members participate) and confront one another on norm violations.
3	15.	We have a "no scapegoating" norm. When things go wrong, it is not one person's fault, but everyone's job to make a new plan.
2	16.	We explain the norms of the group to new members.
3	17.	We feel free to express our feelings (negative and positive).
2	18.	We call attention to discussions which are off-task or stray from the agenda topics.
3	19.	We openly discuss problems in social interaction.
3	20.	We set time aside to process interactions and feelings.
2	21.	We spend time developing a plan to improve interactions.
3	22.	We have arranged for training to increase our small group skills (e.g., giving and receiving criticism, perspective taking, creative problem solving, conflict resolution).
2	23.	We view situations and solutions from various perspectives.
2	24.	We discuss situations from the perspective of absent members.
3	25.	We generate and explore multiple solutions before selecting a particular solution.
2	26.	We consciously identify the decision-making process (e.g., majority vote, consensus, unanimous decision) we will use for making a particular decision.
3	27.	We distribute leadership functions by rotating roles (e.g., recorder, timekeeper, observer).
2	28.	We devote time at each meeting for positive comments.
2	29.	We structure other group rewards and "celebrations."
3	30.	We have identified ways for "creating" time for meetings.
2	31.	We summarize the discussion of each topic before moving on to the next agenda item.
2	32.	We distribute among ourselves the homework/action items.
3	33.	We generally accomplish the tasks on our agenda.
3	34.	We have fun at our meetings.
2	35.	We end on time.

_____ **Total possible points = 100**

Collaborative Teaming, Snell & Janney, © 2000 Paul H. Brookes Publishing Co.

Observing Team Process

Process elements	Positives	Issues and concerns
Informal behaviors: entering the room, seating arrangement, interaction patterns, signs of trust		
Structure of the team meeting: agenda, designated facilitator, sense of purpose, evidence of organization		
Communication: sharing of information, values, perspective-taking, listening, and speaking styles		
Participation by members: shared participation, verbal and nonverbal signs of involvement or withdrawal, invited and encouraged participation		
Problem-solving and decision making processes: clarity of the question, consideration of alternatives, use of consensus, assignments for action, sense of ownership for decision		
Conflict resolution: acknowledgment of differences, open discussion of positions, compromise		
Giving and receiving feedback: by and to individuals, discussion of how team is functioning		
Effectiveness of leadership during meeting: shared leadership, facilitator, timekeeper		
Needs for future team development: current state of development, types of training, experience, and consultation that would help this team achieve the highest stage of development		

(From Garner, H.G. [1997]. *Observing team process.* Unpublished document, Virginia Commonwealth University, Richmond; reprinted by permission.)

Collaborative Teaming, Snell & Janney, © 2000 Paul H. Brookes Publishing Co.

Appendix B

Resources on
Collaborative Teaming

COLLABORATIVE CONSULTATION

Idol, L. (1990). The scientific art of classroom consultation. *Journal of Educational and Psychological Consultation, 1,* 3–22.

West, J.F., & Idol, L. (1990). Collaborative consultation and the education of mildly handicapped and at-risk students. *Remedial and Special Education, 11*(1), 22–31.

COLLABORATIVE TEACHING

Bauwens, J., & Hourcade, J.J. (1995). *Cooperative teaching: Rebuilding the school house for all students.* Austin, TX: PRO-ED.

DeBoer, A., & Fister, S. (1994). *Strategies and tools for collaborative teaching (Participant's handbook).* Longmont, CO: Sopris West.

DeBoer, A., & Fister, S. (1995–1996). *Working together: Tools for collaborative teaching.* Longmont, CO: Sopris West.

Walther-Thomas, C. (1997). Co-teaching: Lasting benefits and persistent problems teams report. *Journal of Learning Disabilities, 30,* 395–407.

Walther-Thomas, C., Bryant, M., & Land, S. (1996). Planning for effective co-teaching: The key to successful inclusion. *Remedial and Special Education, 17,* 255–Cover 3.

COLLABORATIVE TEAMING: GENERAL RESOURCES

Doyle, M.B., York-Barr, J., & Kronberg, R.M. (1996). *Creating inclusive school communities: Module 5. Collaboration: Providing support in the classroom.* Baltimore: Paul H. Brookes Publishing Co.

Ford, A., Messenheimer-Young, T., Toshner, J., Fitzgerald, M.A., Dyer, C., Glodoski, J., & Laveck, J. (1995, July). *A team planning packet for inclusive education.* Milwaukee, WI: The Wisconsin School Inclusion Project.

Friend, M., & Cook, L. (1992). *Interactions: Collaboration skills for school professionals.* New York: Longman.

Katzenbach, J., & Smith, D. (1993). *The wisdom of teams.* Cambridge, MA: Harvard Business School Press.

Lundy, J. (1994). *Teams: Together each achieves more success.* Chicago: Dartnell.

Mardinos, M. (1989). Conception of childhood disability among Mexican-American parents. *Medical Anthropology, 12,* 55–68.

Parker, G. (1994). *Cross-functional teams.* San Francisco: Jossey-Bass.

Rainforth, B., & York-Barr, J. (1997). *Collaborative teams for students with severe disabilities: Integrating therapy and educational services* (2nd ed.). Baltimore: Paul H. Brookes Publishing Co.

Salisbury, C.L., & Dunst, C.J. (1997). Home, school, and community partnerships: Building inclusive teams. In B. Rainforth & J. York-Barr (Eds.), *Collaborative teams for students with severe disabilities: Integrating therapy and educational services* (2nd ed., pp. 57–87). Baltimore: Paul H. Brookes Publishing Co.

Senge, P., Roberts, C., Ross, R., Smith, B., & Kleiner, A. (1994). *Learning to work together: The fifth discipline fieldbook.* New York: Doubleday.

Thomas, C.C., Correa, V.I., & Morsink, C.V. (1995). *Interactive teaming: Consultation and collaboration in special education.* Englewood Cliffs, NJ: Prentice-Hall, Inc.

Thousand, J.S., & Villa, R.A. (1992). Collaborative teaming: A powerful tool in school restructuring. In R.A. Villa, J.S. Thousand, W. Stainback, & S. Stainback (Eds.), *Restructuring for caring and effective education* (pp. 73–106). Baltimore: Paul H. Brookes Publishing Co.

COMMUNICATION AND TEAM DYNAMICS

DeBoer, A. (1995). *Working together: The art of consulting and communicating.* Longmont, CO: Sopris West.

Johnson, D.W., & Johnson, F.W. (1997). *Joining together: Group theory and skills* (6th ed.). Englewood Cliffs, NJ: Prentice Hall.

CONSULTATION

DeBoer, A. (1995). *Working together: The art of consulting and communicating.* Longmont, CO: Sopris West.

FAMILIES AND COLLABORATIVE TEAMING

Dunst, C.J., Johanson, C., Rounds, T., Trivette, C.M., & Hamby, D. (1992). *Characteristics of parent–professional partnerships.* In S.L. Christenson & J.C. Conoley (Eds.), Home–school collaboration: Enhancing children's academic and social competence. (pp. 157–174). Silver Spring, MD: National Association of School Psychologists.

Harry, B., (1992). *Cultural diversity, families, and the special education system: Communication and empowerment.* New York: Teachers College Press.

Soodak, L.C. (in press). Parents and inclusive schooling: Advocating for and participating in the reform of special education. In S.J. Vitello & D. Mithaug (Eds.), *Inclusive schooling: National and*

international perspectives. Mahwah, NJ: Lawrence Erlbaum Associates.

INCLUSION AND TEAMING

McGregor, G., & Vogelsberg, R.T. (1998). *Inclusive schooling practices: Pedagogical and research foundations.* Baltimore: Paul H. Brookes Publishing Co.

McLaughlin, M.J., & Warren, S.H. (1992). *Issues and options in restructuring schools and special education programs.* College Park: University of Maryland and Westat, Inc.

National Center for Children and Youth with Disabilities (NICHCY). (July, 1995). Planning for inclusion. *NICHCY News Digest, 5*(1), 1–31.

Roach, V. (1995). *Winning ways: Creating inclusive schools, classroom, and communities.* Alexandria, VA: National Association of State Boards of Education.

Snell, M.E., Raynes, M., with Byrd, J.O., Cooley, K.M., Gilley, C., Pityonak, C., Stallings, M.A., Van Dyke, R., Williams, P.S., & Willis, C.J. (1995). Changing roles in inclusive schools: Staff perspectives at Gilbert Linkous Elementary. *Kappa Delta Pi Record, 31,* 104–109.

York-Barr, J. (Ed.). (1996). Creating inclusive school communities. Baltimore: Paul H. Brookes Publishing Co.

PROBLEM SOLVING

Giangreco, M.F. (1993). Using creative problem-solving methods to include students with severe disabilities in general education classroom activities. *Journal of Educational and Psychological Consultation, 4,* 113–135.

Giangreco, M.F., Cloninger, C.J., Dennis, R.E., & Edelman, S.W. (1994). Problem-solving methods to facilitate inclusive education. In J.S. Thousand, R.A. Villa, & A.I. Nevin (Eds.), *Creativity and collaborative learning* (pp. 321–346). Baltimore: Paul H. Brookes Publishing Co.

Porter, G.L, & Rioux, M.H. (1994). *Teachers helping teachers: Problem-solving teams that work.* North York, ONT: Roeher Institute.

Pugach, M.C., & Johnson, L.J. (1995). Unlocking expertise among classroom teachers through structured dialogue: Extending research on peer collaboration. *Exceptional Children, 62,* 101–110.

Salisbury, C.L., & Palombaro, M.M. (Eds.). (1993). *No problem: Working things out our way.* Pittsburgh: Allegheny Singer Research Institute, Child and Family Studies Program.

Salisbury, C.L., Evans, I.M., & Palombaro, M.M. (1997). Collaborative problem-solving to pro-

mote the inclusion of young children with significant disabilities in primary grades. *Exceptional Children, 63,* 195–209.

PROGRAM PLANNING FOR INDIVIDUAL STUDENTS

Bateman, B.D., & Linden, M.A. (1998). *Better IEPs: How to develop legally correct and educationally useful programs* (3rd ed.). Longmont, CO: Sopris West.

Forest, M., & Lusthaus, E. (1989). Promoting educational equality for all students: Circles and maps. In S. Stainback, W. Stainback, & M. Forest (Eds.), *Educating all students in the mainstream of regular education* (pp. 43–57). Baltimore: Paul H. Brookes Publishing Co.

Giangreco, M.F., Cloninger, C.J., & Iverson, V.S. (1993). *Choosing options and accommodations for children (COACH): A guide to planning inclusive education.* Baltimore: Paul H. Brookes Publishing Co.

Janney, R.E., & Snell, M.E. (2000). *Teachers' guides to inclusive practices: Modifying schoolwork.* Baltimore: Paul H. Brookes Publishing Co.

Janney, R.E., & Snell, M.E. (2000). *Teachers' guides to inclusive practices: Behavior support.* Baltimore: Paul H. Brookes Publishing Co.

Kincaid, D. (1996). Person-centered planning. In L.K. Koegel, R.L. Koegel, & G. Dunlap (Eds.), *Positive behavioral support* (pp. 439–465). Baltimore: Paul H. Brookes Publishing Co.

Rainforth, B., & York-Barr, J. (1997). *Collaborative teams for students with severe disabilities: Integrating therapy and educational services* (2nd ed.). Baltimore: Paul H. Brookes Publishing Co.

Snell, M.E., & Janney, R.E. (2000). *Teachers' guides to inclusive practices: Social relationships and peer support.* Baltimore: Paul H. Brookes Publishing Co.

RELATED SERVICES AND COLLABORATIVE TEAMING

Giangreco, M.F. (1996). *Vermont Interdependent Services Team Approach (VISTA): A guide to coordinating educational support services.* Baltimore: Paul H. Brookes Publishing Co.

Giangreco, M.F., Edelman, S.W., & Dennis, R.E. (1991). Common professional practices that interfere with the integrated delivery of related services. *Remedial and Special Education, 12*(2), 16–24.

Rainforth, B., & York-Barr, J. (1997). *Collaborative teams for students with severe disabilities: Integrating therapy and educational services* (2nd ed.). Baltimore: Paul H. Brookes Publishing Co.

Index

Page numbers followed by "f" indicate figures; numbers followed by "t" indicate tables.

Teachers' Guides to Inclusive Practices!

These concise, issue-focused books from Martha E. Snell, Ph.D., and Rachel Janney, Ph.D., provide general and special educators with a bridge from inclusion research to inclusive practice, one subject at a time. Focusing on topics essential to inclusive school programs, each teacher-friendly guide briefly summarizes current research and recommended practices then outlines field-tested techniques for working with students who have disabilities. Completed sample forms and photocopiable blank forms accompany discussions of assessment, planning, implementation, and evaluation procedures for students of all ability levels in grades K–8.

Modifying Schoolwork
Full of proven strategies, this guidebook shows educators ways to adapt schoolwork to provide individualized attention to students with a broad range of learning and developmental disabilities.
Stock #3548 · $24.00 · 2000 · 112 pages · 7 x 10 · paperback · ISBN 1-55766-354-8

Collaborative Teaming
This resource explains how to create successful education teams by building teamwork skills, developing problem-solving methods, implementing action plans, teaching collaboratively, and improving communication skills.
Stock #353X · $24.00 · 2000 · 176 pages · 7 x 10 · paperback · ISBN 1-55766-353-X

Social Relationships and Peer Support
This easy-to-read guide offers effective strategies and programs that foster positive social relationships. Staff members will learn how to assess, develop, and teach skills that bolster formal and informal supportive friendships between peers in and out of school.
Stock #3564 · $24.00 · 2000 · 208 pages · 7 x 10 · paperback · ISBN 1-55766-356-4

Behavioral Support
Educators will discover fresh, proactive ideas for helping students develop appropriate behavior skills, form positive relationships, and communicate effectively with peers and adults.
Stock #3556 · $24.00 · 2000 · 120 pages · 7 x 10 · paperback · ISBN 1-55766-355-6